CRCT TEST PREP

6TH GRADE SOCIAL STUDIES

Teaching the Georgia Performance Standards

Dr. Emmett Reid Mullins, Jr.

Glen Blankenship, Ph.D., Consultant

Clairmont Press
Atlanta, Georgia

AUTHOR

Dr. Emmett Reid Mullins, Jr. is the technology coordinator for a school in Gwinnett County, Georgia. He has over twenty-five years of teaching experience and has done extensive work writing supplemental materials for instruction in social studies and technology integration. He is the author of many learning activities at the **mystatehistory.com** website as well as other resources published by Clairmont Press. Dr. Mullins is a graduate of the University of Georgia.

CONSULTANT

Dr. Glen Blankenship, Senior Development Consultant for Clairmont Press, is the Associate Director and Chief Program Officer at the Georgia Council on Economic Education in Atlanta, Georgia. He taught 8th grade Georgia Studies at Renfroe Middle School in Decatur, Georgia. Dr. Blankenship is a frequent presenter at state, regional, and national conferences and consults with school districts across the nation to develop curriculum and improve student learning. He is also a past president of the Georgia Council for the Social Studies and currently serves as the GCSS Historian. Dr. Blankenship earned his B.A. and M.Ed. in Political Science from Georgia State University, and a Ph.D. in Educational Leadership from Emory University.

Editor: Kathy Conway
Design: Cherry Bishop
Production: New Diameter Creative Services Inc.
Maps: New Diameter Creative Serivces Inc.

ISBN: 978-1-56733-099-1

Printed in the U.S.A.
Third Printing

CONTENTS

TO THE STUDENT

You are beginning the study of several important regions of the world: Latin America and Canada, Europe, and Australia. Each of these regions has an interesting history and geography. You will learn how people have shaped the history of each region. You will learn how geography and natural resources have affected how people live. You will also learn about the economies of countries in these regions of the world. Learning more about these parts of the world will help you to be a better citizen of your country.

This workbook will guide you and help you focus on the most important parts of what you need to know. You will be given specific information that will be tested on the Georgia CRCT next spring. The CRCT helps you, your teacher, and our state leaders know that you learned the information and skills that will help our state to continue to grow and prosper in the future.

So get ready to learn about some very interesting parts of our world! You will be given short readings to show you what is important. Then, you will be given some multiple choice questions to answer about the reading to check your learning. Be sure to pay special attention to any questions that you miss. Ask your teacher questions to help you understand why the correct answer was right. This will help you learn the information and be able to use it later.

If you complete this workbook and take the practice tests, you should have a very good score on the CRCT next spring.

Good luck!

INTRODUCTION

All of us want to do well on tests. This book will teach you some techniques to better prepare for tests. After you learn these techniques, you will have the opportunity to practice them as you get ready for the Georgia CRCT.

To become a better test taker, you need to

- Become familiar with the content of the test,
- Become familiar with the format of the test questions,
- Determine if the test is timed, and
- Know if there is a penalty for wrong answers.

CONTENT

Tests are given to find out what you know. To be successful on any test, it is necessary that you know what will be tested. Here are a number of suggestions for preparing for the content of the test.

- Predict what questions will be asked. Look over your notes or assignments or talk with classmates. Think about the information that the teacher emphasized or wrote on the whiteboard or overhead projector. The questions, people, concepts, and so on that are covered in class assignments generally are the things that are tested. Make a list of the important facts and concepts that might be tested.

- Take notes carefully if there is a test review. Note any comments by your teacher such as "This will be on the test," "These are the important people you should know," or "Remember these two points."

- Complete any test review sheet that the teacher might provide. You can use the review sheet as a practice test, or you can make a practice test using the review sheet as a guide.

- Devise methods to study for the test. For example,

  - Make a set of flashcards. Do this by writing a name, date, event, place, vocabulary word, or question on one side of the card. On the other side, write the answer or some information to describe what is listed on the front side of the card.

  - Make an outline of the information. Include major headings, people, events, dates, and so on.

  - Use memory strategies such as mnemonics or graphic organizers (such as concept diagrams, cause and effect charts, Venn diagrams, maps, or timelines) to organize information.

  - Recite the information. Some students are auditory learners and hearing the content helps them to remember.

  - Find a study buddy. Study with a friend or group of friends. Make practice tests for each other or orally ask one another questions.

PACING

It is important to know if a test is timed. Two considerations associated with timed tests are (1) using the allotted time effectively and (2) avoiding text anxiety. There are a number of strategies to help you budget time and, as a result, lessen your anxiety and increase your performance.

One of the biggest problems with timed tests is using the allotted time efficiently. Some students move numerically — from the first question to the last question — on a test. However, the progression of questions often does not move from easy questions at the beginning of the test to more difficult ones at the end. Rather, the degree of difficulty of questions may be random. When you encounter a difficult question, you may spend too much time trying to determine the answer. As a result, the allocated time for the test may elapse before you have completed all the questions.

Through ongoing testing, you can learn to answer the easier questions first. You should skip the harder ones and go back to them at the end of your time. When beginning a test, it is wise to look at the number of items on the test and then figure out how much time you have to answer each one. Following this model ensures that you will answer all the questions you believe you know before time runs out. Try to increase the total number of questions you can complete in a given amount of time.

If the test is not timed, you should work carefully and deliberately. Do not spend an inordinate amount of time on difficult questions, but rather return to those questions later. Do not make random guesses, unless there is no penalty for wrong answers. If there is no penalty, then try to answer all the questions, even if you have not read all of them. When there is a penalty for a wrong answer, answer those questions you know as well as those you can narrow down to two choices. If you have no idea of the answer, do not attempt to answer the question. Later you will learn methods to help you eliminate obviously wrong answers.

Many students have test anxiety, which can increase when the test is timed. The more experience you have with taking tests, the more the anxiety level will decrease. As you feel more comfortable with the content, pacing, and format, you will feel less anxious about the unknown.

COMPLETING ANSWER SHEETS

Many tests require students to bubble in an answer sheet to record their responses. Sometimes, however, students do not clearly understand how to do this simple mechanical process. This lack of understanding can have a bearing on test performance.

Bubbling in an answer sheet requires students to darken a space for their selected response. Many students believe they must fill in the entire space, making it as dark as possible. They spend lots of time, sometimes too much time, darkening in these spaces. In reality, the entire space does not need to be darkened, and it also does not need to be as dark as students sometimes make it.

Ask your teacher for a sample bubble answer sheet and practice filling it in. You may also want to time yourself to see how long it takes to bubble in the answers to a set number of questions. Practice will help you increase the number of bubbles you can darken in a given amount of time.

Another problem with completing answer sheets is that sometimes students skip a question, but they do not skip the corresponding space for its answer. When this happens, the answers to questions are coded incorrectly. Through practice, you can overcome this problem as well. In practice sessions, your teacher may ask you to complete every third or fourth question so you become familiar with skipping answer spaces as well as questions. When you have completed the test, you can go back and check to be sure your answers correctly align with the questions.

You may also want to check the alignment often instead of waiting until you have finished the test. If you only check your answers at the end of the test, you may not have time to make changes, especially if the misalignment began near the beginning.

FORMAT

The test questions on the Georgia CRCT Test are in multiple choice format. Questions that have a multiple choice format are also referred to as selected response questions. These questions, the most common format found on standardized tests, provide a set of choices—one of which is the correct answer. CRCT multiple choice questions contain a phrase or stem followed by 4 choices (selections). Multiple choice formats will ask a student to either answer a question or complete a statement.

When answering multiple choice questions, consider the following suggestions:
- Read the question before looking at the answers.
- If you have an answer, check to see if it is one of the choices. If it is, mark the answer sheet and go on to the next question. If your answer is not one of the choices, discard it and look carefully at the selected responses from which you can choose. Put a mark through choices that are clearly incorrect.

- Identify key words in the stem and selected responses. Check the relationship of the words.
- Locate the verb in the stem. Determine what the verb is asking you to do.
- Note words like *always*, *none*, and *never*. If a choice includes one of these words, it is probably not the correct answer.
- Note words like *often*, *frequently*, and *usually*. If a choice includes one of these words, it is likely to be the correct selection.
- Examine each answer to see how precisely it is written. A precise answer is often the correct one.
- Don't second guess yourself. Generally, your first choice is best.
- Note the use of "All of the above" as a selection. If you know that at least two of the choices are correct, then "All of the above" is probably the correct choice.
- Watch for negative words in the stem. Negative words generally ask you to choose an answer that is not true. When examining a question that contains a negative word, try to find three answers that are correct. This process helps you to narrow down your choices.
- Note similar choices. If two choices are similar, one of them is probably the correct answer. However, if there are two choices that essentially mean the same thing, neither answer is likely to be the correct choice.
- Note selected responses that are complete opposites. Generally, one of the responses is the correct answer.
- Note complex questions. If a question has complex choices, mark each item true or false. This will help you narrow your choices before deciding on the correct answer.

Use the following graphic organizer to analyze a selected response (multiple choice) question. Remember, you should read the sample question and, without looking at the selected responses, answer the question. Check to see if your answer is one of the choices. If it is one of the choices, you would normally mark the answer and move on to the next. For this practice, assume that your answer is not one of the choices. Refer to the list of clues to help you complete the analysis.

Read the stem or question.
Which African country is losing its rainforest most rapidly today?

A. Egypt
   B. Congl
   C. Kenya
   D. Nigeria

Identify key words.
Locate the verb.
Decide what action the verb requires.
Eliminate any choices you know are incorrect.
List the remaining choices.
Make your choice.
Why did you choose that option?

Because multiple choice is the most common test format, especially on standardized tests, it is important to examine a variety of types of questions that test social studies content. Sometimes, before answering questions, you will need to

- Read a long or short passage,
- Use a variety of maps, or
- Interpret data on a graph, table, or chart.

To help you analyze these types of questions, examine the test-taking tips that follow.

Reading a Long Passage

When you are reading a long passage,

- Look at the choices before you read the passage. Knowing what the possible answers are will direct your thinking while you read.
- Read the paragraph and note any key words. Some of the key words might also be found in the selected responses.
- Use the skills you learned for examining multiple choice questions.

Read the following paragraphs and answer the three questions that follow.

Canadians have a country rich in natural resources, or gifts of nature. Some of the most important of these resources are iron ore, nickel, zinc, copper, gold, lead, molybdenum, potash, diamonds, and silver. The large number of rivers and lakes are an excellent source of fish, fresh water, and water for hydroelectric power. Good soil allows farmers to grow enough for the people of Canada, with enough left over to trade with other countries. The forests are a major natural resource, along with abundant wildlife. Coal, oil, and natural gas are also in large supply. Canadians have enough of these energy resources to supply their needs, and they sell the rest to other countries.

Because many of the natural resources of Canada are found in remote areas, Canadians are spread across their country. Small communities can be found across Canada where mining and farming are important. Workers are needed to fish in rivers and at sea. Goods from these types of businesses are shipped by rail or highway to the larger cities for trade with other parts of Canada and the world.

_____1. **Which are important natural resources of Canada?**
   A. coal, oil, water
   B. oil, timber, workers
   C. fish, timber, railroads
   D. highways, natural gas, wildlife

_____2. **Why do Canadians live all across their large country?**
   A. They do not like living so close to one another.
   B. Many of their natural resources are in remote areas.
   C. Cities contain most of the natural resources needed to live.
   D. Natural resources of Canada are mostly within 100 miles of the U.S. border.

_____3. **What types of communities are usually found in areas where mining and farming are important?**
   A. large cities
   B. campgrounds
   C. fishing villages
   D. small communities

Using a Map

A map provides information in a graphic way. Types of maps include topographic, political, raised relief, weather, and natural resource. When reading information on a map,

- read its title to determine the subject and purpose,
- look to see if it has a scale to help you find distances between two or more points,
- examine its key or legend to see what symbols are used and what each represents, and
- look at any other information that is included.

Use the map below to answer the two questions that follow.

Australia

_____1. **Which feature is marked with a "1" on the map?**
   A. Coral Sea
   B. Ayers Rock
   C. Great Barrier Reef
   D. Great Victoria Desert

____2. **Where is the Great Barrier Reef located in relation to Ayers Rock?**
   A. southeast
   B. northeast
   C. southwest
   D. northwest

Interpreting a Graph

There are many types of graphs, including line, bar, and circle. Different types of graphs are used to illustrate different types of data. For example, a *line graph* is most often used to show how something has changed over a period of time. A *bar graph* often is used to make comparisons. A *circle graph* is used to illustrate parts of something to the whole. A circle graph, which usually contains percentages, is also called a pie graph since the parts illustrated might symbolically represent pieces of a pie. The whole circle represents 100 percent.

When you are answering questions about graphs, you should
   • read the title to determine its content,
   • examine the key to see what specific things are included, and
   • look at the specific parts; that is, the pieces of the pie.

Look at the following graph. It combines a line graph and a bar graph. Use the graph to answer the four questions that follow.

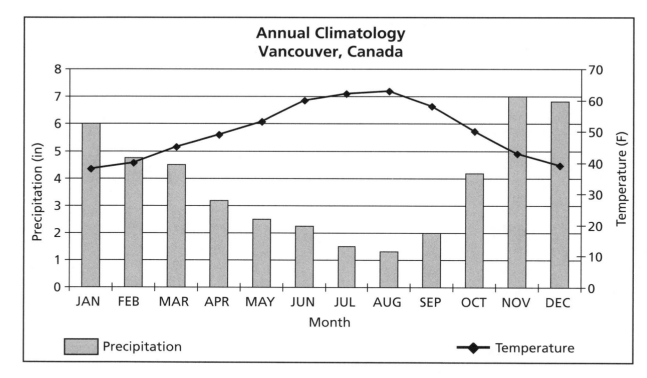

____1. **What month is usually the driest in Vancouver, Canada?**
   A. January
   B. April
   C. August
   D. November

_____ 2. **What month is usually the coldest in Vancouver, Canada?**
A. January
B. April
C. August
D. November

_____ 3. **About how many inches of precipitation does Vancouver have in January?**
A. 4
B. 6
C. 40
D. 60

_____ 4. **Which sentence best summarizes the information in the graph?**
A. Vancouver is hottest and driest in summer.
B. Vancouver is hottest and wettest in summer.
C. Summer and winter have similar temperatures but more rain in winter.
D. Summer and winter have similar precipitation, but it's colder in winter.

Look at the two circle graphs below and answer the four questions that follow.

What Are the Sources of Sulfur Dioxide (SO₂) in the Air?

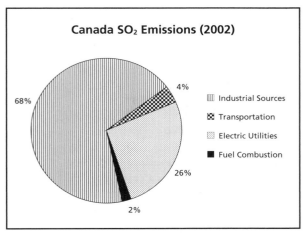

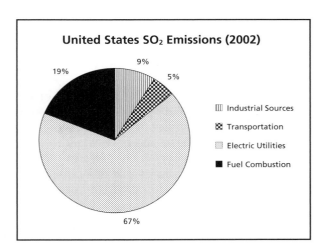

_____ 1. **The purpose of these graphs is to show**
A. that the United States creates more SO_2 pollution than Canada.
B. that Canada creates more SO_2 pollution than the United States.
C. the sources of SO_2 pollution in the United States and Canada.
D. the sources of all air pollution in the United States and Canada.

_____ 2. **Which source of pollution is the greatest producer of SO₂ in the United States?**
A. electric utilities
B. fuel combustion
C. industrial sources
D. transportation (cars, trucks, etc.)

_____3. **What is the second leading source of SO₂ in Canada?**
    A. electric utilities
    B. fuel combustion
    C. industrial sources
    D. transportation (cars, trucks, etc.)

_____4. **How does SO₂ pollution by transportation compare between the two countries?**
    A. They are about the same.
    B. Canada has a much higher percentage.
    C. The United States has a much higher percentage.
    D. There is no SO₂ pollution by transportation in the two countries.

Reading a Chart or Table

A chart or table is a good way to place text into a visual format. Charts are used to categorize data so it is easy to read and understand. Information that would take many pages to put in a text format can be summarized on a chart that may be one page or less.

When you are examining a chart or table, you should
- read the title to determine what the subject is,
- read the column headings and labels,
- draw conclusions from the data, and
- try to identify trends.

Use the passage below and the chart on page 9 to answer the four questions that follow.

Citizen Participation in Autocratic, Oligarchic, and Democratic Governments

People have different rights when it comes to participating in government. In some countries, people hold the power and elect their leaders or rulers. They vote on their laws. Because many people are involved in making decisions, solving a problem or responding to a crisis often takes a long time. In other countries, a small group of people holds power. Those that have wealth, own lots of land, or have military support may form this group. If needed, these groups select one of their own to be the leader. There are also those countries that have only one ruler. This type of ruler may come to power by family bloodlines, like a king or queen, or may be a dictator in power because of military strength. Citizens in countries with these last two types of government have no say in the laws or the government. Such rulers often do not do what is best for their country and
its people.

Copyright © Clairmont Press, Inc. DO NOT DUPLICATE. 1-800-874-8638

	Type of Rule	Who Holds the Power	Who Can Be Elected	Who Can Vote
Autocratic – Czarist Russia was an autocratic government.	Single ruler	Unlimited power for the ruler	No one – citizens have no choice in selecting a ruler	No citizen participation – no elections are held
Oligarchic – Many medieval governments were oligarchic.	Small group of people	Group answers only to each other	No one outside the ruling group – the rulers are selected by the group	No citizen participation – leaders are chosen from within the ruling group and by the group
Democratic – France is an example of a democratic country	Citizens of the country	The voters	Any citizen (with some restrictions like age, not in jail, etc.)	Any citizen (with some restrictions like age, not in jail, etc.)

_____ 1. **In which types of government do citizens have no voting rights?**
A. an autocracy and a democracy
B. an oligarchy and a democracy
C. an oligarchy and an autocracy
D. any of the three types of government

_____ 2. **An autocracy puts the power of the government into the hands of**
A. the citizens.
B. a single person.
C. the representatives.
D. a small group of people.

_____ 3. **How can autocratic rulers come to power?**
A. by voter election
B. by legislative election
C. through their bloodline
D. by representative appointment

_____ 4. **Which statement is true about an oligarchy?**
A. Anyone can lead.
B. Leaders are elected.
C. Laws protect the citizens.
D. A small group of people govern.

Final Thought

In addition to all the specific test-taking strategies that you have learned, the following are general suggestions to help you feel confident and ready when time for the test comes.

The Night Before the Test:

- Review major concepts/objectives.
- Take a break from studying if you get tired.
- Get a good night's sleep.

The Day of the Test:

- Get up early enough to exercise lightly.
- Eat a good, healthy breakfast (avoid sugar and caffeine).
- Wear comfortable clothing to school.
- Arrive at school on time.
- Take any needed materials to the testing site, such as pencils, scrap paper, and a calculator.
- Choose a seat that is free from distractions, for example, in the front of the room or away from the door.
- Take deep breaths if you feel yourself tensing up.
- Listen carefully to any directions. Then, before starting the test, quickly re-read the directions to check for understanding.
- Quickly preview the whole test. Devise a plan to budget your time if the test is timed.
- Be serious. Don't think that any test is unimportant.
- Apply test-taking clues when answering the questions.
- Don't second guess yourself; your first thought is generally best.
- Keep a positive and confident attitude.
- Check your answer sheet periodically to be sure the questions and your answers align properly.
- Reward yourself after the test for a job well done!

Now, go on to page 11. You will read material and answer questions that will help prepare you for the Georgia 6th grade CRCT Test.

LATIN AMERICA AND CANADA

GEOGRAPHIC UNDERSTANDINGS

> **SS6G1 The student will locate selected features of Latin America and the Caribbean.**
>
> a. Locate on a world and regional political-physical map: Amazon River, Caribbean Sea, Gulf of Mexico, Pacific Ocean, Panama Canal, Andes Mountains, Sierra Madre Mountains, and Atacama Desert.

LOCATING PHYSICAL FEATURES OF LATIN AMERICA AND THE CARIBBEAN

In order to learn about Latin America, it is good to know some of the main features of the land and water. Look at the map, and put your finger on the United States. Move your finger south into Mexico. Notice that there is a large body of water on the west side of Mexico–the **Pacific Ocean**. The Pacific Ocean stretches down the entire western side of Central and South America. On the east side of Mexico, there are two smaller bodies of water–the **Gulf of Mexico** and the **Caribbean Sea**. The Gulf of Mexico is north of the Caribbean Sea. It touches both the United States and Mexico. Farther south is the Caribbean Sea. It is bounded on the west and south by Mexico and Central America, on the south by South America, and on the north and east by many islands.

Moving your finger south across Mexico, you will notice a large area of mountains. These are the **Sierra Madre**, which is the chief mountain range of Mexico. After Mexico, your finger will cross many smaller countries in Central America. At the most narrow point, you'll find the country of Panama, home of the **Panama Canal**. Locate this landmark on your map. This canal is a very important shortcut for ships traveling back and forth from the Atlantic to the Pacific Ocean.

As you move your finger further south into South America, look for three main physical features: the **Andes Mountains**, the **Atacama Desert**, and the **Amazon River**. The Andes Mountains run the length of the western side of South America. Find the Andes Mountains. The world's second longest river, the Amazon, runs nearly across the widest part of South America, from the Andes Mountains to the Atlantic Ocean. Further south, along the Pacific side of South America, the Andes Mountains block winds and rains, creating the second driest place on earth, the Atacama Desert.

Use the map below. Choose the best answer for questions 1-4.

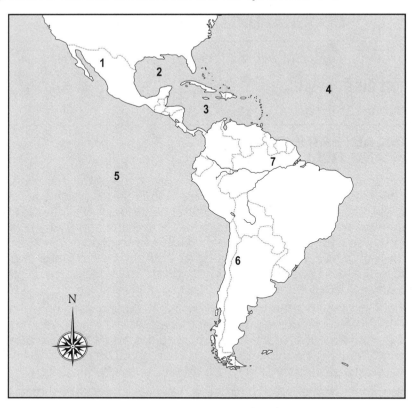

_____ 1. Which is found near the "1" on the map?
   A. Panama Canal
   B. Atacama Desert
   C. Andes Mountains
   D. Sierra Madre Mountains

_____ 2. Which physical feature is found near the "6" on the map?
   A. Amazon River
   B. Pacific Ocean
   C. Atacama Desert
   D. Sierra Madre Mountains

_____ 3. At which number on the map is the Caribbean Sea?
   A. 2
   B. 3
   C. 5
   D. 7

_____ 4. The Amazon River is found at which number on the map?
   A. 1
   B. 6
   C. 7
   D. not shown

LOCATING COUNTRIES IN LATIN AMERICA

There are many countries in Latin America. Use the map to locate a few of them. First, place your finger on the United States. Move it south into the country of **Mexico**. Mexico has a long border with the United States and plays an important role in the economy of the United States. Move your finger south. At the most narrow point of Central America, you will find **Panama**, which is home to the Panama Canal.

As you move your finger further south, you will arrive in South America at the country of **Colombia**. Move your finger eastward to find **Venezuela**, a country that provides oil to many parts of the world. South of Venezuela is **Brazil**, the largest country in South America. West of the central part of Brazil, find **Bolivia**.

In addition to these countries, there are many island-nations. Two important ones are **Cuba** and **Haiti**. To find Cuba, locate Florida in the southeastern United States. South of Florida is a long island stretching to the southeast. This is Cuba. It is bounded on the northwest by the Gulf of Mexico, on the northeast by the Atlantic Ocean, and on the south by the Caribbean Sea. To the southeast of Cuba is the large island of Hispaniola. This island is home to two countries. The western one-third of the island is the country of Haiti.

Latin America

LATIN AMERICA AND CANADA

Use the map below. Choose the best answer for questions 5-8.

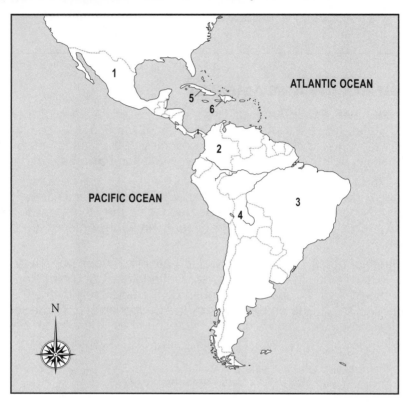

_____ 5. **Which country is found at the "1" on the map?**
   A. Brazil
   B. Bolivia
   C. Mexico
   D. Colombia

_____ 6. **Which country is found at the "4" on the map?**
   A. Brazil
   B. Bolivia
   C. Mexico
   D. Colombia

_____ 7. **Which number on the map marks the country of Cuba?**
   A. 2
   B. 3
   C. 5
   D. 6

_____ 8. **Which number on the map marks the country of Colombia?**
   A. 1
   B. 2
   C. 3
   D. 4

MEXICO CITY AND AIR POLLUTION

In the early twentieth century, Mexico City was known for its clear skies and views of distant snowcapped mountains. Today, Mexico City is known as one of the world's worst areas of air pollution. The air is so bad that children are more likely to have breathing problems and develop lung disease when they grow up. Older adults must stay indoors and limit activity. On most days, the hazy, polluted sky blocks the view to the mountains.

The city is crowded. Over 19 million people live in Mexico City. That's more than double the population of the entire state of Georgia. In this city are thousands of factories and over 3 million cars. The factories and cars send pollution such as lead, sulfur dioxide, and carbon monoxide into the air. Many of the cars are older models. These older cars produce even more pollution than typical new cars.

Geography plays a role in the problems the city faces. The city is built in a bowl-shaped crater of an extinct volcano. The high elevation means that the air is thin, and the exhaust from cars and factories gets trapped in the valley. The intense sunlight helps to push smog even higher. *Smog* is a combination of smoke and thick fog.

The government of Mexico City is working on several solutions to this problem. First, drivers must leave their cars at home one day each week. Citizens are encouraged to ride buses and trains or to carpool to work. Cars are inspected more often. Those with very bad exhaust problems must be repaired. On the days of highest pollution levels, certain factories may be closed.

Because the population continues to grow, Mexico City must continue to find ways to clean its air. The government is working to find ways to improve the fuels used for energy. It is also working to increase the number of cars that produce little or no air pollution.

_____ 9. **How does geography play a role in Mexico City's air pollution problem?**
   A. It is one of the world's largest cities.
   B. The city has views of distant snowcapped mountains.
   C. It lies in a bowl-shaped valley that traps air pollutants.
   D. The cars and factories send pollution such as lead, sulfur, and carbon monoxide into the air.

_____ 10. **What are the main sources of air pollution in Mexico City?**
   A. intense sunlight
   B. the high altitude
   C. factories and cars
   D. cars that produce little or no air pollution

LATIN AMERICA AND CANADA

_____11. **Which solution is a way that the government is trying to reduce pollution in Mexico City?**
   A. ignoring cars with exhaust problems
   B. reducing the number of buses and trains
   C. making sure the population continues to grow
   D. increasing the number of cars that produce little or no air pollution

_____12. **Which solution to Mexico City's air pollution problem would be most challenging to businesses?**
   A. closing factories one day a week
   B. using fuels that produce less pollution
   C. having employees ride trains or buses to work
   D. asking citizens to leave their cars at home one day a week

DESTRUCTION OF THE RAIN FOREST IN BRAZIL

Brazil is the largest country in South America, and the fifth largest in the world, by land area and population. More than half the country is covered by rain forest. This jungle environment is home to more than 40,000 different kinds of plants and thousands of types of animals. Trees in the forest can soar up to 150 feet in the air. The Amazon River and other large rivers carry water from the rain forests across Brazil and into the Atlantic Ocean.

The rain forests of Brazil are valuable in many ways. In the rain forest, humans have found plants that can be used to produce drugs for treating disease. Brazil nuts, cocoa, and rubber are among the products people use as well. The trees themselves can be sold for timber. The forest serves another purpose—creating oxygen! All plants "breathe" carbon dioxide and produce oxygen. It is estimated that 20 percent of the world's oxygen is produced in the rain forests of the Amazon region.

Brazil is home to some native populations that depend on the forest. Many of these rain forest people have had little or no contact with the outside world. They maintain their traditional way of life. These people depend on the rain forest for their food, clothing, shelter, and spiritual life.

This beautiful and important environment is threatened by human activity. Many Brazilians live in poor conditions. One way the people get money for their families is to clear the forest and sell the timber. Humans use chain saws and bulldozers to clear large areas of the forest and haul away the trees. The process is known as **_deforestation_**. The cleared land can be used to start cattle ranches or farms to grow such crops as soybeans. Illegal clearing of the forests increases when the value of crops and cattle go up. In the past ten years, nearly 200,000 square miles of rain forest have been lost due to deforestation. The people, animals, and plants that live in this environment are threatened with extinction.

The government has created laws to control the amount of forest that is cut down. However, little money is spent on enforcing those laws. Environmental groups and governments from around the world are working with Brazil's government to find ways to save the rain forests. They hope to help Brazil's people find ways to use the forests' resources without destroying the rain forest itself.

_____13. **Which is a problem associated with deforestation?**
   A. More oxygen is available on the planet.
   B. Poor people earn money from selling trees.
   C. Native people have too much forest for their needs.
   D. There is less forest to produce goods that humans need.

_____14. **Why does deforestation increase when the value of crops and cattle go up?**
   A. The value of timber goes up.
   B. Laws to protect the rain forest are not enforced.
   C. People think they can make more profit selling cattle and crops.
   D. Environmental groups work with the government only when prices are down.

_____15. **What is the main crop grown in areas of deforestation?**
   A. cocoa
   B. rubber
   C. soybeans
   D. Brazil nuts

_____16. **The world gets about 20 percent of which resource from the Amazon rain forest?**
   A. rubber
   B. oxygen
   C. soybeans
   D. medicine

Use the graph to answer questions 17-20.

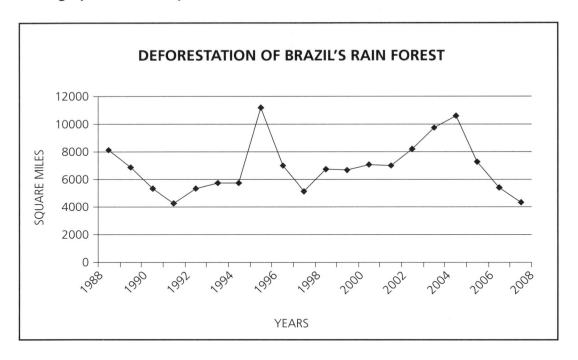

DEFORESTATION OF BRAZIL'S RAIN FOREST

SQUARE MILES

YEARS

_____17. **The purpose of this graph is to show**
A. the amount of land in the Brazilian rain forest.
B. how much forest is left in the Brazilian rain forest.
C. the amount of land protected by deforestation laws in Brazil.
D. how much of the Brazilian rain forest was cut down each year.

_____18. **In what year was the destruction of the rain forest the greatest?**
A. 1991
B. 1995
C. 2004
D. 2007

_____19. **What trend is there in deforestation after 2004?**
A. The amount of deforestation is going up.
B. The amount of deforestation is going down.
C. Deforestation levels have stayed about the same.
D. Deforestation levels are lower than they were in the 1970s.

_____20. **What was the approximate number of square miles lost to deforestation in 1991?**
A. 3,800
B. 4,000
C. 4,200
D. 4,500

OIL-RELATED POLLUTION IN VENEZUELA

Venezuela is one of the largest producers of oil and natural gas in the world. The country is the fifth-largest producer of oil in the world. It has been producing oil for about a hundred years. It is now one of the top four sources of oil for the United States. In fact, about 15 percent of the oil sold in the United States comes from Venezuela. The money from oil sales accounts for about half the money received by the government of Venezuela.

The production of oil and natural gas has come at a cost, however. Along the Caribbean Sea, Venezuela's coast has become polluted with oil. Oil spills and tanker leaks have damaged the environment in the region. They have also hurt the ability of fishermen to earn a living. The country leads South America in the production of the gas carbon dioxide, which is a by-product of burning fossil fuels like natural gas and oil. High levels of carbon dioxide in the air can cause breathing problems for children and the elderly. Other health problems can occur in healthy adults after long exposure to high levels of carbon dioxide. Some scientists believe that increases in carbon dioxide contribute to "global warming." They believe this because carbon dioxide tends to trap warm air at the surface of the Earth instead of letting it rise.

Oil businesses have damaged the environment in another way. Lake Maracaibo is the largest lake in South America. Due to the large amount of oil removed from the nearby areas, the land in the area is changing. The eastern shore of the lake is dropping about three inches a year. The government built a dike to keep the water in the lake from flooding the nearby homes, towns, and farms.

_____ 21. **What problem has been caused by oil production in Venezuela?**
A. About 15 percent of U.S. oil comes from Venezuela.
B. The coast along the Caribbean Sea has been polluted with oil.
C. Lake Maracaibo has become the largest lake in South America.
D. Venezuela is more polluted than other South American countries.

_____ 22. **Why might the Venezuelan government NOT want to stop oil production in the country, even though it causes a lot of pollution?**
A. The government gets about half of its money from the oil business.
B. The government does not care about the damage to the environment.
C. People along Lake Maracaibo are now protected by a dike to prevent flooding.
D. People in Venezuela do not care about the environment as much as other people.

_____ 23. **Who is affected first by carbon dioxide pollution?**
A. healthy adults
B. children and the elderly
C. farmers along Lake Maracaibo
D. fisherman along the Caribbean coast

_____ 24. **Which problem is associated with too much carbon dioxide in the air?**
A. algal bloom
B. breathing problems
C. cooler air trapped at Earth's surface
D. oil slicks on the Caribbean coastline

LATIN AMERICA AND CANADA

LOCATION, CLIMATE, AND NATURAL RESOURCES OF MEXICO

Location of Mexico

Mexico is the second-largest country by size and population in Latin America. It is the largest Spanish-speaking country in the world. The country is located south of the United States. On the west is the Pacific Ocean, and on the east are the Gulf of Mexico and the Caribbean Sea.

Mexico's location between the Pacific Ocean and the Gulf of Mexico and Caribbean Sea allows it the opportunity to trade. There are seven major seaports in Mexico. Oil and other materials from Mexico can be easily shipped around the world to ports along the Atlantic and Pacific Oceans.

Another advantage of Mexico's location is that it is close to the United States. Because the two countries share a border, trade is easier. Railroads and trucks can be used to ship goods. Mexico's main trading partner is the United States.

Climate of Mexico

Mexico has the Sierra Madre Mountains, deserts in the north, tropical beaches, plains, and plateaus. The climate varies according to the location, with some tropical areas receiving more than 40 inches of rain a year. Desert areas in the north remain dry most of the year.

Most people live on the Central Plateau of Mexico in the central part of the country. Mexico City, one of the world's largest cities, is in this region. There is **arable** (farmable) land in this region, and there is usually enough rain to grow a variety of crops. The region has many manufacturing centers, which provide jobs. Over 75 percent of the people in Mexico live in **urban** (city) areas. This allows them to have jobs in manufacturing or service industries. About 25 percent of Mexico's workers are farmers. However, fewer people are choosing to work on farms because of the challenges of little rainfall and unproductive soil as well as little money for modern farm equipment and fertilizers.

Natural Resources of Mexico

The people of Mexico are able to use their **natural resources** (gifts of nature) to trade with other countries. Oil is one of the most important **exports** (goods sold to other countries). Mexico is the tenth-largest oil exporter in the world. It exports about 1.7 million barrels of oil a day. Money from the sale of oil provides about a third of the Mexican government's budget. Mexico is also one of the world's largest exporters of silver. Silver mines in Mexico produce about 15 percent of the silver sold in the world each year. Other exports include fruits, vegetables, coffee, and cotton. The economy is boosted by tourism, too. The country is very close to the United States, so most of the tourists are American. In fact, three-fourths of Mexico's trade with other countries comes from the United States.

_____ 25. **Which metal is mined more in Mexico than anywhere else?**
   A. iron
   B. lead
   C. silver
   D. copper

_____ 26. **Which country has about three-fourths of the trade with Mexico?**
   A. Brazil
   B. Guyana
   C. Venezuela
   D. United States

_____ 27. **Which region of Mexico has the most people?**
   A. Central Plateau
   B. northern deserts
   C. tropical beaches
   D. Sierra Madre Mountains

_____ 28. **Which is a problem for the farmers in Mexico?**
   A. The soil is not very productive.
   B. Many areas have too much rainfall.
   C. There is not enough sunlight to grow crops.
   D. There are few businesses to sell farm equipment.

LATIN AMERICA AND CANADA

LOCATION, CLIMATE, AND NATURAL RESOURCES OF VENEZUELA

Location of Venezuela

Venezuela is a much smaller Latin American country than Mexico. To the north are the Caribbean Sea and the Atlantic Ocean. The country shares borders with Guyana on the east, Brazil on the south, and Colombia on the west.

Venezuela's coastline gives it easy access to trade with other countries. There are four major ports in the country. Oil can be loaded onto tankers and shipped to ports in the United States and Europe. The nearby Panama Canal provides a shortcut to the Pacific Ocean and trade with Asian countries.

Climate of Venezuela

Venezuela lies in the tropics and is just north of the equator. This means that it has a hot, tropical climate all year. Only in high elevations such as the Andes will temperatures fall to the freezing point. Most rain falls from May to October. Along the coast, it is relatively dry with about 16 inches of rain each year. In higher elevations, annual rainfall is over 100 inches a year.

About 88 percent of the people in Venezuela live in urban areas along the coast in the northern part of the country. Although there is a lot of poverty, many professionals live in these urban areas, including doctors, lawyers, teachers, businessmen, and government employees. These people give the country a large middle class. About 75 percent of Venezuelans make their living in service jobs such as education, health care, and hotel, transportation, and trade businesses. **Service jobs** are those that involve providing services to people rather than products.

Natural Resources of Venezuela

Other Venezuelans make their living fishing in Lake Maracaibo, South America's largest lake, and along the coast of the Caribbean Sea. There is little arable land, so farming provides jobs for only 10 percent of the population.

The oil industry provides other jobs. Venezuela is the sixth-largest oil exporter in the world. It produces 2.8 million barrels of oil a day. Its location on the ocean gives it easy access to trade with countries around the world. About 90 percent of the money the government makes on trade with other countries comes from the oil business. In fact, half of the government's money comes from the oil business. The government has used this money to improve health care and education services, especially in poor communities. It has also used the money to make improvements in roads and telephone networks.

Venezuela and Mexico have common problems. For instance, millions of their citizens live in poor conditions. They have little or no health care, and their children do not have an opportunity for a good education. In addition, both countries depend on oil production for a large part of their trade. When the price of oil goes down, it is difficult for the government to pay its bills and help its people. The environmental cost of the production of oil is a problem, too. Pollution caused by oil will affect the land and air in these countries for many years to come.

_____29. **What is a major reason that few Venezuelans are farmers?**
    A. There is too much rain.
    B. There is little arable land.
    C. Venezuela trades with Guyana, Brazil, and Colombia for food.
    D. Venezuela is able to buy the food it needs from other countries.

_____30. **Which is a negative result of Venezuela's oil business?**
    A. Health care services have improved.
    B. Pollution has damaged the air and land.
    C. Education for poor children has improved.
    D. Road and telephone networks have been expanded.

_____31. **How has Venezuela's location helped its trade with other countries?**
    A. Venezuela is in the northern part of South America.
    B. The countries of the Caribbean Sea can trade with nearby Venezuela.
    C. The countries of Guyana, Brazil, and Colombia share a border with Venezuela.
    D. Venezuela has a coastline with ports on the Caribbean Sea and the Atlantic Ocean.

_____32. **Most people in Venezuela live in what type of area?**
    A. rural
    B. urban
    C. half live in urban areas, half in rural
    D. this information has not been collected

Use the information from the reading and the following table to answer questions 33-37.

Comparing Mexico and Venezuela

	Mexico	Venezuela
Location	• at southern border of the United States • coasts on the Pacific Ocean, Gulf of Mexico, and Caribbean Sea • northernmost country of Latin America • very mountainous with large central plateau • land varies from warm tropical beaches to dry deserts • most land is too dry and rugged to grow crops; only about 12% is arable • earthquakes and volcanic activity	• in northeast part of South America • coasts on Caribbean Sea and Atlantic Ocean • just north of the equator • mountains in the north, central plains, with plateaus and low mountains in the south • about 3% arable land; most lands better for pastures than crops
Climate	• tends to be dry and warm, although it varies by region • hottest June-August • wettest June-August	• hot, tropical climate • cooler in the mountains • rain varies by region (16 inches on the coast; over 100 inches in the mountains)
Natural Resources	petroleum, natural gas, silver, copper, gold, lead, zinc, and timber	petroleum, natural gas, iron ore, gold, bauxite, other minerals, hydropower, diamonds
Population	about 113,000,000	about 28,000,000
Area	about 760,000 square miles	about 350,000 square miles
Where People Live	• Urban: 77% • Rural: 23% • nearly 20% of the people live in the area of Mexico City • 2nd most populous country in Latin America • largest Spanish-speaking country in the world	• Urban: 93% • Rural: 7% • Caracas is the largest city • most people live in the northern highlands, along the coast
Trade	• mix of new and old industries • recently expanded railroads, airports, and electric generating plants • 7 major seaports • exports: manufactured goods, oil and oil products, silver, fruits, vegetables, coffee, and cotton • tourism	• 90% of money made on exports comes from oil • 4 major seaports • other exports: bauxite and aluminum, steel, chemicals, agricultural products, basic manufactures • tourism

_____33. **Which statement BEST describes the population of Mexico and Venezuela?**
   A. The countries have about the same population.
   B. The countries do not have information on their population.
   C. Mexico has about four times the number of people of Venezuela.
   D. Mexico has about one-fourth the number of people of Venezuela.

_____34. **The warm climate of Mexico and Venezuela is MOST helpful to which of its industries?**
   A. oil
   B. fishing
   C. tourism
   D. health care

_____35. **Why do most Mexicans and Venezuelans live in urban areas?**
   A. Rural areas do not have good climates.
   B. There is much arable land in these countries.
   C. There are more jobs in the factories and businesses of the cities.
   D. Rural areas have more opportunity for good education and health care.

_____36. **What is the major source of income in both Mexico and Venezuela?**
   A. oil
   B. tourism
   C. manufactured goods
   D. agricultural products

_____37. **What is one problem with depending on oil exports for most of a country's income?**
   A. Most countries produce the oil they need.
   B. Most countries do not need to purchase oil.
   C. When the price of oil goes up, the country cannot afford to sell oil.
   D. When the price of oil goes down, the country begins to run low on money.

LATIN AMERICA AND CANADA

LOCATION, CLIMATE, AND NATURAL RESOURCES OF BRAZIL

Location of Brazil

Brazil is the largest country in Latin America in both population and land area. Brazil is located on the eastern side of South America along the coast of the Atlantic Ocean. Brazil shares a border with nearly every other country in South America. The Amazon River and other large rivers stretch across most of Brazil.

Brazil's location on the Atlantic Ocean and its closeness to the Panama Canal greatly influence its trade with other countries. Brazil's exports can be shipped through any of the seven major seaports on the coast. Cars and other transportation equipment are traded to other countries. Exports also include iron ore and shoes. The United States is Brazil's most important trading partner. China, Argentina, Germany, and the Netherlands also buy goods from Brazil.

Tourism is a growing industry in Brazil. The Amazon rain forest draws many visitors. Its animals, plants, and other natural wonders cannot be found anywhere else in the world. Brazil's sandy beaches and warm climate are another attraction. Cities such as Rio de Janeiro and São Paulo have attractions and festivals that bring visitors from around the world.

Climate of Brazil

The country's location on the equator gives it the climate needed to support one of the world's largest regions of tropical rain forest. The climate is mostly hot and tropical. In the south, further from the equator, the climate is temperate (mild).

Most Brazilians live along the eastern, coastal areas of their country. Good roads do not extend into the vast Amazon rain forest region of the interior of the country. As a result, 80 percent of the people live within 200 miles of the ocean. Brazil's cities are clustered in this area too. About 30 percent of the people work in health care, education, or government jobs. Another 30 percent work in businesses such as transportation, communication, and trade. Nearly 12 percent of the workers find jobs in manufacturing. Because these jobs tend to be found in urban areas, nearly 85 percent of Brazilians live in urban environments.

Natural Resources of Brazil

Only 7 percent of the land in Brazil is arable, but Brazil makes the most of this resource. Twenty percent of the workers in Brazil are farmers. They produce one-third of the world's coffee, and they lead the world in the production of oranges, papayas, and sugar cane. Soybeans and soybean products are important products for trade with other countries. Only the United States exports more farm products than Brazil.

_____38. **Where do most Brazilians live in their country?**
   A. in the interior
   B. along the Amazon river
   C. in the Amazon rain forest
   D. along the eastern, coastal area

_____39. **The climate of Brazil allows farmers to export all of these crops EXCEPT**
   A. wheat
   B. coffee
   C. oranges
   D. sugar cane

_____40. **Which natural resource is an important export for Brazil?**
   A. cars
   B. shoes
   C. iron ore
   D. sugar cane

_____41. **Why does Brazil have a fast-growing tourism industry?**
   A. Most Brazilians live in urban areas and need jobs.
   B. Most Brazilians live within 200 miles of the coast.
   C. Brazil has many cities scattered across the country that tourists enjoy visiting.
   D. Brazil has many natural wonders that cannot be found anywhere else in the world.

_____42. **How does Brazil's location help it trade with other countries?**
   A. There are seven major seaports along the Atlantic coast.
   B. The Amazon River allows ships to travel inland to the Andes.
   C. Brazil shares a border with nearly every other South American country.
   D. Brazil is able to purchase from other countries goods that it cannot make on its own.

LOCATION, CLIMATE, AND NATURAL RESOURCES OF CUBA

Location of Cuba

Cuba is an island nation 90 miles south of the state of Florida. It is bounded by the Gulf of Mexico on the northwest, the Atlantic Ocean on the northeast, and the Caribbean Sea to the south. The island is a little more than 700 miles long, and it ranges from 135 miles at its widest point to only 20 miles at the narrowest point. Cuba is the largest island in the West Indies.

Most Cubans (76 percent) live in urban areas. Twenty percent of them live in the capital and largest city, Havana. Many workers in the urban areas have jobs in manufacturing. A large number have jobs in service professions such as education, health care, government, and tourism. Cuba's location on ocean trading routes has been an important influence on its history and current economy.

Climate of Cuba

Cuba's climate is tropical but moderated by tradewinds. There is a rainy season from May to October, and there is a dry season from November to April. The tropical climate means that Cuba is warm to hot all year long. Winds help move the air and provide relief from the heat.

Cuba's location and climate also make it a target for hurricanes. The warm tropical waters provide energy for the storms, which begin on the coast of Africa. As the storms move west, they often move across islands in the Caribbean, including Cuba. Hurricane season runs from June 1 through November 30.

Natural Resources of Cuba

Twenty-eight percent of Cuba's land is arable. Cuba makes good use of this land by growing not only crops for its own people but also crops to sell to other countries. For centuries, sugar cane plantations have been a major source of income for Cuba. This is true today, with sugar being the most important export of the country. Coffee, fish, fruits, and tobacco products are traded to other countries as well. Cuba is known for its cigars. This tobacco product is highly prized by many people and provides a good income to the country. Cuba's location on the ocean gives it easy access to rich fishing waters. Fishing provides food for Cubans, and it gives the country another product to export.

One of the fastest-growing industries is tourism. Cuba has a beautiful, natural landscape and wonderful beaches. Tourists from Canada, Europe, and Latin America bring money to the island and provide jobs for the people. Hotels are being built or renovated to attract even more tourists.

Cuba is a **communist** country. That means the government owns or controls most farms and businesses. The communist government of the Soviet Union helped to support Cuba for many years. When the Soviet Union collapsed in 1991, Cuba faced difficult times. Cuba's trade with other countries does not bring in enough money to meet the needs of its people. Today, Venezuela sells oil to Cuba at a reduced price, but Cuba cannot sell enough goods to buy everything its people need. In order to save energy, the government sometimes orders businesses and factories to close. The government also orders **blackouts**, or times when all electricity to a region is cut off.

_____43. **What has been the major export for Cuba for the past two hundred years?**
   A fish
   B. fruits
   C sugar
   D. coffee

_____44. **Which industries are helped MOST by Cuba's location on the ocean?**
   A. tourism and fishing
   B. fishing and tobacco
   C. sugar and health care
   D. tourism and health care

_____45. **Which product does Venezuela provide at a reduced cost to Cuba?**
   A oil
   B. fish
   C. wheat
   D. sugar cane

_____46. **The large amount of arable land is MOST helpful to which industry in Cuba?**
   A. fishing
   B tourism
   C. farming
   D. manufacturing

_____47. **Which country supported Cuba until 1991?**
   A. Canada
   B. Venezuela
   C. Soviet Union
   D. United States

LATIN AMERICA AND CANADA

Use information from your reading and the following table to answer questions 48-52.

Comparing Brazil and Cuba

	Brazil	Cuba
Location	• eastern side of South America, bordering the Atlantic Ocean • the equator crosses the northern part of the country • mostly flat to rolling lowlands; some plains, hills, mountains • largest country in Latin America • about 7% arable land	• Caribbean island about 90 miles south of Florida • Gulf of Mexico to the northwest and Atlantic Ocean to the northeast • mostly flat to rolling plains; rugged hills and mountains in the southeast • largest island in the West Indies • about 28% arable land
Climate	• mostly hot, tropical • temperate (mild temperatures) in the south	• tropical; moderated by trade winds; dry season (November to April); rainy season (May to October)
Natural Resources	bauxite, gold, iron ore, manganese, nickel, phosphates, platinum, tin, uranium, petroleum, hydropower, timber	cobalt, nickel, iron ore, chromium, copper, salt, timber, silica, petroleum, arable land
Population	about 203,000,000	about 11,000,000
Area	about 3,300,000 square miles	about 43,000 square miles
Where People Live	• Urban: 87% • Rural: 13% • most populated country in Latin America • largest Portuguese-speaking country in the world • most Brazilians live along the coast; 80% live within 200 miles of the ocean • nearly all cities and large towns are in the coastal area	• Urban: 76% • Rural: 24% • Havana is the largest city • about 20% of Cubans live in Havana
Trade	• 7 major seaports • exports: transport equipment, iron ore, soybeans, footwear, coffee, autos, and sugar • the United States is the largest trading partner • tourism	• 3 major seaports • exports: sugar, nickel, tobacco, fish, medical products, citrus, coffee • Venezuela is the largest trading partner • tourism

_____48. **Who is Brazil's largest trading partner?**
   A. Cuba
   B. Guyana
   C. Venezuela
   D. United States

_____49. **A similarity between Brazil and Cuba is that, in both countries, people tend to live in**
   A. rural areas.
   B. urban areas.
   C. away from the ocean.
   D. farming communities.

_____50. **A difference between Brazil and Cuba is that Brazil**
   A. has a much larger population than Cuba.
   B. has a much smaller population than Cuba.
   C. does not allow people to live near the coast.
   D. does not want people to move inland into the rain forest.

_____51. **How do the land areas of Cuba and Brazil compare?**
   A. Cuba is over 700 miles long.
   B. Cuba is about half the size of Brazil.
   C. The countries are about the same size.
   D. Brazil is about eight times the size of Cuba.

_____52. **In which industries do Cuba and Brazil compete with each other for trade with other countries?**
   A. coffee, sugar, tourism
   B. Brazil nuts, tobacco, nickel
   C. iron ore, soybeans, footwear
   D. tobacco, autos, medical products

LATIN AMERICA AND CANADA

THE BLENDING OF ETHNIC GROUPS IN LATIN AMERICA AND THE CARIBBEAN

The cultures of Latin America are diverse. Each region has its own character, which reflects its history. The languages, customs, beliefs, and even the foods from an area are a result of its history. Latin America also has diversity in its races. Europeans, Africans, and Native Americans were the largest groups. Members of these groups have intermarried and developed unique cultures over time.

Many of the Europeans that came to the New World in the sixteenth and seventeenth centuries forced the native people to work on plantations or in mines. Disease and death followed, and most of the natives on the islands were wiped out. However, in Central and South America, many Native Americans were able to preserve their cultures by moving to remote mountain or forest regions.

In order to get workers, Europeans brought Africans to the New World and forced them to work as slaves. Descendants of these people live there today. There are also people of mixed ancestry. **Mulattoes** in Brazil, Panama, and the West Indies are numerous. Their ancestors were both African and European. Most of the people in Venezuela are **mestizos**. Their ancestors were both European and Native American.

The main religion in Latin America and the Caribbean is Roman Catholic. However, the practices of Native Americans and Africans have blended with Roman Catholic beliefs. Unique festivals such as the "Day of the Dead" in Mexico are one result. This holiday coincides with the Catholic All Saints' Day. The Day of the Dead blends Native American beliefs about the afterlife with Roman Catholic beliefs. Religions based on African traditional beliefs are also present. Cuba, for instance, has groups that practice **Santeria**. In Peru and Bolivia, many native people continue their traditional beliefs and ceremonies.

The groups in Latin America are proud of their heritage. There are some problems, though. People with European ancestors often have more important jobs, better education and health care, and more money than others. Native Americans, blacks, and mestizos have begun to demand equality in their countries. In Bolivia, for instance, a Native American was elected president for the first time in 2005.

_____ 53. **What are the three main sources of the cultural groups of Latin America and the Caribbean?**
A. Africans, Mulattoes, Catholics
B. Africans, Europeans, Native Americans
C. Mestizos, Native Americans, Europeans
D. Native Americans, Mulattoes, Europeans

_____ 54. **In Latin America and the Caribbean, people with which ethnic background often have better jobs and more money?**
A. African
B Mestizo
C. European
D. Native American

_____55. **How is the "Day of the Dead" an example of blended culture?**
   A. It is celebrated by traditional African cultures.
   B. A Roman Catholic holiday is given a new name in Mexico.
   C. The Roman Catholic holiday is celebrated in a way which includes Native American traditions.
   D. The traditional Native American belief is celebrated in the same way that it has been for thousands of years.

_____56. **What is one cause for the blending of cultures in Latin America and the Caribbean?**
   A. Men and women from different ethnic groups intermarried.
   B. Native Americans adapted their beliefs to the beliefs of other people.
   C. The rugged land of Central and South America kept the people apart.
   D. People from different ethnic groups enjoyed learning about other cultures.

> **SS6G4 The student will describe the cultural characteristics of people who live in Latin America and the Caribbean.**
> b. Explain why Latin America is a region based on the languages of Portuguese and Spanish.

THE REGION OF "LATIN AMERICA" AND ITS RELATIONSHIP TO SPANISH AND PORTUGUESE LANGUAGES

Christopher Columbus made his first famous voyage to the New World in 1492. He was working for the king and queen of Spain trying to find a quick and safe passage to China. He hoped such a passage would be profitable to him and the Spanish king and queen. Of course, we now know that Columbus did not reach China or anywhere in Asia. He had, in fact, "discovered" continents unknown to the Europeans at that time.

Over the next two hundred years, Spain, its neighbor Portugal, and other European countries sent ships to explore these new lands. The Spanish explored, conquered, and settled areas of Florida, Mexico, and large parts of Central and South America. The Spanish also claimed many islands of the West Indies. Portugal's claim was Brazil. This land stretched from the Atlantic Ocean across South America to the Andes Mountains. It covered most of the vast Amazon River region. The Spanish and Portuguese spread their culture and religion across the region and developed communities that were similar to their home countries.

The Portuguese and Spanish followed similar patterns in their history in the region. Each conquered the native population and attempted to use these people as a source of slave labor. Africans were later imported as slaves to work in mines and large farms such as sugar cane plantations.

The British colonies in North America fought for independence from their mother country, **Great Britain**. In the same way, the regions of Central and South America fought for independence from Spain and Portugal. Spain lost Mexico in the early 1800s. By 1898, Puerto Rico, the last Spanish colony in the New World, had been ceded to the United States.

French, English, Dutch, and hundreds of native languages are spoken in Central and South America and the Caribbean. Despite this fact, the term **Latin America** was started in the 1800s to group the countries that spoke mostly languages based on the ancient Latin language (Spanish and Portuguese). The shared history and culture, and the dominance of Portuguese and Spanish languages, have made the term **Latin America** one that unites Central and South America and the Caribbean based on its two primary languages. The English language is based on an ancient German language. So, English-speaking countries of North America are not included in the term **Latin America**.

_____**57.** **What are the two primary languages of Latin America?**
    A. English and French
    B. French and Spanish
    C. Portuguese and English
    D. Spanish and Portuguese

_____**58.** **On what common language are the languages of Spain and Portugal based?**
    A. Spanish
    B. Portuguese
    C. ancient Latin
    D. ancient German

_____**59.** **Why does the term *Latin America* fit as a description for the regions of Central and South America and the Caribbean?**
    A. The people in these countries speak Latin.
    B. The countries share similar histories and culture.
    C. The people in these countries speak languages that come from Latin.
    D. The countries share similar histories and culture, and they mostly speak languages based on Latin.

_____**60.** **Which countries are included in the term *Latin America*?**
    A. all countries that speak Latin
    B. countries located in North America
    C. countries in Central and South America and the Caribbean
    D. countries in Central and South America, but not those in the Caribbean

Map of European Claims in America 1763

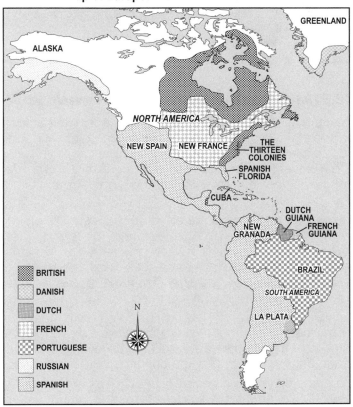

61. Which European counties claimed the most territory in South America in 1763?
A. France and Spain
B. Portugal and Spain
C Brazil and La Plata
D. Portugal and the Netherlands (Dutch)

62. Which European countries claimed small portions of South America in 1763?
A. Portugal and Spain
B. Brazil and La Plata
C. New Granada and La Plata
D. the Netherlands (Dutch) and France

63. Which modern-day countries are located in the land labeled New Spain?
A. Spain and Portugal
B. United States and Brazil
C. Mexico and United States
D. Mexico and North America

64. The region labeled New Spain was claimed by what country?
A. Spain
B. Brazil
C. Portugal
D. Great Britain

> **SS6G4 The student will describe the cultural characteristics of people who live in Latin America and the Caribbean.**
> c. Evaluate how the literacy rate affects the standard of living.

LITERACY AND THE STANDARD OF LIVING IN LATIN AMERICA

A *literate* person is one who can read and write. Literacy is a major factor in whether a person is able to get a job and be successful in the workplace. The countries of Latin America have improved the *literacy rate* of their people. On average, 89 percent of the people in Latin America and the Caribbean are literate. That leaves an *illiteracy rate* of 11 percent. The *standard of living* (the "economic level" achieved by a person, family, or country) is often lower in countries where the illiteracy rate is high.

In some cultures, it is believed to be more important for boys to have an education than girls. This fact is shown in the fact that 12 percent of girls are illiterate in this region while only 9 percent of boys are illiterate. In some countries, the difference between boys' and girls' literacy rates is very large. In other countries, the illiteracy rates are about the same. Either way, the goal of most governments is to have 100 percent literacy among their people. Many governments, missionaries, and aid groups come to the poorest of these countries to assist the people in educating all their children.

One reason that many of the poor cannot learn to read and write is because their communities cannot afford to pay for teachers and schools. Having these basic skills, however, is important. Without the basic skills of reading and writing, workers are stuck in the lowest-paying jobs. Countries with large numbers of illiterate workers cannot build and operate modern industries.

A cycle of poverty can develop in which people cannot get an education, so they can only get low-paying jobs. Because they can only get low-paying jobs, they cannot get enough money to pay for their children's education. The standard of living remains low for these families because their education level remains low.

_____ 65. **When a person is literate, that means that the person can**

    A. read and write.

    B. get a good job.

    C. have a greater standard of living.

    D. pay for his or her child's education.

_____ 66. **Which is often an effect of a high literacy rate?**

    A. a higher illiteracy rate

    B. lower education levels

    C. a lower standard of living

    D. a higher standard of living

67. Why do some countries have higher literacy rates for boys than for girls?

   A. Boys enjoy learning to read and write more than girls do.

   B. Girls enjoy learning to read and write more than boys do.

   C. Some cultures believe that it is not as important for girls to learn to read and write as it is for boys.

   D. Some cultures believe that it is not as important for boys to learn to read and write as it is for girls.

68. An illiterate person is most likely to have all of the following EXCEPT

   A. a large home.

   B. a low-paying job.

   C. a lower standard of living.

   D. children who cannot read and write.

Use the following graph to answer questions 69-72.

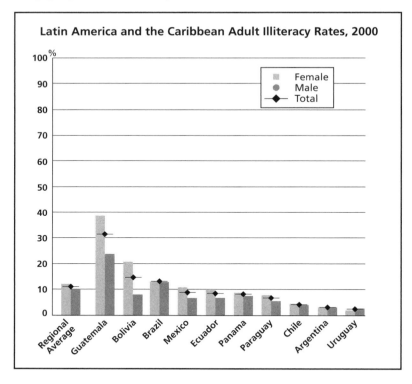

Latin America and the Caribbean Adult Illiteracy Rates, 2000

Legend:
- Female
- Male
- Total

_____69. **Which country has the best rates of literacy for its people?**
A. Brazil
B. Uruguay
C. Argentina
D. Guatemala

_____70. **Which country has the greatest difference between boys' and girls' literacy rates?**
A. Brazil
B. Uruguay
C. Argentina
D. Guatemala

_____71. **If a businesswoman wanted to build a factory and have educated workers, which country would be the best choice?**
A. Brazil
B. Bolivia
C. Mexico
D. Guatemala

_____72. **Which county has a literacy rate better than the regional average?**
A. Chile
B. Brazil
C. Bolivia
D. Guatemala

SS6G5 The student will locate selected features of Canada.

a. Locate on a world and regional political-physical map: the St. Lawrence River, Hudson Bay, Atlantic Ocean, Pacific Ocean, the Great Lakes, Canadian Shield, and Rocky Mountains.

LOCATING PHYSICAL FEATURES OF CANADA

In order to learn more about Canada, start by learning its location. Look at the map that follows and put your finger on the United States. Move your finger north, and you'll land in Canada! From Canada's point of view, its entire southern border is with the United States. Notice the three oceans around Canada. The Atlantic Ocean is on the east. The Pacific Ocean is on the west. To the north is the **Arctic Ocean**. **Hudson Bay** extends far into Canada and connects to the Atlantic Ocean. Along the western border is the U.S. state of Alaska.

Canada has many rivers. One of the most important is the **St. Lawrence River**. It stretches from Lake Ontario to the Gulf of St. Lawrence on the Atlantic side of the country. Look on the map and find the eastern point of Lake Ontario. Follow the river eastward, and you will pass Montreal and Quebec City before reaching the Gulf of St. Lawrence. This river was important to Canada's history because it allowed explorers to travel deep into North America by water. It is an important natural resource today as a source of water and as a trade route.

Canada is home to many lakes. The **Great Lakes** form part of the border with the United States. Lake Superior, Lake Huron, Lake Erie, and Lake Ontario are split between the United States and Canada. Lake Michigan is entirely within the United States.

The **Canadian Shield** covers a large part of eastern and central Canada. It has ancient rock just below and sometimes sticking out of the soil. The area is known for its thin, rocky soil and rough, rolling landscape. This region has many lakes and rivers and is rich in minerals.

On the west, the **Rocky Mountains** are an impressive feature. These mountains stretch over 3,000 miles, from British Columbia in Canada to New Mexico in the United States. Mount Robson is the tallest peak in the Canadian Rockies at nearly 13,000 feet.

Study each of the landforms and features that were mentioned and learn their locations on the map. Knowing the location of important places will help you better understand the people that live in those places.

Canada

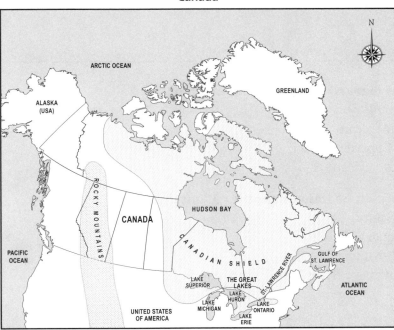

Use the information in the passage and the following map to answer questions 73-76.

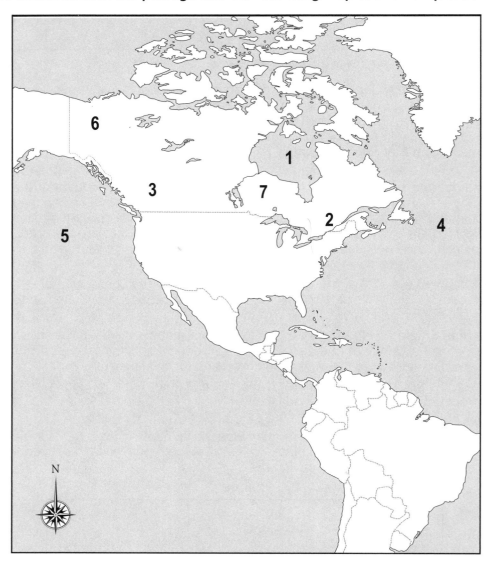

____73. **Which is marked with a "1" on the map?**
   A. Hudson Bay
   B. Pacific Ocean
   C. Lake Superior
   D. Atlantic Ocean

____74. **Which would be found near the "3" on the map?**
   A. Lake Huron
   B. Canadian Shield
   C. Rocky Mountains
   D. St. Lawrence River

_____75. **Which number is closest to the St. Lawrence River?**
   A. 2
   B. 3
   C. 6
   D. 7

_____76. **Which would be found near the "7" on the map?**
   A. Lake Huron
   B. Canadian Shield
   C. Rocky Mountains
   D. St. Lawrence River

_____77. **Which country borders Canada?**
   A. Cuba
   B. Mexico
   C. Panama
   D. United States

_____78. **Which area is known for its rolling, rocky land covering eastern and central Canada?**
   A. Lake Huron
   B. Canadian Shield
   C. Rocky Mountains
   D. St. Lawrence River

LOCATION OF CANADA

Canada is the largest country in the Western Hemisphere in land area. It is the second-largest country by land area in the entire world. Its southern border stretches across the northern United States. It is bounded by three oceans: the Atlantic on the east, the Arctic on the north, and the Pacific to the west. Alaska forms part of Canada's western border. From a polar point of view, the country is in an important position between the United States and Russia.

The population of Canada, about 33 million, is small compared to its land area. Mexico has about three times the number of people of Canada. The United States has about nine times the number of people of Canada. Most Canadians live on the southern border with the United States. About 90 percent of Canadians live within 100 miles of the border with the United States. Most of these live toward the east and central parts of the country.

Most Canadians live in cities or towns. Only about 20 percent of the people live in rural areas. Just over half of the population lives in one of four zones. The **Golden Horseshoe** zone lies around the southern end of Lake Ontario and includes Toronto. About one-fourth of all Canadians live in this zone. Another one-fourth of Canadians live in the three areas of Montréal, British Columbia's Victoria region and southern Vancouver Island, and the Calgary-Edmonton area.

The Great Lakes and the St. Lawrence River provide important trade routes into central Canada from the Atlantic Ocean. Excellent railroads and highways carry goods shipped to either coast. There are nine major seaports that help the country to trade with other countries around the world.

_____79. **Which country is the second largest in the world in land area?**
A. Alaska
B. Russia
C. Canada
D. United States

_____80. **Which statement is true about where people in Canada live?**
A. They mostly live in rural areas.
B. Most people live in the Toronto area.
C. They live north of Ontario and Quebec.
D. Most Canadians live within 100 miles of the U.S. border.

_____81. **Which statement best describes Canada's population?**
A. Mexico has a smaller population than Canada.
B. The United States has a smaller population than Canada.
C. Canada has a large population compared to the size of its land area.
D. Canada has a small population compared to the size of its land area.

CLIMATE OF CANADA

Although Canada is a large country, the climate of the country keeps most of its people living in just a few areas. Most of the southeastern part of Canada has a humid continental climate. This zone is between the subtropical climate to the south and the subarctic climate in the north. It has warm to hot summers and cold winters. There can be up to 60 inches of precipitation a year. Snowfall can exceed 100 inches a year in some parts of eastern Canada. The climate in the southern and central parts of the country allows for a long growing season. Canada's central plains are important source of canola, wheat, and other grains.

The area along the Pacific coast has a temperate climate. The ocean cools the region in summer and keeps it warmer in winter. This region can get over 100 inches of rain a year. Most of this precipitation comes in winter.

Moving northward, Canada becomes much colder. Few Canadians live in the northern regions for this reason. The subarctic and arctic regions of Canada have long, cold winters and short, cool summers. It's possible to have temperatures below freezing even in the summer.

_____82. **What climate feature keeps most Canadians living in the southern part of their country?**
A. The south has over 100 inches of rain a year.
B. The south has over 100 inches of snow a year.
C. The north has very little precipitation each year.
D. The north has very cold winters and cool summers.

_____83. **Which part of Canada has subarctic and arctic climates?**
A. east
B. west
C. north
D. south

_____84. **The humid continental climate that covers a large part of Canada helps the country with which type of business?**
A fishing
B. mining
C. farming
D. shipping

NATURAL RESOURCES OF CANADA

Canadians have a country rich in **natural resources** (gifts of nature). Some of the most important of these resources are iron ore, nickel, zinc, copper, gold, lead, molybdenum, potash, diamonds, and silver. The large number of rivers and lakes are an excellent source of fish, fresh water, and hydroelectric power. Good soil allows farmers to grow crops for the people of Canada with enough left over to trade with other countries. The forests are a major natural resource along with abundant wildlife. Coal, oil, and natural gas are in large supply as well. Canadians have enough of these energy resources to supply their needs and sell the rest to other countries.

Because many of the natural resources of Canada are found in remote areas, Canadians are spread across their country. Small communities are found across Canada where mining and farming are important. Workers are needed to fish in rivers and at sea. Goods from these types of businesses are shipped by rail or highway to the larger cities for trade with other parts of Canada and the world.

_____85. **Which are important natural resources of Canada?**
   A. coal, oil, water
   B. oil, timber, workers
   C. fish, timber, railroads
   D. highways, natural gas, wildlife

_____86. **Why do Canadians live all across their large country?**
   A. They do not like living so close to one another.
   B. Many of their natural resources are in remote areas.
   C. Cities have most of the natural resources they need to live.
   D. Natural resources of Canada are mostly within 100 miles of the U.S. border.

_____87. **What types of communities are usually found in areas where mining and farming are important?**
   A. large cities
   B. campgrounds
   C. fishing villages
   D. small communities

_____88. **Why is it good for Canada that it has enough oil and natural gas to sell?**
   A. It can help other countries that don't have these resources.
   B. Canadians don't need as much oil and natural gas as people in other countries do.
   C. It can supply its own energy needs and doesn't have to depend on other countries.
   D. Canadians use more oil and natural gas than people in other countries but it costs them less.

SS6G6 The student will explain the impact of location, climate, distribution of natural resources, and population distribution on Canada.

b. Describe how Canada's location, climate, and natural resources impact trade.

HOW CANADA'S LOCATION, CLIMATE, AND NATURAL RESOURCES IMPACT TRADE

Canada's location in the world helps it to be a leader in world trade. Canada is uniquely located on three oceans: the Arctic, the Atlantic, and the Pacific. This gives the country wonderful opportunities to trade with both Europe and Asia. From a polar point of view, the vast country of Russia is nearby. When sea lanes are open, travel across the Arctic Ocean is possible. Canada has nine major ports and numerous smaller ones. These ports allow goods to be shipped into and out of Canada easily without having to travel through other countries. Canada's rivers help traders as well. The St. Lawrence River served as a highway for early European explorers. Today, the Great Lakes and St. Lawrence Seaway network allow goods to be shipped to and from the central part of Canada to the Atlantic Ocean. A major benefit for Canada is its location north of the United States. The two countries share over 3,000 miles of border. Trade across this long border is relatively easy, and Canadian businesses depend on easy trade of their goods and services to make their businesses successful. About 80 percent of Canada's exports come to the United States.

The climate of Canada helps the country trade with other countries. Though much of the northern part of the country has a rough, cold climate, the southern part is good for farming. A long growing season and good rainfall helps Canada produce canola, wheat, and other grains in large quantities. These are exported to other countries and traded for goods and services that are not available in Canada. Even though the climate overall is colder than the United States, it is not so harsh that trade cannot take place in the winter. An excellent system of highways, railroads, and air transportation has been built and adapted to the colder climate.

Canada's natural resources are very important to its ability to trade with other countries. Canada sells oil and natural gas, fish, agricultural products, and timber to other countries. Electricity is made at hydroelectric power plants along Canada's rivers. Extra energy not needed by Canadians is sold to the United States. About 5 percent of the land in Canada is arable. However, because there is so much land, that 5 percent is actually a large amount of land. The rich soil helps to produce valuable crops consumed in Canada and traded to other countries.

_____89. **Which condition makes it easy for Canada to trade with the United States?**

A. The countries share a border over 3,000 miles long.

B. Canada has easy access to seven major ports on three oceans.

C. The countries have abundant natural resources and a long growing season.

D. Canada has many natural resources and goods that are not available in the United States.

_____90. **Which geophysical area is most important to help businesses in central Canada move goods to countries in Europe?**

A. the Canadian Shield

B. the Rocky Mountains

C. the ports on the Pacific Ocean

D. the Great Lakes and the St. Lawrence Seaway

_____ 91. **Why is timber an important natural resource for export by Canadian businesses?**
    A. There are more trees available than the Canadians can use themselves.
    B. There are fewer trees in Canadian forests than in most forests of the world.
    C. Many countries in the world trade with Brazil to get the timber that they need.
    D. Many countries in the Western Hemisphere trade only with Latin American countries.

_____ 92. **How are Canadians able to produce enough food for their own use and still have food to sell to other countries when only 5 percent of the land is arable?**
    A. Canadians do not eat as much food as other people.
    B. Canadians buy most of their food from other countries.
    C. Canada is a very large country, so 5 percent arable land is quite a lot of land.
    D. Canada has lots of technology that they use to grow more crops on a small amount of land.

Use the graph to answer questions 93-96.

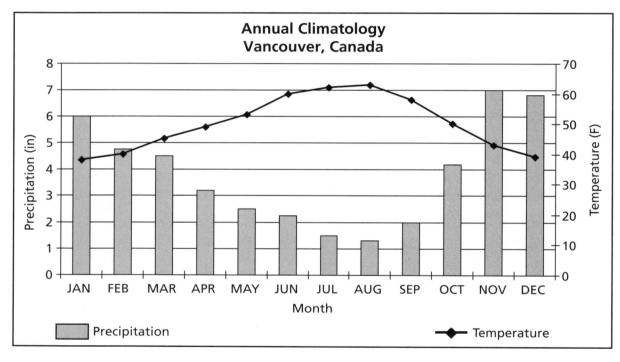

_____ 93. **What month is usually the driest in Vancouver, Canada?**
    A. April
    B. August
    C. January
    D. November

_____ 94. **What month is usually the coldest in Vancouver, Canada?**
    A. April
    B. August
    C. January
    D. November

LATIN AMERICA AND CANADA

_____95. **About how many inches of precipitation does Vancouver have in January?**
   A. 4
   B. 6
   C. 40
   D. 60

_____96. **Which sentence BEST summarizes the information in the graph?**
   A. Vancouver is hottest and driest in summer.
   B. Vancouver is hottest and wettest in summer.
   C. Summer and winter have similar temperatures but more rain in winter.
   D. Summer and winter have similar precipitation, but it's colder in winter.

> **SS6G7 The student will discuss environmental issues in Canada.**
>
> a. Explain the major environmental concerns of Canada regarding acid rain and pollution of the Great Lakes, the extraction and use of natural resources on the Canadian Shield, and timber resources.

Canada faces a number of environmental issues. It has many natural resources that it can use for its people and for trade to other countries. Some of the natural resources are renewable, and some are nonrenewable. The country must find ways to carefully manage both types of resources so that the environment is not damaged. Industries help Canada have a good economy with a high standard of living. However, factories are a source of pollution. Canada must find ways to keep its industry alive without destroying its environment.

ACID RAIN

Factories and automobiles produce many pollutants. Depending on what a factory makes, it can put many different pollutants into the air. Coal-burning power plants, cars, and trucks are also polluters of the air. Sulfur dioxide, carbon dioxide, and nitrogen oxides are especially dangerous. When these pollutants are put into the air, they mix with the water molecules and turn the water acidic. Clouds or rain droplets that are acidic are called **acid rain.**

Acid rain causes many problems in the environment. Acid levels can become similar to the levels of acid in vinegar. This level of acid can kill plants, damage or kill trees, and pollute lakes and rivers enough to kill the fish. Property can be damaged too. In some cities, acid rain has dissolved the stone used in statues. The statues of people, for instance, lose their crisp facial features and begin to look smoothed and worn down.

Canada has passed laws to limit pollution. The government has worked with factory owners to build factories that do not pollute the air. Laws have been passed requiring automobiles to produce less pollution. The government also encourages Canadians to walk, ride bikes, or take the bus instead of driving their cars. Canada cannot solve this problem alone, however. In parts of southern Canada, 50-75 percent of the pollution that causes acid rain comes from the United States. Wind patterns tend to move the pollution from the United States north into Canada.

_____97. **Rain mixes with which substances to become acidic?**
   A. sulfur dioxide, oxygen, hydrogen
   B. hydrogen, oxygen, carbon dioxide
   C. water molecules, carbon dioxide, hydrogen
   D. sulfur dioxide, carbon dioxide, nitrogen oxide

_____98. **Which are sources of chemicals in acid rain?**
   A. forests
   B. walkers
   C bicycles
   D. coal-burning power plants

_____99. **Canada has to work with the United States to solve the problem of acid rain because the United States**
   A. is the source of much of Canada's air pollution.
   B. purchases many of the goods that Canada produces in its factories.
   C. has reduced the amount of acid rain and understands how to solve the problem.
   D. is careful to keep air pollution from leaving the United States and entering Canada.

Use the statements below to answer question 100.

1. Fish in lakes die.
2. Forests begin to die.
3. Bicycle use increases.
4. Stone statues begin to lose their features.

_____ 100. **Which statements are problems that result from acid rain?**
   A. 1, 2, 3
   B. 2, 3, 4
   C. 1, 2, 4
   D. 1, 3, 4

WHAT ARE THE SOURCES OF SULFUR DIOXIDE (SO$_2$) IN THE AIR?

Use the two graphs to answer questions 101-104.

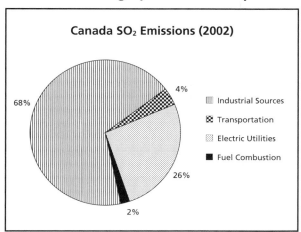

Canada SO$_2$ Emissions (2002)

68%
4%
26%
2%

- Industrial Sources
- Transportation
- Electric Utilities
- Fuel Combustion

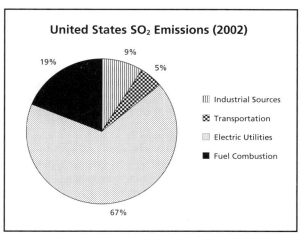

United States SO$_2$ Emissions (2002)

9%
5%
19%
67%

- Industrial Sources
- Transportation
- Electric Utilities
- Fuel Combustion

____ **101. The purpose of these graphs is to show**
   A. the sources of SO$_2$ pollution in the United States and Canada.
   B. that the United States creates more SO$_2$ pollution than Canada.
   C. that Canada creates more SO$_2$ pollution than the United States.
   D. the sources of all air pollution in the United States and Canada.

____ **102. Which source of pollution is the greatest producer of SO$_2$ in the United States?**
   A. electric utilities
   B. fuel combustion
   C. industrial sources
   D. transportation (cars, trucks, etc.)

____ **103. What is the second leading source of SO$_2$ in Canada?**
   A. electric utilities
   B. fuel combustion
   C. industrial sources
   D. transportation (cars, trucks, etc.)

____ **104. How does SO$_2$ pollution from transportation compare between the two countries?**
   A. They are about the same.
   B. Canada has a much higher percentage.
   C. The United States has a much higher percentage.
   D. There is no SO$_2$ pollution from transportation in the two countries.

LATIN AMERICA AND CANADA

POLLUTION OF THE GREAT LAKES

Industries and people in Canada depend upon the water from the Great Lakes. They use the water to drink. They also use it in the processes of their factories. Since the Great Lakes are shared between the United States and Canada, it is important for the two countries to work together to keep the lakes' environment clean and healthy.

By the 1970s, the Great Lakes were becoming well known for their water pollution. In some places, fishing was unsafe. In other places, there were no fish alive! The factories around the Great Lakes had been using the lakes as their inexpensive dumping ground. In 1972, the governments of the two countries signed an agreement to begin reduction of **phosphorus**. This chemical is used in fertilizer, pesticides, toothpaste, detergents, and explosives. It is bad for lakes because, in large quantities, it can cause a rapid increase in algae called an **algal bloom**. One result from algal blooms is the eventual death of plant and animal life in the area of the bloom.

The Great Lakes Water Quality Agreement between the United States and Canada was signed in 1971 and renewed in 2002. The goal of the agreement is to restore the lakes' environment and prevent further damage. The countries are working to make sure that chemicals that could poison animals and people are not put into the lakes. The countries are also working to reduce the amount of human wasted dumped into the lakes.

_____ 105. **The first Canadian-American plan to clean the Great Lakes was to reduce which chemical?**
A. detergent
B. fertilizer
C. pesticide
D. phosphorus

_____ 106. **Why does the Canadian government have to work with the U.S. government to clean up the Great Lakes?**
A. The two countries share the water in the lakes.
B. The two countries put different types of pollution in the lakes.
C. Animals and plants in the lakes depend on people to clean up the water.
D. Animals and plants in the lakes are not important to the people of either country.

_____ 107. **Which people are likely to be against the Great Lakes Water Quality Treatment Agreement?**
A. fishermen who catch fish in the lakes
B. homeowners who live along the lakes
C. factory owners in the area of the lakes
D. people who get their drinking water from the lakes

EXTRACTION AND USE OF NATURAL RESOURCES ON THE CANADIAN SHIELD

The Canadian Shield is a large area of uplands surrounding Hudson Bay. This region covers most of the eastern half of Canada. The soil in the region is thin and rocky. Beneath the soil is one of Canada's most valuable resources–minerals. The mines in this region produce gold, silver, copper, zinc, lead, iron ore, uranium, and nickel. In fact, the most valuable minerals available in Canada are in the Canadian Shield. About 1.5 million people make their living in the mining industry in Canada–many of them in the Canadian Shield.

Mining can be messy work. The land around mines can be damaged and the environment ruined. Blasting and digging with heavy machinery are common activities in mining areas. *Slag*, or leftover rock from the smelting process, is often dumped in any convenient place. Mining processes can spew sulfur dioxide, SO_2, into the air, producing acid rain and killing nearby vegetation and lake animals. Chemicals from the mines that are dumped into rivers and streams can poison the water and kill animal and plant life.

The Canadian Shield's minerals are also near the most populated areas of Canada. Pollution related to mining can have an impact on the large metropolitan areas to the south. The government has made new rules about mining. Some of the new rules reduce the amount of pollution allowed in waterways. Canada's government hopes to keep its fish alive and safe to eat without shutting down important mining industries.

_____ 108. **Where in Canada are the most valuable minerals found?**

    A. Hudson Bay

    B. Canadian Shield

    C. Golden Horseshoe

    D. St. Lawrence Seaway

_____ 109. **Which is a benefit of mining in Canada?**

    A. Valuable mining lands are located near cities.

    B. Waterways are polluted in the process of mining.

    C. Over 1.5 million people work in the mining industry.

    D. Sulfur dioxide (SO_2) is spewed into the air and lands in waterways.

_____ 110. **Why is the Canadian Shield important to the economy of Canada?**

    A. It contains large, valuable mineral deposits.

    B. Mining operations look for new deposits of minerals.

    C. It is close to many of the large metropolitan areas of Canada.

    D. There are many ways that the environment can be damaged by mining.

THE TIMBER INDUSTRY IN CANADA

Vast forests cover almost half the land in Canada. Canadians have made this natural resource important to the economy. Loggers cut the trees and then send them to mills. These mills use the timber to make a variety of products including lumber, plywood, and wood pulp for making many kinds of paper.

Forests serve an important role in the environment. Animals and plants depend on the forests to live. Forests also serve to provide oxygen to the atmosphere and to filter out pollutants in the air. Forests serve as homes for wildlife and areas for human recreation.

Citizens in Canada are concerned that logging will destroy the forests and the benefits that it brings. A major concern for many Canadians is **clear-cutting**. Most timber companies cut all the trees in a given area, leaving large treeless gaps in the forest. Results of clear-cutting include reduced water quality, erosion, and loss of wildlife habitat. Heavy machinery can leave the forest floor compacted. This makes it hard for new growth to start. Some environmental groups want companies to leave small trees and seedlings. They also want to see smaller groups of trees removed instead of hundreds of acres of trees at a time.

The government and industry are working together to try to manage the use of the forests. Hundreds of millions of seeds and seedlings are planted each year. Billions of dollars are spent managing and protecting the forests. Over $100 million is spent each year by the logging industry to protect wildlife and their habitats.

_____ **111. Forests cover about how much land in Canada?**
   A. one-half
   B. one-third
   C. one-fourth
   D. three-fourths

_____ **112. Which is a problem related to clear-cutting?**
   A. Soil is turned up.
   B. Erosion of soil stops.
   C. Timber companies save money.
   D. Wildlife loses large areas of habitat.

_____ **113. What is the government of Canada doing to protect the forests?**
   A. planting seeds and seedlings
   B. spending billions of dollars selling forests
   C. encouraging clear-cutting to keep lumber costs down
   D. providing new homes for wildlife and new areas for human recreation

CIVICS/GOVERNMENT UNDERSTANDINGS

SS6CG1   The student will compare and contrast various forms of government.
a. Describe the ways government systems distribute power: unitary, confederation, and federal.

Every country has a government that is set up in its own distinct way. One thing that a country has to decide is how to organize the government and distribute power. The power of the government can be organized so that there is one central government that controls all other governments in the country. Power can also be spread out so that there is not one central government but many smaller governments in the country working at different levels. Governments in each country are different, but there are three main ways they are organized to spread their power: unitary government, confederation government, and federal government.

UNITARY GOVERNMENT

In a ***unitary*** form of government, a central government operates all levels of government in the country. This single government assigns power to provincial or state governments and to local governments. For example, a leader in such a government might have the power to choose the governor of a region or the mayor of a town. This kind of central government can give power to a legislature in an area to govern itself. Then, it could decide to dissolve that legislature and control the region again directly.

There are many countries in the world organized in this way. In the western hemisphere, Cuba and Bolivia are two examples. In Europe, Great Britain and France are examples of countries with unitary governments. Counties in England, for example, are similar to states in the United States. However, English counties have leaders that report to the central government in London. The power of these leaders is limited to whatever duties they have been assigned by the central government.

Unitary government is not the structure of the United States government. Our Congress, for example, does not have the power to dissolve the Georgia legislature or appoint a new governor for Georgia if the current one needs replacement. Georgia itself has a unitary government, however. The state has the power to create cities and counties or to break up counties and dissolve county and city governments, if it so desires.

_____ **114. How is power distributed in a unitary government?**
   A. One ruler makes all the decisions for a country.
   B. Smaller units of government, like counties, control the central government.
   C. A central government assigns power and duties to smaller units of government within the country.
   D. The central government does not have much power over the smaller units of government in the country.

_____ **115. Which could happen in a country with a unitary government?**
   A. Each of the counties in the country creates its own money.
   B. A state government removes the president of the country and picks a new president.
   C. The national government removes the governor of the state and picks a new governor.
   D. Each of the states in a country writes its own laws, which may be different from the laws of the other states.

LATIN AMERICA AND CANADA

- Bolivia
- Cuba
- France
- Great Britain

_____ 116. **How are these countries alike?**

    A. They have a unitary style of government.

    B. They do not have a unitary style of government.

    C. The countries do not have a strong central government.

    D. The countries have one leader to follow in the government.

CONFEDERATION GOVERNMENT

Some countries might agree that they would be better able to solve problems or provide for their people if they worked together. They might sign a treaty or a constitution under which the countries agree to defend each other, to sign treaties with other countries, to trade with other countries, or to agree to a common currency. Such a group would be called a **confederation government**. A usual feature of the confederation is that membership is voluntary. A country can decide to leave at any time. Decisions by the confederation government may not be considered as law unless most, or all, of the member countries agree.

Confederations are not commonly found among governments in the twenty-first century. This is because there are several problems with them. They often have little power, because a very high percentage of the membership must agree to decisions made. Individual countries can often have a veto of any decision. Changes in the constitution of the confederation also require all members to agree. Considering the challenge of getting this much agreement, it's not surprising that confederations generally have a weak central government.

The United States tried this type of government under the Articles of Confederation. From 1777 to 1787, the states considered themselves to be separate countries. Each had more power than the confederation government. The weak central government became a problem because Congress could make decisions and laws but had no power to enforce them. Although Congress could not tax, it could request money from the states. The states could choose to send money, or not. The Articles of Confederation was replaced by the Constitution, which provided for a federal form of government.

_____ 117. **What is one problem with a confederation government?**

    A. The central government is too strong.

    B. The central government has too many taxes.

    C. The central government cannot have an army to defend itself.

    D. The central government can create laws but might not be able to enforce them.

_____ 118. **In a confederation, government power lies with**

    A. the people.

    B. a constitution.

    C. the central government.

    D. the governments of the member countries.

119. What is the MOST LIKELY reason a country would join a confederation with a weak central government?

A. The country is afraid it will be attacked.

B. The country does not want to have strong partners.

C. The country wants to keep most of the power for itself.

D. The country wants to send tax money to the central government.

FEDERAL GOVERNMENT

In a *federal* form of government, power is divided between the central government and small divisions, such as states. A document such as a constitution may describe the rights, responsibilities, and duties of the central government and the states. In this system, the central government can be quite powerful, but it does not have the ability to dissolve the states or choose the leaders in a state. Power to change the constitution may reside with the people directly, with the states, or with the people's representatives in the central government.

Many countries use this form of distributing government power. In the western hemisphere, Brazil, Canada, Mexico, the United States, and Venezuela are examples of countries with a federal system. A federal system does not mean that there is more or less personal freedom for the people of the country. It just explains how power is distributed.

In the United States, the federal government has powers that the states do not have, such as the power to declare war and sign treaties with other countries. Georgia cannot, for example, declare war on another country. States do have some powers that the federal government does not. For example, the federal government does not have the power to choose the governor of Georgia or create new counties in the state. Power to do those things is held by the state of Georgia and its people.

120. Which type of government divides power between the central government and smaller units such as states?

A. unitary

B. federation

C. totalitarian

D. confederation

121. What defines the rights, responsibilities, and duties of the central government and the states in a federal government?

A. the people

B. a constitution

C. the central government

D. governments of the states

122. Which could happen in a country with a federal government?

A. Each of the states in the country has its own governor and legislature.

B. The central government removes the governor of the state and picks a new governor.

C. A state government removes the president of the country and picks a new president.

D. Each of the states in a country writes its own laws, which may be different from the laws of the other states.

LATIN AMERICA AND CANADA

CITIZEN PARTICIPATION

In each country, the people have different rights to participate in the government. In some countries, any citizen can run for office or vote in elections. In other countries, there are restrictions placed on who can run for office and who can vote. There are also countries where no citizen can vote and there are no elections.

Autocratic Governments

An **autocratic government** has a single ruler with unlimited power. The word **autocracy** comes from the Greek words **autos** (meaning "self") and **kratos** (meaning "power"). The people in such a country have no ability to participate in the selection of the ruler or in the creation of laws. One benefit of this type of government is that decisions for a country can be made quickly. However, the needs of the people may be ignored or unheard. The leader may make poor or selfish decisions that work against the well-being of the people.

Examples of this type of government can be found in countries where rule is by a dictator or king with absolute power. The ancient Inca of South America had this type of government. Their ruler had absolute power over everyone in his empire.

Oligarchic Governments

Another type of government is "rule by a few." This is called an **oligarchy,** from the Greek words **oligos** (meaning "few") and **arkhos** (meaning "leader"). Under this system, a country is ruled by a small group of people. An advantage to this system is that decisions can be made relatively quickly. Compared to an autocratic system, oligarchies have more heads to think through problems and should be able to make better choices. However, like autocratic systems, the people do not have a voice, and poor and selfish decisions by leaders may work against the well-being of the other citizens.

Democratic Governments

A **democratic** form of government puts the power of the government in the citizens of the country. The word **democracy** comes from the Greek words **demos** (meaning "people") and **kratos** (meaning "power"). All citizens have the opportunity to be a leader, and all citizens have the opportunity to vote for leaders and laws. Advantages of this system include the fact that all citizens are involved in the decision-making process of the government, and all groups in the country are represented. Democratic governments can often be slow to make decisions since people must discuss and vote on issues. Also, every citizen may not have the information to be truly informed on all matters to make decisions.

In the twenty-first century, most democratic countries are **representative democracies**. In this type of democracy, the citizens of the country elect representatives to make decisions. A representative democracy allows citizens to choose leaders for a certain length of time. After that time, elections are held to choose new leaders. The United States is an example of a representative democracy. A **direct democracy** requires a vote by all citizens for every decision by the government.

LATIN AMERICA AND CANADA

Most countries in the world are officially labeled democracies. However, this does not mean that there are open and free elections in all of these countries. Cuba, for example, labels itself as a democracy. However, when elections are held, the Communist Party approves the candidates for each position. It is not possible for a person to be elected to office without the approval of the Communist Party. In Canada, citizens are allowed to run for a position in the House of Commons with few restrictions. Citizens vote for these law-making leaders. From among these people, a prime minister is selected to head the government. The queen or king of the United Kingdom is Canada's head of state. She or he requests that the prime minister select a governor general to represent her or him in the government.

123. **In which form of government would the "will of the people" MOST likely be the rule of law?**
    A. autocracy
    B. oligarchy
    C. direct democracy
    D. representative democracy

124. **Which form of government puts the power of the government in a single person?**
    A. autocracy
    B. oligarchy
    C. direct democracy
    D. representative democracy

125. **What is one disadvantage of a direct democracy?**
    A. Every citizen has the right to vote on issues.
    B. All groups in a country are represented when decisions are made.
    C. Decision making can be slow since many people's views must be heard.
    D. No one person has all the power, so poor or selfish decisions are less likely to be made by the government.

126. **Which is true about democracies?**
    A. Elections for leaders are a part of few democracies.
    B. There are many different ways to set up a democracy.
    C. Kings or queens rule autocratically in a democratic government.
    D. Laws created in a democracy are more likely to protect the parliament.

TWO PREDOMINANT FORMS OF DEMOCRATIC GOVERNMENTS

Democratic forms of government vary by country. Citizens take part in the government by voting on laws or electing leaders to make decisions. In a direct democracy, all citizens have the right to assemble and create the laws and make the decisions. Town meetings in some New England towns are like this. In a country with millions of citizens, this model is not practical. Instead, citizens elect leaders to make the decisions for the country. There are two main types of democratic government: parliamentary and presidential.

Parliamentary System

The parliamentary form of government is the most common type of democratic government. In a ***parliamentary system***, citizens elect members of parliament called **MP**s. The MPs choose a leader from among themselves called the ***prime minister***. The prime minister is the chief executive of the country. The ***chief executive*** heads the military, enforces laws, and keeps the country running day to day. The prime minister leads the lawmaking body—parliament. MPs are elected to serve for a certain amount of time, but the parliament can be dissolved and elections held again if the prime minister feels the government is not working well. If MPs believe that the prime minister is not making good decisions, they can vote to have new elections.

The country may have a king or queen with little ruling power or a president who serves as the head of state. In a parliamentary system, the ***head of state*** is the symbolic leader of the country. Australia, Canada, and the United Kingdom are examples of countries with a parliamentary system. The king or queen of the United Kingdom is the head of state for each of these countries.

Presidential System

In a ***presidential system***, the citizens elect the members of the legislature and the chief executive known as the president. The president serves as the head of state, runs the government on a day-to-day basis, and heads the military. However, the president does not make the laws. The legislature has the job of making laws. The president serves for a fixed amount of time; then elections are held again. The legislature does not have the power to force an early election, and the president does not have the power to dissolve the legislature. The United States, Mexico, and most South American countries have presidential democracies.

_____ 127. **How is the president in a presidential democracy like the prime minister in a parliamentary democracy?**

    A. They are both in charge of the legislature.

    B. Each leader is elected directly by the citizens of the country.

    C. They are both in charge of the military and the day-to-day operations of the country.

    D. Each leader is elected to serve for a fixed term, which cannot be changed by the legislature.

_____ 128. **Which is TRUE of a parliamentary democracy?**

    A. The prime minister is head of state.

    B. The president is the chief executive.

    C. The prime minister is the chief executive.

    D. The president is the head of the legislature.

_____ **129. A presidential democracy is used in which country?**
   A. Australia
   B. Canada
   C. Mexico
   D. United Kingdom

_____ **130. A parliamentary democracy is used in which country?**
   A. Brazil
   B. Canada
   C. Mexico
   D. Venezuela

_____ **131. Which is TRUE about how the president in a presidential democracy is different from the prime minister in a parliamentary democracy?**
   A. The prime minister is the head of state for the country, but the president is not.
   B. The prime minister is the chief executive and head of the military, but the president is not.
   C. The prime minister is elected directly by the people, but the president is elected by the legislature.
   D. The prime minister is chosen from among the members of parliament, but the president runs for office separately.

LATIN AMERICA AND CANADA

Government of the Federative Republic of Brazil

The government of Brazil is a federal government. Power is divided between the central government and the state and local governments. The government is very large. Brazil is a presidential democracy. The citizens elect the president, and they elect the members of the legislature, which is called the Congress.

Citizens of Brazil have many freedoms, and they also have the right to vote. Men and women who are 16-17 years old may choose to vote. Citizens who are 18-70 years old are required by law to vote. Those over 70 may choose to vote. There are many political parties. Most parties have particular beliefs that attract followers. Others center on particular people.

Brazil is a country that enjoys an average level of freedom compared to other countries in the world. Personal property rights are not always protected, and the court system cannot be trusted to help people in all cases.

_____ **132. What type of government exists in Brazil?**
  A. communist
  B. monarchy
  C. presidential democracy
  D. parliamentary democracy

_____ **133. Which term describes how political power is distributed in Brazil?**
  A. federal government
  B. unitary government
  C. aristocratic government
  D. confederation government

_____ **134. One way that Brazil's government is different from the U.S. government is that it**
  A. has a president as chief executive.
  B. does not allow 16-year-olds to vote.
  C. requires citizens aged 18-70 to vote.
  D. has a legislature called the Congress.

LATIN AMERICA AND CANADA

GOVERNMENT OF THE UNITED MEXICAN STATES

The government of Mexico is a federal government. Power is divided between the central government and the state and local governments. Mexico is a presidential democracy. The citizens elect the president who can serve one 6-year term. They also elect the members of the legislature, which is called the Congress.

Citizens of Mexico have many freedoms, and they also have the right to vote. Men and women who are citizens aged 18 years or over may choose to vote. There are many political parties. Most parties have particular beliefs that attract followers. Others center on particular people.

Mexico is a country that enjoys an average level of freedom compared to other countries in the world. The court system is managed by the central government, and is not totally independent of the president.

_____ 135. **What type of government exists in Mexico?**
   A. monarchy
   B. communist
   C. parliamentary democracy
   D. presidential democracy

_____ 136. **Which term describes how political power is distributed in Mexico?**
   A. federal government
   B. unitary government
   C. aristocratic government
   D. confederation government

_____ 137. **One way that Mexico's government is different from the U.S. government is that**
   A. the president is the chief executive.
   B. the legislature is called the Congress.
   C. citizens 18 years old and over may vote.
   D. presidents can only serve one 6-year term.

GOVERNMENT OF THE REPUBLIC OF CUBA

The government of Cuba is a unitary government. Power organized from a strong central government controls each of the smaller units in the country. Cuba is a communist dictatorship. The citizens do not elect the president. The president is appointed by the National Assembly of People's Power. Citizens may vote for members of the National Assembly of People's Power, but only for candidates approved by the Communist Party of Cuba. The Communist Party controls the central government and all aspects of smaller units of government.

Citizens of Cuba have few freedoms. Men and women who are citizens aged 16 years or over may choose to vote, but they have few options. Only one political party is allowed. It has been controlled by Fidel Castro and his brother Raúl since 1959.

Cuba is one of the least free countries in the world. The government controls nearly all aspects of life. There is little opportunity to own personal property. The government is large and controls almost all businesses, factories, and farms.

_____ **138. What type of government exists in Cuba?**
A. monarchy
B. dictatorship
C. presidential democracy
D. parliamentary democracy

_____ **139. Which term describes how political power is distributed in Cuba?**
A. federal government
B. unitary government
C. aristocratic government
D. confederation government

_____ **140. Which statement about political parties is true about Cuba?**
A. There are many political parties.
B. There is only one legal political party.
C. The leader of a political party cannot be president.
D. Those running for office may not be in the Communist Party.

Use the following chart to answer questions 141-143.

A Comparison of the National Governments of Brazil, Mexico, and Cuba

	Brazil	Mexico	Cuba
Full Name	Federative Republic of Brazil	United Mexican States	Republic of Cuba
Chief Executive	president (elected for 4-year term; 2 term limit)	president (elected to 6-year term; 1 term limit)	president (unlimited terms); also serves as first secretary of the Communist Party
Distribution of Power	federal	federal	unitary
Citizens' Role	16-17-year-olds and those over 70 may vote; 18-70-year-olds are required to vote	must be 18 years or older to vote	must be 16 years or older to vote
Citizens' Level of Personal Freedom (1 = most free; 159 = least free) World Average is 57.	59	52	157
Legislature	Congress	Congress	National Assembly of People's Power
Political Parties	many; people are free to join any they wish	many; people are free to join any they wish	one: Cuban Communist Party PCC; membership is very restricted

Level of personal freedom calculated by the State of World Liberty Project. The scale examines freedom to travel and trade, protection of personal property rights, freedom to conduct business, and taxation level. The United States is ranked very free with a score of 8.

141. **Citizens of which country are considered to have the least freedom?**
    A. Cuba
    B. Brazil
    C. Mexico
    D. United States

142. **Which country requires most adults to vote?**
    A. Cuba
    B. Brazil
    C. Mexico
    D. United States

143. **Which pair of countries have governments that are most similar?**
    A. Brazil and Cuba
    B. Mexico and Cuba
    C. Brazil and Mexico
    D. Cuba and United States

> **SS6CG3** **The student will explain the structure of the national government of Canada.**
>
> a. Describe the structure of the Canadian government as a constitutional monarchy, a parliamentary democracy, and a federation, distinguishing the role of the citizen in terms of voting and personal freedoms.

STRUCTURE OF THE CANADIAN GOVERNMENT

The government of Canada is a **constitutional monarchy**. The monarch (king or queen) of the United Kingdom is the head of state and traditional symbolic leader of the country. The king or queen has little real power. The constitution of Canada explains how the government is organized. The constitution also explains the rights of the citizens of Canada. The constitution includes limits on the power of the king or queen of the United Kingdom.

Canada has a parliamentary democracy. In a parliamentary democracy, citizens elect members of parliament called MPs, who in turn elect the prime minister. The prime minister is the chief executive of the country and heads the military, enforces laws, and keeps the country running day to day. The prime minister also leads the parliament. MPs are elected to serve for a certain amount of time, but the parliament can be dissolved and elections held again if the prime minister feels the government is not working well. If MPs believe that the prime minister is not making good decisions, they can vote to have new elections.

Canada also has a federal government. Power is divided between the central government and ten provinces. Canada's provinces can write their own laws and elect their own leaders. Parliaments in the provinces are organized in a way similar to the parliament of Canada. Instead of choosing a prime minister, provincial parliaments choose a **premier**.

Citizens of Canada have many freedoms, and they also have the right to vote. Men and women who are citizens aged 18 years or older may choose to vote. There are several political parties. The main political parties are Bloc Quebecois, Conservative Party of Canada, Green Party, Liberal Party, and New Democratic Party.

Canada has a level of personal freedom that is among the highest in the world. Citizens have the freedom to travel and trade. Personal property rights are protected by laws and enforced by an excellent court system.

_____ **144. What type of government exists in Canada?**

      A. monarchy

      B communist

      C. presidential democracy

      D. parliamentary democracy

_____ **145. Which term describes how political power is distributed in Canada?**

      A. federal government

      B. unitary government

      C. aristocratic government

      D. confederation government

____ **146. One way that Canada's government is different from the U.S. government is that Canada**

    A. has a federal form of government.

    B. allows citizens 18 years old and over to vote.

    C. elects leaders to make laws and run the government.

    D. has a monarch—that is a king or queen—as head of state.

____ **147. Which describes a right of the people in Canadian provinces in the federal system of Canada?**

    A. They can choose a new viceroy.

    B. They can print their own money.

    C. People can elect a new king or queen.

    D. People can elect their representatives to provincial parliaments.

LATIN AMERICA AND CANADA

ECONOMIC UNDERSTANDINGS

> **SS6E1** **The student will analyze different economic systems.**
> a. Compare how traditional, command, and market economies answer the economic questions of 1-what to produce, 2-how to produce, and 3-for whom to produce.

Scarcity is the limited supply of something. Every country must deal with the problem of scarcity. No country has everything that its people want and need. Therefore, every country must develop an **economic system** to determine how to use its limited resources to answer the three basic economic questions.

1. *What* goods and services will be produced?
2. *How* will goods and services be produced?
3. *Who* will consume the goods and services?

The way a society answers these questions determines its economic system. Three types of economic systems exist to answer these questions: traditional, command, and market.

TRADITIONAL ECONOMY

In a **traditional economy**, the customs and habits of the past are used to decide what and how goods will be produced, distributed, and consumed. In this system, each member of the society knows early in life what her or his role in the larger group will be. Because jobs are handed down from generation to generation, there is very little change in the system over the generations. In a traditional economy, people are depended upon to fulfill their traditional roles. If some people are not there to do their part, the system can break down. Farming, hunting and gathering, and cattle herding are often a part of a traditional economy.

An example of a traditional economy can be found in some native cultures of South America. For example, the Yanomamo Indians in Brazil and Venezuela have such an economy. The men, women, and children have specific jobs that involve raising their food in small gardens or hunting and gathering food from the Amazon rain forest. Each village is able to meet its needs with the resources that it gathers from the forest or from the crops grown in small gardens. The Yanomamo do not have a central government to tell the people what to grow. The government does not tell the Yanomamo what to gather or what to kill for food in the forest. The Yanomamo also do not have a system of buyers and sellers. The food grown in the village is not sold to villagers or to outsiders.

_____ 148. **What would be the MOST important factor in deciding what job you would do if you lived in a traditional economy?**
   A. the job your parents had
   B. how smart you were in school
   C. the types of factories in your area
   D. careers that you were most interested in

_____ 149. **What types of activities are often a part of traditional economies?**
   A. farming, herding livestock, hunting and gathering
   B. choosing careers, plantation farming, seeking new markets
   C. building new factories, expanding farms, selling goods to other tribes
   D. attracting buyers for traditional crafts, hunting wild animals, farming

150. Customs and habits are most important to which type of economy?
   A. mixed
   B. market
   C. command
   D. traditional

COMMAND ECONOMY

In a centralized ***command economy***, government planning groups make the basic economic decisions. They determine such things as which goods and services to produce, the prices, and wage rates. Individuals and corporations generally do not own businesses or farms themselves. These are owned by the government. Workers at a business are told what to produce and how much to produce in a given time. This is called a ***quota***. The government's goal is to assign quotas to all workers. The expectation is that when all workers meet all quotas, everyone in the country will be able to have the goods they need when they need them.

There are problems and benefits in this type of economy. One problem with the system is trying to predict exactly what goods people will need. For example, the government may think that building tractors is important. More tractors could mean that farmers can grow more crops. More crops mean that more people have the food they need. However, if factories are busy making tractors, they might not be making enough shoes. The people may end up with plenty of food but no shoes to wear.

A benefit of this economy is that prices are controlled and people know exactly how much everything will cost. For example, food prices are always kept low because food is a basic need of all people. The cost of clothing and housing is kept low as well. Health care and education are provided by the government at no cost. The cost of things that are considered luxuries, such as televisions or computers, may be very high since these are not considered basic needs. Wages for different jobs are also set by the government.

Cuba is a country that has a centralized command economy. The government owns all factories and most farms. About 90 percent of the people in Cuba work for the government. The Cuban government sets quotas for the farms and factories, and it tries to make sure that everyone's needs are met by setting the right quotas. Cuba trades goods to other countries for the goods that it cannot provide on its own. For instance, sugar cane is grown in large quantities. The sugar produced is sold to other countries in order to purchase oil and natural gas. Unfortunately, Cuba cannot sell enough sugar to pay for the oil and natural gas it needs. Sometimes the government has to close factories or shut off power in parts of the country to save energy.

151. In which type of economic system does the government control what a factory produces and what price it will charge for those products?
   A. mixed
   B. market
   C. command
   D. traditional

152. What is one problem faced by a command economy?
   A. Education is offered at no cost.
   B. Food prices are set at a low level.
   C. The price of housing is set at a low level.
   D. Shortages of goods may occur if the government cannot predict what the people need.

_____ **153. In a command economy, who usually owns the farms and factories?**
A. individuals
B. corporations
C. the government
D. farm and factory workers

_____ **154. What is one problem that Cuba faces in using a command economy?**
A. Ninety percent of the people work for the government.
B. Cuba cannot afford to buy the oil and natural gas it needs.
C. The country cannot grow enough sugar cane to supply its people.
D. Factories and businesses must close down from time to time because the workers produce too many goods.

MARKET ECONOMY

In a decentralized **market economy**, decisions are guided by changes in prices that occur between individual buyers and sellers in the marketplace. Other names for market systems are **free enterprise**, **capitalism**, and **laissez-faire**. In a market economy, businesses and farms are generally owned by individuals or corporations. Each business or farm decides what it wants to produce.

Market economies have benefits and problems. A benefit is that consumers can usually find the goods they want. They are free to earn as much money as they are able in order to buy the goods and services they want. Businesses are free to find new ways to make better products and lower prices. A problem is that if a company does not manage its money well, it can go out of business, and the workers lose their jobs and incomes.

Mexico is an example of a Latin American country with a market economy. Individuals and corporations own most of the businesses and farms in Mexico. They employ people to build a variety of goods that are sold in Mexico and other countries. Individuals and corporations also sell services to people. These individuals and corporations are free to decide what to sell. The government provides some laws to make sure that businesses run smoothly and fairly. The Mexican government does not set prices for goods and services, and it does not own the businesses and farms.

_____ **155. In which economic system do consumers make economic decisions based on changes in prices that occur between buyers and sellers?**
A. mixed
B. market
C. command
D. traditional

_____ **156. Which statement describes a part of a market economy?**

    A. All the stores in a country have prices set by the government.

    B. People purchase a factory to build a new type of energy-saving car.

    C. The government orders a factory to produce 100 more televisions a day.

    D. A farmer is given direction from the government about which crops to grow.

_____ **157. What is one problem of a market economy?**

    A. Prices for goods can get high very quickly if demand goes up but the supply does not change.

    B. The price of goods is set by the government, so people know exactly how much things will cost.

    C. People know that they will always have a job because the government owns all the businesses and farms.

    D. There can be shortages of goods if the government does not predict which goods will be needed by people.

_____ **158. Which describes the economic system in Mexico?**

    A. Individuals cannot own a business or farm in Mexico.

    B. Corporations are not allowed to do business in Mexico.

    C. Individuals and corporations own most of the businesses in the country.

    D. The government owns and manages the businesses and farms in Mexico.

LATIN AMERICA AND CANADA

MIXED ECONOMY

There are no pure command or market economies. To some degree, all modern economies have characteristics of both systems and are often referred to as ***mixed economies***. However, most economies are closer to one type of economic system than another.

In a truly free market economy, for example, the government would not be involved at all. There would be no laws to protect workers from unfair bosses. There would be no rules to make sure that credit cards were properly protected. Many societies have chosen to have some rules to protect consumers, workers, and businesses. These rules reduce the freedoms that businesses have, but they also protect the workers and consumers.

Mixed economies come in many forms. Cuba is considered a command economy. However, the Cuban government does allow some farmers to sell extra farm goods after they have met their quotas. These small farmers are allowed to keep extra money that they make selling these farm goods.

Mexico is considered a market economy. However, the government owns and operates the energy companies. In Brazil, the market economy is used for most businesses and farms. However, the government owns and controls some large industries such as steel production.

The diagram below illustrates this point. On the left is the pure command economy. Cuba's government controls nearly all businesses. There are a few people who are allowed some freedom to operate their own businesses. Brazil, on the other hand, is mostly a market economy. The government does have rules to govern business, and it owns some industry such as steel production. In the United States, the government makes laws to govern businesses. However, the government does not own businesses and does not control production or prices.

Types of Economies

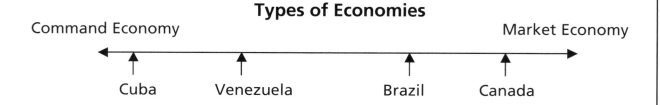

Command Economy   Market Economy

Cuba   Venezuela   Brazil   Canada

_____ 159. **Which statement describes the economy of Brazil?**

A. Brazil has a pure market economy.

B. Brazil has a pure command economy.

C. Brazil is mostly a market economy, but the government does control some businesses.

D. Brazil is mostly a command economy, but the government allows some farmers to sell some of their goods on their own.

160. An economy that is a blend between a command economy and a market economy is said to be

    A. hybrid.

    B. mixed.

    C. centralized.

    D. decentralized.

161. Which country in the diagram has the economic system closest to a pure market economy?

    A. Cuba

    B. Brazil

    C. Canada

    D. Venezuela

162. What is one of the main differences described between the economies of Canada and Brazil?

    A. Brazil's government owns and controls a few industries such as steel.

    B. Brazil's government does not make any laws to control businesses.

    C. The Canadian government does not make any laws to control businesses.

    D. The Canadian government owns and controls industries such as steel.

_____ **164. Which country has the <u>least</u> freedom to do business?**

    A. Cuba

    B. Brazil

    C. Canada

    D. about the same in each

_____ **165. In which countries do buyers and sellers come to agreement on prices in order to trade?**

    A. Brazil and Cuba

    B. Cuba and Canada

    C. Canada and Brazil

    D. Canada, Cuba, and Brazil

_____ **166. Which issue would make Canada a more desirable place to start a business than Brazil?**

    A. Starting a new business does not take very long.

    B. Companies have freedom to decide what to produce.

    C. Property rights are protected by strong laws and courts.

    D. All of the above.

LATIN AMERICA AND CANADA

> **SS6E2** **The student will give examples of how voluntary trade benefits buyers and sellers in Latin America and the Caribbean and Canada.**
> a. Explain how specialization encourages trade between countries.

SPECIALIZATION ENCOURAGES TRADE IN THE ECONOMY

Mrs. Estrada works at a shoe factory. In this factory, she runs a machine that sews the leather parts of the shoes together. She has done this job for a long time, and she is an expert at it. Because she is an expert, she has found ways to improve the machine that she uses. She has also learned skills that help her do her job faster. She knows exactly what to do if there is a problem of any kind. We can say that Mrs. Estrada is "specialized" in her work. She does not work on gathering, processing, or cutting the leather for the shoes. She does not work on manufacturing the soles of the shoes. She does not make laces. Mrs. Estrada does her part of the process very well, and that helps the business run better.

Because the people in Mrs. Estrada's shoe factory have **specialized** in their part of the shoe-making process, the entire company works better. The factory has a "division of labor." The work is divided into different parts and each worker is allowed to become an expert in her or his part of the work. More shoes are made when each specialized worker finds ways to improve the process and learns how to do the job more quickly. The shoe factory is specialized, too. It is not trying to also make belts, purses, or some other goods. The owners are focusing their business on trying to produce more shoes in less time for less cost.

Countries may specialize in the production of certain goods just as the people in the shoe factory were specialized. Most countries do not produce all of what they consume. Instead, they focus on producing certain goods. They trade those goods for goods they need from other countries.

_____ **167. In which part of her business was Mrs. Estrada specialized?**
   A. sewing the leather on shoes
   B. repairing the sewing machines
   C. getting leather to the shoe factory
   D. making laces of different sizes for different types of shoes

_____ **168. Which is an example of specialization?**
   A. A business makes many different types of goods.
   B. A country buys all the goods it needs from other countries and does not produce any of its own.
   C. A factory focuses on producing one or two types of goods and leaves the production of other goods to other factories.
   D. A violin maker completes the process of making a violin from cutting a tree for wood to producing his own strings.

_____ **169. What is an advantage of specialization?**
   A. Factories cannot produce goods as quickly.
   B. Workers do not become experts in their jobs.
   C. A factory can produce more goods in less time and for less money.
   D. Businesses cannot sell as many types of goods when they specialize.

> **SS6E2 The student will give examples of how voluntary trade benefits buyers and sellers in Latin America and the Caribbean and Canada.**
> b. Compare and contrast different types of trade barriers, such as tariffs, quotas, and embargos.

BARRIERS TO TRADE: TARIFFS, QUOTAS, AND EMBARGOS

Trade is the voluntary exchange of goods and services among people and countries. Trade and voluntary exchange occur when buyers and sellers freely and willingly engage in market transactions. When trade is voluntary, both parties benefit and are better off after the trade than they were before the trade.

Sometimes people complain about trade. They say that too much trade with other countries causes workers to lose jobs. Countries sometimes try to limit trade by creating **trade barriers**. The most common types of trade barriers are tariffs and quotas. A **tariff** is a tax on imports. **Imports** are goods purchased from other countries (exports are goods sold to other countries). A **quota** is a specific limit placed on the number of imports that may enter a country.

Another kind of trade barrier is an **embargo**. An embargo is a government order stopping trade with another country. An embargo might be enacted to put pressure on another country. For example, the United States put an embargo against Cuba. The U.S. government hoped to put pressure on Cuba to change from a communist country to a democratic one.

Should countries create trade barriers that limit trade? It is true that some workers in certain industries may be hurt by trade. For example, some U.S. clothing workers have had to change jobs during the past thirty years because many clothes now are imported from other countries. However, this trade allows people in the United States as a whole to buy clothing at lower prices. This results in a higher standard of living for people in the United States and for our trading partners.

170. **Which type of trade barrier involves adding a special tax onto goods brought into the country?**
     A. tariff
     B. quota
     C. embargo
     D. voluntary exchange

171. **In order to help U.S. car companies sell more cars, some people want to put a limit on the number of cars that can be imported from other countries. This is an example of a(n)**
     A. tariff.
     B. quota.
     C. embargo.
     D. voluntary exchange.

172. **Which situation might keep an embargo against a country from being successful?**
     A. The country is able to find other trading partners.
     B. The country does not need to trade with other countries.
     C. People in the other country suffer because trading has stopped.
     D. People in the other country don't care whether their country trades with other countries.

SS6E2 The student will give examples of how voluntary trade benefits buyers and sellers in Latin America and the Caribbean and Canada.

c. Explain the functions of the North American Free Trade Agreement (NAFTA).

THE NORTH AMERICAN FREE TRADE AGREEMENT

In 1994, the governments of the United States, Canada, and Mexico signed an agreement called the North American Free Trade Agreement, or **NAFTA**. This agreement took away all tariffs on goods traded among the three countries. Leaders said that by taking away the tariffs, trade among the countries would increase. A large free-trade zone would lead to an increase in the standard of living for all people in the three countries.

NAFTA did other things besides making the world's largest free-trade zone. It created special rules for protecting artists from having their work copied illegally. Rules were added to make sure that people in the three countries could trade fairly with each other and would have to follow similar laws.

Many people feared NAFTA. In the United States, many believed that companies would move their factories to Mexico because labor costs were lower there. This would mean a loss of jobs for American workers. Opponents were also concerned that there would be an increase in air and water pollution in Mexico and in the southwest United States.

_____ 173. **A main purpose of NAFTA was to**

    A. increase trade by creating a large free-trade zone.

    B. create tariffs between Canada, Mexico, and the United States.

    C. decrease the standard of living for some people while raising it for others.

    D. keep people in one country from buying goods from the other two countries.

_____ 174. **Which issue did some people think would be a problem related to NAFTA?**

    A. increases in immigrants from Mexico to the United States

    B. decreases in income to governments because of lower tariffs

    C. increases in pollution in Mexico and the southwest United States

    D. decreases in the standard of living for the people of the three countries

_____ 175. **Which problem did many Americans believe would result from NAFTA?**

    A. American factory workers would lose jobs.

    B. The countries would not have a strong central government.

    C. More immigrants would come to the United States from Mexico.

    D. Rules about trading fairly between different countries would be removed.

LATIN AMERICA AND CANADA

INTERNATIONAL TRADE AND EXCHANGING CURRENCIES

Currency is the money people use to make trade easier. In the United States, we use U.S. dollars (USD or $) to buy goods and services. When we work at a job, we are paid in dollars. In other countries, different currencies are used. The chart below gives examples of some of the currencies used by different countries. Most of the time, when you are in another country, you cannot buy goods and services with currency from your own country. So what do you do? You trade it in, or exchange it.

Sample Currencies in the Americas

	Name of Currency	Abbreviation	Symbol
Canada	dollar	CAD	$ or C$
Mexico	peso	MXN	$ or Mex$
United States	dollar	USD	$
Cuba	peso	CUP	Cu$
Brazil	real	BRL	R$

Trading with other countries requires trading for different currencies. For example, a California farm company sells almonds to Brazil. The Brazilians have **reals** (the Brazilian currency) to spend, but the Californians need U.S. dollars. A Brazilian company that sells television sets to the United States wants to end up with reals, not dollars. Somewhere along the way, dollars have to be exchanged for reals; reals also have to be exchanged for dollars.

Foreign exchange markets buy and sell international currencies. An **exchange rate** is the price of one nation's currency in terms of another nation's currency. Foreign exchange markets help individuals and companies by making it easier to trade all around the world. For instance, a Canadian company that builds cars needs to pay its workers in Canadian dollars. A buyer in Mexico has **pesos** (the Mexican or Cuban currency) to spend. An exchange of currency must be made in order for the deal between the car maker and the car buyer to work.

_____ **176. What is the money people use in a country called?**
   A. trade
   B. currency
   C. exchange
   D. voluntary

_____ **177. What is the currency of Mexico?**
A. euro
B. peso
C. real
D. dollar

_____ **178. What is one reason for people to exchange currency?**
A. to make more money by trading currency
B. most people want to use American dollars to trade
C. because different countries have different currencies
D. to buy and sell goods and services with other countries

> **SS6E3** **The student will describe factors that influence economic growth and examine their presence or absence in Latin America.**
> a. Explain the relationship between investment in human capital (education and training) and gross domestic product (GDP).

HUMAN CAPITAL AND THE GROSS DOMESTIC PRODUCT

The **Gross Domestic Product (GDP)** of a country is the total value of all the final goods and services produced in a country in one year. The GDP is one way to tell how rich or poor a country is. It can also be used to tell if the economy of a country is getting better or getting worse. Raising the GDP of the country can mean a higher standard of living for the people in the country.

To increase the GDP, countries must invest in **human capital**. This resource includes education, training, skills, and health of the workers in a business or country. If the workers in a country are uneducated or untrained, they will be limited in the kind of work they can do. An unskilled workforce limits the types of industry that can develop. If workers are unhealthy, they cannot produce the goods and services that are needed. Businesses and countries that want to be successful must pay attention to investing in human capital. Successful businesses help to increase the GDP of a country and improve the standard of living for all.

_____ **179. Which is an example of investment in human capital?**
A. trucks
B. factories
C. education
D. highways

_____ **180. It is important for a country to invest in human capital because businesses**
A. need money in order to pay their workers.
B. enjoy workers getting extra training and job opportunities.
C. are more successful when the workers have good training and health care.
D. are not responsible for the training and health care of the workers they employ.

181. What is an example of human capital?

    A. a country's standards of living

    B. the cash a business has to spend

    C. the workers of a business or country

    D. the buildings, equipment, and property of a business

182. Which is MOST likely to be in a country with a high literacy rate?

    A. a low standard of living

    B. a high standard of living

    C. little investment in human capital

    D. too much investment in capital resources

> **SS6E3 The student will describe factors that influence economic growth and examine their presence or absence in Latin America.**
>
> b. Explain the relationship between investment in capital (factories, machinery, and technology) and gross domestic product (GDP).

CAPITAL INVESTMENTS AND THE GROSS DOMESTIC PRODUCT

As stated earlier, the Gross Domestic Product (GDP) of a country is the total value of all the final goods and services produced in a country in one year. Raising the GDP of the country can mean a higher standard of living for the people in the country.

To increase the GDP, countries must invest in **capital goods**. Capital goods include the factories, machines, technologies, buildings, and property needed for a business to operate. If a business is to be successful, it cannot let its equipment break down or have its buildings fall apart. New technology can help a business produce more goods at a lower cost.

Here's an example. The TransCanada Sock Company makes wool socks. They are using the same equipment they have used for thirty years. The company makes good socks, and customers are satisfied with the quality and price. A new company, Great White North Wool Socks, opens. This company has invested in new technology that reduces the cost of wool socks. Customers are satisfied with the quality of the new socks, and they like the lower price. TransCanada Sock Company has a problem. They are losing customers to the new company. They decide to buy newer and better equipment so they can make more socks for a cheaper price. They are investing in capital goods.

183. Which activity is an example of investing in capital goods by a company?

    A. constructing a new factory

    B. throwing away old delivery trucks

    C. giving workers more time off to rest

    D. training workers to do their jobs better

184. How does investment in capital goods by companies help increase GDP?

    A. The GDP of a country goes down when companies make more money.

    B. Companies that invest in capital goods are able to provide a better place for their workers to work.

    C. Highly trained workers help the company be more profitable by finding ways to help the company work better.

    D. When a company invests in capital goods, it can produce more goods at a better price and increase the profit that it makes.

Use the following table to answer questions 185-187.

Top 10 Countries by Gross Domestic Product (GDP)

Rank	Country	GDP
1	United States	$13,840,000,000,000
2	Japan	$4,384,000,000,000
3	Germany	$3,322,000,000,000
4	China	$3,251,000,000,000
5	United Kingdom	$2,773,000,000,000
6	France	$2,560,000,000,000
7	Italy	$2,105,000,000,000
8	Spain	$1,439,000,000,000
9	Canada	$1,432,000,000,000
10	Brazil	$1,314,000,000,000

Source: CIA World Factbook (2007)

_____ **185. Which Latin American country is in the top 10 list of countries by Gross Domestic Product?**
   A. Brazil
   B. Spain
   C. Canada
   D. United States

_____ **186. What was the approximate GDP of Canada in the year 2007?**
   A. $1 trillion
   B. $1.4 trillion
   C. $14.3 trillion
   D. $143.2 trillion

_____ **187. How does the GDP of the United States compare to the GDP of Brazil?**
   A. They are about the same.
   B. Brazil's GDP is about ten times larger than that of the United States.
   C. The GDP of the United States is about ten times larger than Brazil's.
   D. The United States has the largest GDP of all the countries in the world.

THE ROLE OF NATURAL RESOURCES IN A COUNTRY'S ECONOMY

A country has different kinds of resources that can help its people produce goods and services. *Human resources* are the education and skills that people have to produce goods and services. *Capital resources* are the things like machines and equipment that people need to produce goods and services. *Natural resources* are sometimes thought of as "gifts of nature." Natural resources include forests, like the Amazon rain forest in Brazil. They include fertile soil such as the plains of southern Canada. Water is another natural resource. Venezuelans use their water resources by damming rivers and creating hydroelectric power.

Natural resources are important to countries. Without natural resources of their own, countries must import the natural resources that they need. This adds to the cost of goods and services. A country is better off if it can use its own natural resources to supply the needs of its people. If a country has lots of natural resources, it can trade them to other countries for goods and services. It can also use the natural resources to create goods that can be traded to other countries. In Latin America, countries with the most natural resources tend to have a higher standard of living than those with few natural resources.

Venezuela, for example, produces more oil and natural gas than its people need. The country is able to sell this resource to countries that do not have enough oil and natural gas. Venezuelans can use the money from this trade to purchase other goods and services that are not available in their country. For instance, Venezuela exports oil and natural gas to Europe, and automobiles built in Europe are imported to Venezuela.

_____ **188. Which item is an example of a natural resource?**

    A. furnaces

    B. education

    C. natural gas

    D. automobiles

_____ **189. How does having natural resources help the economy of a country?**

    A. The country is able to produce all the goods and services that it needs.

    B. Companies can export natural resources without having to create goods to sell.

    C. The country saves money because it does not have to import natural resources needed by the people.

    D. Companies spend more money because they must buy the natural resources needed to create more goods.

_____ **190. Which natural resources are the greatest help to the economies of some countries in Latin America?**

    A. forests, oil, water

    B. steel, natural gas, fertile soil

    C. fertile soil, forests, mountains

    D. forests, hydroelectric power, oil

LATIN AMERICA AND CANADA

THE ROLE OF THE ENTREPRENEUR IN THE ECONOMY

In some countries, people and companies have the right to start their own businesses. These people hope that they can create a business that will be successful. To be successful, the business must earn a profit. The business must sell goods or services to generate *income*. It will also have costs related to the business called *expenses*. The company is successful if its income is greater than its expenses. The difference is called *profit*.

The person who starts a business is called an *entrepreneur*. Entrepreneurs are people who risk their own money and resources because they believe their business idea will earn a profit. The entrepreneur must organize the business well for it to be successful. The entrepreneur brings together natural, human, and capital resources to produce goods or services to be provided by the business.

In Latin America, Chile is a country that is good for entrepreneurs. Laws that protect businesses are enforced. Businesses can start quickly, and there are few barriers. On the other hand, Cuba is a country in which it is nearly impossible to be an entrepreneur. Only a few privately owned farms and businesses are allowed. There are many laws that restrict trade, and a business owner faces many limits on earning a profit. One effect of the good environment for business is that Chile has one of the highest GDP levels in Latin America. Cuba, on the other hand, ranks near the bottom.

Entrepreneurs play an important role in the economy of a country. As they work to make their businesses profitable, they hire more workers, giving more people jobs. The tax money that comes from their businesses helps the government. Goods and services provided by entrepreneurs encourage trade within a country, which provides more jobs and more money. Entrepreneurs trading with people in other countries bring in goods and services that are not already available.

_____ **191. What are entrepreneurs?**
- A. businesses owned by the government
- B. people who start their own businesses
- C. businesses that are organized to be successful
- D. people who own farms and businesses that do not want to make a profit

_____ **192. In which country are entrepreneurs of least importance?**
- A. Cuba
- B. Chile
- C. Canada
- D. United States

_____ **193. Which is a way that entrepreneurs help increase a country's GDP?**
- A. writing laws to protect personal property
- B. creating businesses that give people jobs
- C. closing businesses that are making too much money
- D. working to decrease the amount of goods and services sold in a country

Use the following diagram to answer questions 194-196.

The Role of Entrepreneurs in a Business

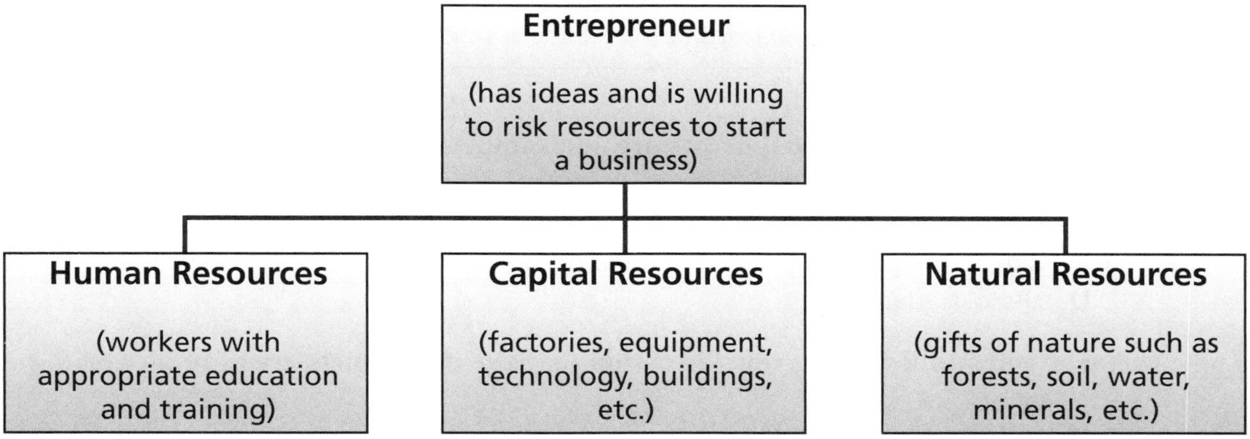

Entrepreneur

(has ideas and is willing to risk resources to start a business)

Human Resources	**Capital Resources**	**Natural Resources**
(workers with appropriate education and training)	(factories, equipment, technology, buildings, etc.)	(gifts of nature such as forests, soil, water, minerals, etc.)

_____ 194. **The box for "Entrepreneur" is at the top of the diagram because it shows that the entrepreneur is**
- A. first in the alphabet compared to the other words.
- B. dependent on other people to make the business successful.
- C. most important in organizing all other resources for a successful business.
- D. interested in making sure that the people in the business are well trained for the job.

_____ 195. **Which part of the diagram explains the role of the person who pulls together the other parts to make a business successful?**
- A. Entrepreneur
- B. Capital Resources
- C. Human Resources
- D. Natural Resources

_____ 196. **Why are natural resources, capital resources, and human resources on the same level of the diagram?**
- A. to show they are equally important to a business
- B. to show that natural resources are more important than human resources
- C. because the diagram looked better with the shapes organized in a straight row
- D. because the entrepreneur is the most important part of the business organization

Use the information in the box to answer questions 197-198.

> Two sisters start a company selling fancy T-shirts. The sisters use their home as the place to start their business. They purchase plain T-shirts from a company in Mexico. They purchase cool sparkles from a company in Brazil. The women hire other women to attach the sparkles to the T-shirts in fancy patterns.

_____ **197. The women sewing the sparkles are an example of**
  A. entrepreneurs.
  B. capital resources.
  C. human resources.
  D. natural resources.

_____ **198. The soil and water to grow the cotton to make the T-shirts are examples of**
  A. entrepreneurs.
  B. capital resources.
  C. human resources.
  D. natural resources.

SS6E4 The student will explain personal money management choices in terms of income, spending, credit, saving, and investing.

PERSONAL MONEY MANAGEMENT CHOICES

All of us make choices about managing money. Everyone must make choices about what to do with their income. Younger students probably have income from allowances, gifts, or for doing jobs at home. Older students may have jobs and receive income in their paychecks.

Saving and Investing

People really have only two choices about what to do with income: spending money now on goods and services or saving it for the future. **Savings** is the income that is not spent after people buy things they need or want. To help people make decisions about using their income, they can develop a budget. A **budget** is a spending-and-savings plan for an individual or an organization, based on estimated income and expenses.

Saving becomes a form of investing. **Investing** refers to putting money aside now in order to receive a greater benefit in the future. Often that greater benefit takes the form of **interest**, a fee for the use of money. For example, a person might have a savings account at a bank that earns interest. A checking account usually earns little or no interest. It is used simply as a safe place for people to keep their money until it is spent.

Financial investment refers to the decisions individuals make to invest money in things such as bank accounts, certificates of deposit, stocks, bonds, and mutual funds. Financial investment is important to gaining personal wealth. **Real investment** or **physical capital investment** refers to the decisions businesses make to purchase equipment or perhaps a factory. It also includes the purchase of new homes by consumers. The amount of real investment is critical to economic growth. Financial investment and real investment are connected, but they are not the same. When you hear someone talking about "investment," be clear in your own mind whether it is financial investment or real investment.

Credit

Credit refers to the ability to borrow money. When people borrow money, they understand they have to pay the money back plus interest. Generally, it is better to borrow money when the interest rate is low.

Some forms of credit used by consumers are car loans, home mortgage loans, and credit cards. Businesses also use credit regularly, either by borrowing from a bank or issuing corporate bonds. Government uses credit when it borrows money to finance a budget deficit. Government credit may be in the form of savings bonds or treasury notes. Those who can borrow moderate or large sums of money at a reasonable rate of interest are sometimes said to have *good credit*, while those who cannot borrow such amounts at such rates are said to have *bad credit*.

Credit is extremely useful to the economy. Most people would find it difficult to buy a house if they couldn't borrow the money. Many people use credit to further their education. In addition, people often use short-term credit in the form of credit cards as a simple and convenient way to pay for purchases. Businesses would be unable to build new factories if they had to save all the money first.

However, too much borrowing can be a problem for households, businesses, and governments. Making interest payments on the amount borrowed to buy a house to live in, a car to drive, or a factory to produce goods can make good sense. But credit should not be used to pay in the present for goods that were completely consumed in the past. People must be careful if the loan lasts longer than the item bought with it.

_____ **199. What is an advantage of a savings account over a checking account?**

    A. Savings accounts are easier to get.

    B. Savings accounts pay a higher rate of interest.

    C. Savings accounts can be used to guarantee loans.

    D. Savings accounts provide more protection for your money.

_____ **200. The BEST time to borrow money is when**

    A. interest rates are low.

    B. when a person has a good credit rating.

    C. when a person wants to purchase an expensive item.

    D. when a person has a good job so he or she can repay the loan.

_____ **201. Which condition causes people to use less credit?**

    A. They have other debts.

    B. Interest rates are high.

    C. They have no collateral.

    D. They have no savings account.

_____ **202. What is credit?**

    A. the ability to borrow money

    B. a type of card used to get money from a checking account

    C. a useful tool for borrowing more money that you can afford to repay

    D. a way to borrow money that is only used by businesses and the government

_____ **203. Which is an example of a "real" investment?**
   A. piggy bank
   B. a new house
   C. savings account
   D. stock mutual fund

_____ **204. Which is true of buying goods with credit?**
   A. Loans should last longer than the item being purchased.
   B. Credit is useful for buying very expensive items such as cars and houses.
   C. Credit is good for paying for things in the future that were used in the past.
   D. When people buy something with credit, they usually have to pay back less than they borrowed.

Use the words in the box to answer question 205.

> • stocks
> • bonds
> • mutual funds
> • certificates of deposit

_____ **205. Which statement explains what these items have in common?**
   A. They are ways to invest extra money.
   B. They are things that wealthy people purchase.
   C. Banks sell them as a way to improve their profits.
   D. They are bought by people as a way to save money.

HISTORICAL UNDERSTANDINGS

> **SS6H1 The student will describe the impact of European contact on Latin America.**
> a. Describe the encounter and consequences of the conflict between the Spanish and the Aztecs and Incas and the roles of Cortes, Montezuma, Pizarro, and Atahualpa.

AZTEC CIVILIZATION

The Aztec civilization was the most powerful in central and southern Mexico at the time of European exploration. The Aztec controlled the area around their capital city of **Tenochtitlan**, now Mexico City. Their borders stretched from the Gulf of Mexico to the Pacific Ocean. They controlled lands as far south as present-day Guatemala.

The Aztec were known for their artwork and architecture. They constructed a beautiful capital city on islands in a large lake. A pyramid temple was at the center of this great city.

An important part of the culture of the Aztec was the sacrifice of animals and humans. People who were conquered by the Aztec were required to pay large taxes. They also had to provide people to offer as sacrifices to the Aztec gods.

The Aztec had a complex and rich society. They had a mathematical system to keep up with their empire. They had two different calendar systems to organize their empire. They had a farming system that was very efficient. They used irrigation to keep their crops growing even during dry periods.

The Aztec civilization ended in 1521 when it was conquered by the Spanish. The Spanish destroyed much of the Aztec building and artwork. They destroyed the city of Tenochtitlan and built Mexico City in its place. Today, some of the art and buildings of the Aztec have been re-discovered. A modern version of the Aztec language, **Nahuatl**, is still spoken by thousands of people in Mexico.

_____ 206. **What was the capital of the Aztec empire?**
   A. Nahuatl
   B. Mexico City
   C. Montezuma
   D. Tenochtitlan

_____ 207. **What was the language of the Aztec?**
   A. Mexican
   B. Nahuatl
   C. Spanish
   D. Montezuman

_____ 208. **Which items show the Aztec had advanced knowledge?**
   A. farms, calendars, taxes
   B. calendars, taxes, human sacrifices
   C. irrigation systems, calendars, mathematics
   D. animal sacrifices, mathematics, irrigation systems

_____ 209. **What did the Spanish do to the Aztec art and architecture after they conquered the Aztec?**
   A. destroyed it
   B. preserved it
   C. adapted it for their own use
   D. shipped it back to Spain to sell

LATIN AMERICA AND CANADA

HERNÁN CORTÉS

Hernán Cortés was a Spanish **conquistador** (conqueror). He is famous for conquering the Aztec Empire in Mexico in 1519-1521. After this victory, the Spanish began to settle in Mexico. The Spanish stayed in Mexico for the next three hundred years.

Cortés was born in Spain in 1485. As a young man, he heard stories of the expeditions of Christopher Columbus and the riches that were to be found in the Indies. When Cortés was 19, he sailed to the New World, where he got a job as a clerk. He learned how colonies were run. (A **colony** is a foreign area controlled by a country and contributing to its wealth.) He also made many contacts with Spanish explorers. After Cuba was conquered, Cortés was made mayor of one of the towns.

In 1518, Cortés was told to take a group of ships to Mexico. He was ordered to conquer the powerful Aztec. He landed in Mexico in 1519 with eleven ships, five hundred soldiers, and one hundred sailors. Cortés was worried that some of his men would be frightened by the Aztec. To make sure that no one tried to go back to Cuba, Cortés had all the ships burned. Success or death were the only options.

Cortés trained his men for several months. He made friends with nearby Indians who did not like the Aztec. By the time he marched to the Aztec capital city of Tenochtitlan, he had over 1,500 fighters. Over 1,000 were native people who wanted to fight the Aztec.

The ruler of the Aztec was Montezuma II. For unknown reasons, he welcomed Cortés into the city. Cortés and his men took Montezuma captive. Cortés believed that he could control the Aztec by keeping their leader hostage. Cortés was able to rule the lands of central Mexico for some months before problems began.

A fight started between Cortés's men and the Aztec while Cortés was away. When Cortés returned, battles had to be fought to win back Tenochtitlan. In 1521, Cortés led a military victory over the Aztec. From this time forward, the Spanish sent more troops and settlers to Mexico. They tore down the buildings of the Aztec and destroyed Tenochtitlan. In its place, they built Mexico City. For the next three hundred years, Mexico was under Spanish control.

_____ **210. Cortés is most famous for which deed?**
   A. conquering the Aztec empire
   B. becoming mayor of a Cuban town
   C. starting construction of Mexico City
   D. becoming friends with native people

_____ **211. What did Montezuma do to Cortés and his men as they approached Tenochtitlan?**
   A. killed them all
   B. welcomed them
   C. captured them for human sacrifice
   D. took the Spanish troops as hostages

_____ **212. Which was a result of the defeat of the Aztec?**
   A. Mexico City was burned.
   B. Tenochtitlan was destroyed.
   C. Aztec artwork was collected.
   D. The Spanish left Mexico and did not return.

_____ 213. **What did Cortés do to Montezuma after the two met?**
   A. killed him
   B. took him hostage
   C. invited him to visit Cuba
   D. offered a sacrifice to the Aztec gods

_____ 214. **About how long was Spanish rule in Mexico after Cortés conquered the Aztec?**
   A. 3 years
   B. 30 years
   C. 3 months
   D. 300 years

MONTEZUMA II

Montezuma II was an Aztec ruler from about 1500 to 1520. He is most famous for ruling the Aztec when their land was invaded by the Spanish conquistador, Hernán Cortés.

Montezuma had spread the Aztec empire over a large part of central and southern Mexico. The Native Americans conquered by Montezuma had to pay him high taxes. They also had to send humans for sacrifice in the temples of the Aztec. Because of the taxes and sacrifices, Montezuma was unpopular with those he conquered. Montezuma was popular with his own people, however, and was considered a great ruler.

When Cortés and his army came to Tenochtitlan, Montezuma was alerted. Some people believed that Cortés was a god-like being. Montezuma ordered that Cortés and his men be welcomed into the city. They were given grand gifts of gold. Some believe that Montezuma acted this way in the hope that Cortés would take the gifts and leave. Instead, Cortés took Montezuma hostage and ruled for some time while Montezuma was a prisoner in his own palace.

In 1520, a fight broke out between Spanish troops and Aztec warriors. The battle grew, and somehow Montezuma was killed. Both Aztec and Spanish mourned the loss of the great leader of the Aztec.

_____ 215. **Who was the ruler of the Aztec when Cortés arrived in Mexico?**
   A. Cortés
   B. Pizarro
   C. Atahualpa
   D. Montezuma

_____ 216. **What did Montezuma give Cortés when they met?**
   A. gifts of gold
   B. a human sacrifice
   C. a pyramid in Tenochtitlan
   D. an area of land to rule in the south

_____ 217. **What had Montezuma done before the arrival of Cortés that made him a great leader in the eyes of his people?**
   A. started irrigation for farms
   B. expanded the territory of the Aztec
   C. built new pyramids in Tenochtitlan
   D. offered sacrifices to the Aztec gods

_____ **218. What did Montezuma get from people he conquered?**
    A. gifts to give to the Spanish
    B. taxes and irrigation for farms
    C. taxes and humans for sacrifice
    D. gold for the temple of the Aztec gods

INCA CIVILIZATION

The Inca lived along the western coast of South America. Their lands stretched over 2,000 miles from present-day Colombia south to Chile. Their empire was centered at their capital in **Cusco**, Peru. They also controlled lands in present-day Argentina, Bolivia, and Ecuador.

The Inca were known for many great achievements. They made beautiful gold, silver, and bronze pieces. Their leader even had rooms of gold and silver in his palace. They were known for skillfully made textiles. The Inca built a network of roads to quickly move around their empire. Terraces built on the mountainsides helped the Inca farm on difficult lands. Although it is not totally understood today, they had a system of mathematics and accounting. These achievements helped the Inca become the wealthiest of the native peoples in the New World.

Historians believe that the Inca Empire began in the early 1400s. They were in a time of expansion when the Spanish arrived. The Inca leader was killed, and, without a clear leader, the Inca people were unable to push back the Spanish.

The Spanish settlers wiped out much of the Inca culture and ruled for nearly three hundred years. Today, however, there is still evidence of the Inca. Their language, **Quechua**, is still spoken, and their terraces are still used for farming. Textiles made today are similar to those made five hundred years ago.

_____ **219. About how far was it from the northern tip to the southern tip of the Inca Empire?**
    A. 500 miles
    B. 1,400 miles
    C. 1,532 miles
    D. 2,000 miles

_____ **220. What evidence is there today of the Inca Empire in Peru?**
    A. The Quechua language is still spoken.
    B. There are still rooms of gold and silver.
    C. There is an Inca emperor in charge of Peru.
    D. The Inca system of accounting and mathematics is still in use.

_____ **221. Where was the capital of the Inca Empire?**
    A. Cusco
    B. Bolivia
    C. Cajamarca
    D. Machu Picchu

Use the following map to answer questions 222-224.

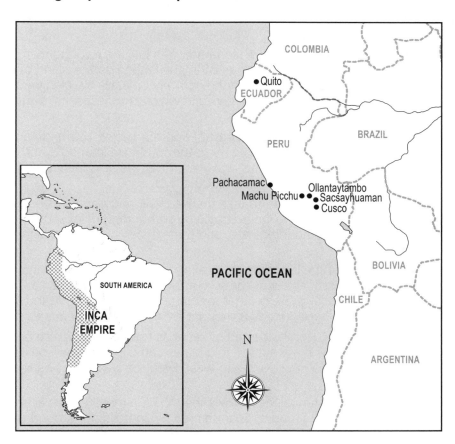

222. **Which modern country includes land that was part of the Inca Empire?**
    A. Peru
    B. Brazil
    C. Panama
    D. Venezuela

223. **Which was the northernmost city of the Inca Empire?**
    A. Cusco
    B. Quito
    C. Cajamarca
    D. Machu Picchu

224. **Which question can be answered using the map?**
    A. Which ocean bordered the Inca Empire?
    B. Who was the ruler of the Inca Empire in 1530?
    C. Which native tribes lived near the Inca Empire?
    D. What languages were spoken in the Inca Empire?

FRANCISCO PIZARRO AND ATAHUALPA

Francisco Pizarro was a Spanish conquistador. He is famous for conquering the Inca Empire in South America between 1531 and 1533.

Pizarro was born in Spain in 1475. He was a pig farmer as a boy. As a young man, he joined a ship traveling to the New World. In 1502, at the age of 27, he landed on the island of Hispaniola. He learned a lot about exploration and conquering the native people. He traveled with Vasco Núñez de Balboa on his famous exploration of Central America in which Europeans first sighted the Pacific Ocean.

In 1523, he led a voyage to explore the west coast of South America, south of Panama. He came across some Indian traders, who told of a rich country to the south. He learned that these people were the Inca and that they lived in the area of what is now Peru. Over the next few years, Pizarro went back to Spain to get permission to invade and conquer the Inca.

The Spanish king gave Pizarro permission to take the Inca land and claim it as part of Spain. He made Pizarro a **viceroy** (governor) over the lands stretching six hundred miles south from Panama. He also gave him three ships, about two hundred men, and three dozen horses to make his plan work. Pizarro began his mission in 1531.

Atahualpa was the last ruler of the Inca Empire. Inca land stretched two thousand miles along the Pacific Coast of South America. Atahualpa was the son of the Inca emperor Huayna Capac. After his father's death, Atahualpa fought against his brother for control of the empire. Atahualpa won the battle and became Sapa Inca. The *Sapa Inca* was thought to be a living descendant of the sun god.

The Sapa Inca was very wealthy. He was carried by servants from place to place on a special chair called a *litter*. He wore gold jewelry and ate from gold plates and cups. He was considered to be almost a god. Each day, he was given new clothes to wear. Even the walls of his palace were gold and silver.

Pizarro learned the location of Atahualpa. In November 1532, a meeting was arranged between the two men at Cajamarca. The small group of Spanish men hid in buildings around the town. They hid their guns, cannons, and horses. Atahualpa arrived with thousands of men.

Atahualpa walked into a trap. When Pizarro came out, the Spanish began shooting their cannons and guns, which were unknown to the Inca. This startled and frightened the Inca warriors, and the guards around Atahualpa were killed. Pizarro captured Atahualpa and demanded a ransom. The Inca brought 24 tons of gold and silver in exchange for the life of Atahualpa. The gold and silver were melted into bars, and most were sent back to Spain for the king. However, Atahualpa was not released.

Atahualpa was executed on August 29, 1533, by Pizarro and his men. Atahualpa's death ended the empire of the Inca. Even though some warriors still fought, the empire was gone because it had no recognized leader.

The Spanish settlements in Peru began to grow. Gold and silver continued to be taken from the Inca and shipped back to Spain. Pizarro grew wealthy. He founded the city of Lima and built a palace there. Some of the other Spanish leaders were jealous of Pizarro's wealth. They tried to take over his palace in 1541. Pizarro was killed in the attack. For nearly 300 years, the Spanish ruled the lands once held by the Inca.

_____ **225. The king of Spain rewarded Pizarro for his plan to conquer the Incas by**
        A. making him viceroy.
        B. allowing him to travel with Balboa.
        C. building him a palace in Lima, Peru.
        D. letting him keep all the gold he found.

226. **Which choice puts the following events in the correct order?**

> 1. Pizarro learns that the Inca emperor is very wealthy.
> 2. The Inca emperor, Atahualpa, is executed.
> 3. Pizarro attacks the Inca emperor.
> 4. The Spanish king allows Pizarro to attack the Inca.

    A. 1, 3, 2, 4
    B. 1, 4, 3, 2
    C. 4, 1, 3, 2
    D. 4, 3, 2, 1

227. **Pizarro conquered the Inca Empire because he**
    A. defeated the emperor's army in battle.
    B. killed the emperor in an attack on Cusco.
    C. went back to Spain to get permission to attack.
    D. surprised the emperor's army and took the emperor hostage.

228. **Who was the last Sapa Inca?**
    A. Huascar
    B. Atahualpa
    C. Huayna Capac
    D. Francisco Pizarro

229. **What did Atahualpa hope to keep when he gave away 24 tons of gold and silver to Pizarro?**
    A. his life
    B. his family
    C. his palace
    D. his empire

230. **What happened to the gold and silver taken by Pizarro from the Incas?**
    A. It was sent to the king of Spain.
    B. It became a part of Pizarro's palace in Lima.
    C. The Spanish sent it home to be divided among their families.
    D. Most of it was given back to the Incas after Pizarro was killed.

LATIN AMERICA AND CANADA

THE IMPACT OF THE COLUMBIAN EXCHANGE ON LATIN AMERICA AND EUROPE

Christopher Columbus "discovered" the New World in 1492. This event started an exchange between the Old World (Europe) and the New World (the Americas). As the Spanish spread their empire, the **indigenous population** (or native people) began to decline. The Europeans introduced Africans in the New World as slaves. The Africans also became a part of this exchange. Today we know this as the **Columbian Exchange**, since it began as a result of Columbus's discovery.

One important part of the Columbian Exchange was the exchange of food plants. Cocoa, corn, potatoes, peppers, and tomatoes grew in Central and South America. The Spanish and Portuguese discovered these foods and took them back to Europe. European crops brought from Europe and Africa to the New World included coffee, peaches, sugar, and wheat. Farming changed in the New World. Large plantations with slave labor were started. Sugar cane was one important plantation crop.

The indigenous population was defeated by diseases that were also part of the Columbian Exchange. The Europeans brought with them many diseases that the native people had not seen before. Their bodies did not have immunity (natural resistance) to the diseases, and their healers did not know how to treat the diseases. Some of the diseases brought to the New World were influenza, measles, smallpox, and typhoid fever. Between 50 and 75 percent of the population of some native tribes may have lost their lives to these diseases.

Europeans introduced certain animals to the New World. These included pigs, cows, goats, and bees. The horse was a culture-changing animal. It allowed native people to travel further and faster. The horse was useful in battle and hunting. Horses helped the indigenous people spread their territory and trade with other tribes.

_____ **231. Which animal helped native people hunt and trade over a larger area?**
   A. pig
   B. goat
   C. horse
   D. sheep

_____ **232. What was the Columbian Exchange?**
   A. sending food and people from the Old World to the New World
   B. sending animals and plants from the Old World to the New World
   C. the moving of animals, plants, people, and diseases from Central and South America to North America
   D. the moving of animals, plants, people, and diseases from the Old World to the New World and from the New World to the Old

_____ **233. Which foods came to Europe from Central and South America?**
   A. peaches, coffee, corn, wheat
   B. coffee, peaches, sugar, wheat
   C. coffee, sugar, cocoa, peaches
   D. corn, peppers, potatoes, tomatoes

Use the statements in the box to answer the next question.

> 1. Coffee and sugar were introduced.
> 2. Diseases from Europe killed a large part of the population.
> 3. The horse changed the life and culture of many indigenous people.
> 4. Indigenous people began plantations to grow sugar cane and coffee.

_____ **234. Which items identify results of the Columbian Exchange?**

A. 1, 2, 4

B. 1, 2, 3

C. 1, 3, 4

D. 2, 3, 4

> **SS6H2 The student will explain the development of Latin America and the Caribbean from European colonies to independent nations.**
> a. Describe the influence of African slavery on the development of the Americas.

THE INFLUENCE OF AFRICAN SLAVERY ON THE DEVELOPMENT OF THE AMERICAS

Finding cheap labor was a goal of the Europeans in America in the 1500s. Gold and silver found by conquistadors made Spain and Portugal wealthy. The wealth also made them powerful countries. At first, these metals could be taken from the native people. As these supplies were used up, the Europeans decided to try to set up mines to get more. As more Europeans came to the Americas, some tried to find ways to grow crops that could be sold in Europe. Sugar cane grew well in the Caribbean and in the tropics of Central and South America. The sugar cane was used to make sugar, molasses, and rum. Both of these projects required a large and cheap labor force.

The native people were not a good choice for labor. Millions died from diseases brought by the Europeans. More died because of violence with the Europeans. Natives that were forced to farm or work in mines faced harsh conditions. Many of them died as well. Many of the indigenous people simply retreated into the mountains or into the jungles. The Europeans then looked to Africa for labor.

Africans were brought to the Americas by ship. For many, the difficult journey ended in death by starvation or disease. Once they arrived in the New World, the Africans were forced to work on plantations or in mines. Long working hours, poor housing, and poor nutrition made life difficult. Children born to the Africans were considered slaves too. They faced a lifetime of work with no chance of freedom.

For about three hundred years, businesses that depended on slavery grew. The laborers—slaves—grew in numbers as the plantations expanded. Most of them lived in the tropical areas near the coast where large farms could be built.

This labor force helped to build many of the countries of Latin America, but most of the wealth was sent back to Europe. As different countries gained freedom from Europe in the 1800s, they ended slavery.

Today, the descendants of the African slaves are a part of the culture of Latin America. Most of the descendants live in the areas where plantation farming was important. Intermarriage of people from different continents has produced a diverse culture. People with only African ancestors or people with both African and European ancestors (mulattoes) live in large numbers in these countries. For instance, about 60 percent of Cubans and nearly 50 percent of Brazilians are in these groups.

235. **Where did Europeans in the sixteenth century find a cheap labor source for work in the New World?**
A. slaves from Africa
B. settlers that came from Europe
C. peasants from Spain and Portugal
D. indigenous people of Central and South America

236. **Which is one reason Europeans chose slaves from Africa as a labor source in the New World?**
A. The New World had diseases that did not affect African workers.
B. European workers did not know how to do farm and mining work.
C. Indigenous people were in short supply due to warfare and diseases.
D. Settlers from Europe did not know how to operate large plantations.

237. **When did slavery end for most parts of Latin America?**
A. after the slaves revolted
B. as countries got independence from Europe
C. after the kings of Spain and Portugal outlawed slavery
D. when the people of the country voted to free the slaves

238. **What is one effect of slavery that influences Latin America today?**
A. Slavery exists in few Latin American countries.
B. Many Latin Americans have ancestors from Africa.
C. Latin America has no people with ancestors from Africa.
D. The people of Latin America accept slavery as part of their lives.

239. **Slavery helped to build the countries of Latin America, but much of the wealth was shipped to Europe. Today, one effect of that situation is**
A. many Latin American countries are very poor.
B. Latin American countries do not have good workers.
C. people in Latin America are trying to move to Europe.
D. there are few people in Latin America with African ancestors.

SS6H2 The student will explain the development of Latin America and the Caribbean from European colonies to independent nations.

b. Describe the influence of the Spanish and the Portuguese on the language and religions of Latin America.

THE INFLUENCE OF THE SPANISH AND THE PORTUGUESE ON LANGUAGE AND RELIGION IN LATIN AMERICA

Languages in Latin America

As the Spanish and Portuguese conquered the indigenous people, they spread their language and religion. The Spanish language is still in use in the lands claimed and ruled by Spain. This includes most of Central and South America and the Caribbean Islands. The Portuguese language is the official language of Brazil. Portugal ruled Brazil from the 1500s until 1822. Because Portugal is such a large country in area and population, almost as many people in Latin America speak Portuguese as Spanish.

The Europeans spread their language across Latin America. Spanish and Portuguese were the official languages. They were the languages of government, business, and power. To be successful, people in these regions had to know these languages. Other languages did not die, however. The indigenous people of Central and South America moved into the mountains and into the jungles. Many of their languages were preserved. Quechua, language of the Incas, still is spoken by 10 million people in western South America. Almost 2 million Aymara people of the Andes and Altiplano region speak the Aymara language. It is even an official language of Bolivia. African languages survived in some places. Haitian Creole, for instance, is a blend of French and African languages. Still, for the millions of people living in Latin America in the twenty-first century, Spanish and Portuguese are the most important languages for business, government, and culture.

Religion in Latin America

The religion of South America is mostly Roman Catholic. During the colonial period, the governments of Spain and Portugal, whose official religion was Roman Catholic, paid for missionaries to go to the New World. Priests, friars, and monks set up missions all over Latin America. Their job was to convert the indigenous people to Christianity. They also ministered to the Europeans who moved to the area. The governments of Spain and Portugal supported the missionaries with money to build missions and churches. They sometimes supported them with protection by the army.

Indigenous people were often forced to say they were accepting Christianity. However, they often continued to practice their traditional beliefs. Some people mixed their traditional beliefs with beliefs of the Catholic Church.

_____ 240. **Which two European countries contributed most to the languages of Latin America?**
A. England and Spain
B. Spain and Portugal
C. France and Portugal
D. England and Portugal

_____ 241. **Spanish and Portuguese are important in Latin America because they are**
A. the only official languages.
B. the two main spoken languages.
C. spoken by everyone in Latin America.
D. understood by government workers and businessmen.

_____ 242. **What is the most common religion of Latin America?**
A. Creole
B. Aymara
C. Quechua
D. Roman Catholic

_____ 243. **How did the Spanish government have an influence on the spread of the Roman Catholic Church in the New World?**
A. The Catholic Church controlled Spain.
B. Spanish royalty did not support the Catholic Church.
C. It paid to build missions to bring Christianity to the native population.
D. Churches from other parts of the world did not send missionaries to the New World.

244. What was the main job of the priests, friars, and monks sent by Spain to the New World?
   A. find food and shelter for the poor
   B. convert the Indians to Christianity
   C. build missions to serve the settlers
   D. minister to the armies of the Spanish king

Use the following table to answer questions 245-247.

Percent of Population that is Roman Catholic in Select Latin American Countries (1910 & 2005)

	1910	2005
Brazil	96	85
Cuba	90	56
Mexico	99	92
Venezuela	96	87

Source: International Bulletin of Missionary Research

245. Which question could be answered using the table?
   A. What percent of Mexicans is Roman Catholic today?
   B. What is the most common religion in Latin America?
   C. Which Latin American country has the greatest number of Roman Catholics?
   D. Which of the four countries had the highest percent of Roman Catholics in 1910?

246. Which country had the largest decline in percent of people that were Roman Catholic?
   A. Cuba
   B. Brazil
   C. Mexico
   D. Venezuela

247. Which statement best summarizes the information in the table?
   A. Each country shown has had a decrease in the percent of population that is Roman Catholic.
   B. Each country shown has had an increase in the percent of population that is Roman Catholic.
   C. The four countries listed have about the same percentage of their population that were Roman Catholics.
   D. The number of Roman Catholics in Latin America has gone down over the 95- year period that this information covers.

The governments of Spain and Portugal ruled most of Latin America for nearly three hundred years. In that time, there were numerous battles for control of the lands. At times, the people who were being ruled by the Europeans grew restless. They thought about what it would be like to be free. The American Revolution in 1776 gave some in Latin America the idea that they too could be free. In 1789, the French Revolution showed that the kings and queens of Europe could be overcome. These events encouraged Latin Americans in the belief that they might be able to overcome their European rulers.

TOUSSAINT L'OUVERTURE

Toussaint L'Ouverture was a famous black freedom fighter. He was a major leader of the slave revolts in Saint Domingue (present-day Haiti). He was later made governor of Saint Domingue.

François-Domingue Toussaint was born a slave in the mid-1700s. His father had been a free African who was captured and sold into slavery in Saint Domingue. He told his son about freedom and what life was like before his capture. Toussaint was lucky because the plantation owner allowed him to learn to read and write. Toussaint read every book that he could. He read books that were popular in France. These books had ideas about freedom and equality for all men.

In 1789, the French Revolution occurred. The new government in France granted freedom to all free blacks and mulattoes (those with African and European ancestors). However, the plantation owners in Saint Domingue were furious. In 1791, the French government changed its mind and took back the freedom it had given to blacks and mulattoes. This time, the slaves were furious. Toussaint led a slave army and defeated the French troops.

By 1793, the French government abolished slavery altogether. Toussaint then led his men against invading British and Spanish troops. During this time, he was nicknamed Toussaint L'Ouverture, or "opening," because he seemed to be able to find openings in the defenses of his enemies. In the end, Toussaint L'Ouverture was left in charge of Saint Domingue even though it was officially a French colony.

In 1802, the French emperor Napoleon sent troops to regain control. Some thought that he also wanted to reinstate slavery. Toussaint L'Ouverture was invited to a meeting with a French general to discuss a peace treaty. Instead, Toussaint was captured, arrested, and sent to France. He was imprisoned and died shortly after. Within two years, the people of Saint Dominigue declared their independence and renamed their country Haiti.

____ **248. Toussaint L'Ouverture was famous for his role in gaining independence for which country?**
A. Cuba
B. Haiti
C. Mexico
D. Venezuela

____ **249. Which country's government imprisoned Toussaint L'Ouverture?**
A. Haiti
B. Spain
C. France
D. Great Britain

____ **250. Which important goal did Toussaint L'Ouverture want to achieve?**
A. freedom for the slaves in Saint Dominigue
B. improved production on sugar cane plantations
C. control of the French, Spanish, and British armies in the Caribbean
D. a meeting with the French government in France to get better working conditions

____ **251. Which childhood event allowed Toussaint L'Ouverture to learn ideas about freedom and equality?**
A. He made a trip to France.
B. The French Revolution occurred.
C. He worked on the plantation with his family.
D. His owner allowed him to learn to read and write.

SIMON BOLIVAR

Simon Bolivar was a leader in the wars for independence in South America. He and other leaders fought against Spanish rule. They wanted independence for all the people in Latin America. Bolivia, Colombia, Ecuador, Panama, Peru, and Venezuela won their independence through his efforts.

Bolivar was born in 1783, in Caracas, in what is now Venezuela. He was from a wealthy family. He had an excellent education and read many books with ideas on freedom and equality. He lived at the time of the French Revolution and through that learned of the defeat of the French royal family.

From 1810 to 1824, Bolivar led different groups of troops against Spanish rule. He fought in the lands that are now Venezuela, Colombia, and Panama. He was able to finally defeat the Spanish in 1824 and end Spanish rule in South America. The country of Bolivia was named for Bolivar, and he wrote a constitution to organize the country.

Bolivar is known as "The Liberator" in South America. He is also sometimes called the "George Washington of South America." He became dictator and tried to create a single, large South American country called Gran Colombia. It covered the entire northern part of South America. Fights among different groups caused the different countries to break up. Bolivar became infected with tuberculosis and died from the disease in 1830.

_____ 252. **Simon Bolivar was known as the liberator for which people?**

    A. Mexicans

    B. Spanish soldiers

    C. South Americans

    D. Indigenous people

_____ 253. **Which country got its independence because of Simon Bolivar's efforts?**

    A. Canada

    B. Mexico

    C. Venezuela

    D. United States

_____ 254. **Which country's revolution encouraged Bolivar to fight for independence?**

    A. Spain

    B. France

    C. Mexico

    D. Venezuela

_____ 255. **Which country did Bolivar and his fellow patriots fight against?**

    A. Spain

    B. France

    C. Mexico

    D. Venezuela

MIGUEL HIDALGO

Miguel Hidalgo is known as the father of Mexican independence. He was a priest who led a peasant army against the Spanish army in Mexico, which was then called New Spain. His force won some victories, but Hidalgo did not live to see independence.

Hidalgo was born in 1753. His family saw that he got a good education. As he grew up, he read books with ideas on freedom and equality. He saw that there was not equality for the peasant workers in Mexico. He also saw that those born in Spain got special treatment, compared to citizens born in Mexico. After training to be a priest, he worked among the native people and peasants.

In 1808, France invaded Spain, and the king was removed. This created problems in Mexico. People were not sure they supported the new French government. Others did not support the old Spanish government. A third group thought it was time for Mexico to be independent. Hidalgo and his friends were for the third choice.

In 1810, Hidalgo was warned that he was going to be arrested. Those loyal to the French government had turned him in. On September 16, instead of running away, he ran to his church and rang the bell. People from the countryside came in. Instead of having a church service, the people got a speech. In this speech, Hidalgo said it was time for Mexico to be free.

At first, thousands of people followed Hidalgo. They won several victories against the Spanish army. However, they did not have training, and they did not have many weapons. Eventually, the Spanish army pulled its forces together and mounted an attack. They defeated a group of the rebels and captured Hidalgo. He was tried for treason and found guilty. He was executed by Spanish soldiers on July 30, 1811, but the war for independence continued. Mexico did not win its independence for another ten years. In 1821, Spain withdrew the last of its troops from Mexico.

_____ **256. Miguel Hidalgo was known as the father of independence for which country?**
A. Peru
B. Bolivia
C. Mexico
D. Venezuela

_____ **257. What job did Miguel Hidalgo have in Mexico?**
A. priest
B. soldier
C. general
D. peasant

_____ **258. What event caused people in Mexico to begin to think about independence?**
A. France took over Spain and removed the king.
B. Mexico had many peasants who were unhappy.
C. Spain sent additional troops to fight against Hidalgo.
D. Thousands of people followed Hidalgo after his speech.

> **SS6H3 The student will analyze important 20th century issues in Latin America and the Caribbean.**
>
> a. Explain the impact of the Cuban Revolution.

THE IMPACT OF THE CUBAN REVOLUTION

Cuba is an island nation located ninety miles south of Florida. For most of the twentieth century, it had political problems. Leaders came to power and then were thrown out by others. At the same time, American businesses were trading with Cuba. American companies owned a large amount of land in the country. Most of Cuba's sugar cane crop was sold to America. In the late 1950s, a change in leadership took place there. Fidel Castro became dictator, creating the only communist country in the western hemisphere. Castro's power was such that he ruled for nearly fifty years.

In the late 1950s, Fulgencio Batista was ruler of Cuba. He had been elected president at one time, but he later made himself dictator. That meant that he ruled without any controls on his power. Many people in Cuba were unhappy with his rule. There was much poverty. Education and health care were not good for most Cubans. Fidel Castro led a group of rebels against Batista. Because Batista was so unpopular, many followed Castro. Castro defeated the Batista government and made himself dictator in 1959.

Castro began right away to organize a communist government. He declared that all the property belonging to Americans now belonged to the government. All farms, factories, and businesses owned by Cubans also became government property. Castro had people who supported Batista arrested. Most were executed by firing squad. Some spent decades in prison. Cubans no longer had the right to protest against the government. Cuban newspapers, radio, and television were shut down. The government became the only source for news. Churches were closed, and all church property was taken by the government.

Because of these harsh events, the United States placed an embargo on Cuban goods. That meant that Cuba's sugar cane crop could not be sold to the United States. The **Soviet Union** became friends with Cuba. They bought the country's sugar cane each year. They also supplied weapons and other goods to the Cubans. The Soviets helped to educate young Cubans and trained their military.

Under Castro's rule, the Cuban people had some benefits. Hospitals and schools were improved. Women and blacks became better educated and had better jobs. However, most parts of people's lives were controlled by the government. People who practiced their Christian religion were discriminated against. Although everyone was guaranteed a wage, the income of most Cubans was low. The country was one of the poorest in the region. Its people lived in one of the least free countries in the world.

Castro's government and the U.S. government did not get along well. The United States did not like having a communist country so close to Florida. Americans who owned land and businesses in Cuba did not like the loss of their property. The United States decided to keep the pressure on Cuba. It did not allow travel by Americans to or from Cuba. It also tried to keep other countries from trading with the Cubans.

Cuba tried to spread communism into Latin America. It supported revolutionary ideas in many countries by providing military training, money, and weapons. One event, the **Cuban Missile Crisis**, almost started a nuclear war. In 1962, Cuba gave the Soviet Union permission to build a missile launching complex. Missiles launched from the site could reach U.S. cities. U.S. President John F. Kennedy demanded the missiles be removed. A tense time followed. Finally, the Soviets agreed to remove the missiles, and the United States said it would not invade Cuba.

Relations between the United States and Cuba have not improved much in the past fifty years. There is still an embargo on goods from Cuba. Americans, however, can send money to their families in Cuba. In the early 1980s and again in the 1990s, there were periods in which large numbers of Cubans escaped their island for America. The United States had been accepting Cubans who escaped. However, thousands were being "allowed" to escape. This caused a strain on relations between the two countries. In 1994, the United States agreed to allow 20,000 Cubans a year to enter the United States. The Cubans agreed to stop allowing so many Cubans to "escape."

____ 259. **Who took over as dictator of Cuba in 1959?**
    A. Fidel Castro
    B. Raul Castro
    C. John F. Kennedy
    D. Fulgencio Batista

____ 260. **What type of government did Castro create in Cuba?**
    A oligarchy
    B. communist
    C. democratic
    D. confederacy

____ 261. **What was one reaction the United States had to Cuba taking over property owned by Americans?**
    A. The United States threatened a nuclear attack.
    B. The United States put an embargo of Cuban goods.
    C. The United States wanted Cuba to trade with other countries.
    D. An agreement was reached to limit the number of Cubans entering the United States.

____ 262. **Which country helped Castro build Cuba into a communist country?**
    A. Mexico
    B. Venezuela
    C. Soviet Union
    D. United States

____ 263. **What almost caused a nuclear war between the United States and the Soviet Union?**
    A. Kennedy did not like the leader of the Soviet Union.
    B. The Soviet Union wanted to show the Cubans that they were strong friends.
    C. Castro allowed the Soviet Union to build a nuclear missile launch complex in Cuba.
    D. The United States wanted the sugar cane crop that the Soviet Union was buying from Cuba.

> **SS6H3 The student will analyze important 20th century issues in Latin America and the Caribbean.**
>
> b. Explain the impact and political outcomes of the Zapatista guerrilla movement in Mexico.

THE IMPACT AND POLITICAL OUTCOMES OF THE ZAPATISTA GUERRILLA MOVEMENT IN MEXICO

The **Zapatistas** are a group of Mexicans who support improved rights and living conditions for Mexico's indigenous people. The group is named after Emiliano Zapata, who lived in the early twentieth century and fought for the rights of native people. In the late twentieth century, the Zapatistas were known for harassment and sabotage against the government.

On January 1, 1994, the North American Free Trade Agreement (NAFTA) came into effect. This was an agreement to allow free trade between Canada, Mexico, and the United States. Some people in Mexico did not like this plan. They thought that NAFTA would allow cheap farm goods to come into Mexico from the United States. The farmers in Mexico would not be able to compete with the cheaper food.

On the day NAFTA took effect, a group of Mexicans called the Zapatistas took over several towns in their part of Mexico. The army was sent in to remove the Zapatistas. Fighting lasted for several weeks. A cease-fire finally ended the fighting. The Zapatistas did not go away, however.

Agreements between the Zapatistas and the government have not solved the problems the people have with the government. The Zapatistas have control of some small parts of southern Mexico. The Zapatistas argue that the indigenous people of Mexico need more help to improve health care, housing, education, and jobs. The Zapatistas have formed friendships with groups in other countries that have similar goals.

_____ **264. The Zapatistas did not like NAFTA because they believed it would**

A. mean U.S. factories would move to Mexico.

B. force Mexicans to move to the United States.

C. hurt businesses in Canada and the United States.

D. cause poor Mexican farmers to go out of business.

_____ **265. Which group do the Zapatistas support?**

A. Canadian farmers

B. U.S. factory workers

C. indigenous people of Mexico

D. poor farmers in North America

_____ **266. Which is an area of concern for the Zapatistas?**

A. religion

B. housing

C acid rain

D. deforestation

_____ **267. What did the Zapatistas do to show they were against NAFTA?**

A. attacked government troops in Mexico City

B. took over several towns in southern Mexico

C. formed friendships with groups in other countries with similar goals

D. worked with the government on agreements to improve the rights of poor Mexicans

THE INFLUENCE OF THE FRENCH AND THE ENGLISH ON THE LANGUAGE AND RELIGION OF CANADA

The Europeans who settled Canada came mainly from Great Britain and France. The English and the French explored and established settlements across North America. They brought their languages and religions with them. Conquered Indian tribes were pushed aside, destroyed, or isolated. In time, Canada came to be ruled by **Great Britain**. There were many French-speakers, however, in the province of Quebec. Religion was different in Quebec, too. Most of Canada was non-Catholic Christian. The French-speaking people of Quebec were mostly Roman Catholic.

Great Britain got control of Canada in 1763 as a result of the French and Indian War. The British rule of Canada lasted into the twentieth century. During those years, settlers moved across the continent. The English-speakers of Canada stretched from coast to coast. Today, nearly 70 percent of Canadians speak English as their first language. English is one of the official languages of government and business in the country.

The effects of French settlement remain, however. Although only 20 percent of the population speaks French as its first language, 81 percent of the people in Quebec have French as their first language. Only about 8 percent of Quebec's citizens speak English as a first language. French is the official language of business and government in Quebec. Advertising can be in both French and English. However, the English portion must come after the French part, and the English words must be of smaller size. Because of the distinct society of French-speakers in the country, French is an official language of Canada. All government documents are written in French and English.

Religion in Canada is a result of its history too. The French settlers were Roman Catholic. English settlers tended to be non-Catholic Christians. Today, about 80 percent of people in Quebec are Catholic. In Canada as a whole, the number is about 44 percent. Although other religions are practiced, the main religions are those that were brought from the mother countries.

_____ 268. **Which are the official languages in Canada?**
  A. English and French
  B. Portuguese and Spanish
  C. Spanish and French Creole
  D. Canadian and French-Canadian

_____ 269. **Which pair of European countries contributed most to the languages of Canada?**
  A. England and Spain
  B. Spain and Portugal
  C. England and France
  D. France and Portugal

_____ 270. **What is the most common religion of Quebec?**
  A. Hindu
  B. Jewish
  C. Roman Catholic
  D. Protestant Christian

LATIN AMERICA AND CANADA

_____ **271. Which statement describes why English is the most common language of Canada?**

A. France did not send settlers to Canada.

B. English is an easier language to learn than French.

C. The French did not rule Canada during its settlement.

D. Great Britain ruled Canada for most of its period of settlement and expansion.

HOW CANADA BECAME AN INDEPENDENT NATION

Great Britain colonized lands around the world. In North America, the thirteen colonies declared their independence and fought a war with Great Britain to secure it. They created the United States of America. Other colonies fought for their freedom, too. Some colonies were able to get their independence through peaceful means. Canada was one of those countries.

Canada became part of Great Britain in 1763. This was a result of Great Britain's defeat of France in the French and Indian War. The country expanded, and pioneers and settlers found ways to use the resources of the country. By the mid-1860s, people in Canada wanted to be united. They asked the British Parliament to create a constitution allowing for increased self-government. Some Canadians worried that the United States might invade parts of Canada to gain new lands.

The British North America Act of 1867 put together the provinces of New Brunswick, Nova Scotia, Ontario, and Quebec, and the new constitution titled the country the Dominion of Canada. The country was allowed to have its own parliament and prime minister. It was **not** allowed to make treaties with other countries, and it had to be a part of the military of the United Kingdom (Great Britain and Northern Ireland). The **monarch**, king or queen, would be the same for Canada and Great Britain.

This system worked well for many years. However, many Canadian soldiers were used by the United Kingdom in World War I. The loss of life was very high. Canadians decided they wanted more control in foreign affairs. After the war was over, Canadians began to work toward independence. In 1931, the British Parliament granted independence to Canada. It was 1982 before the final links were broken between the British Parliament and the Canadian government. The two countries still share the same monarch.

_____ **272. Which was allowed for Canada by the British North America Act of 1867?**

A. Canada could choose the governor-general.

B. Canada could sign treaties with other countries.

C. A Canadian parliament could make laws for the country.

D. Canada could elect its own monarch separate from Great Britain.

_____ **273. What part of the British North America Act of 1867 were Canadians opposed to after World War I?**

A. sharing the same monarch

B. having one parliament for two countries

C. having their own parliament and prime minister

D. use of Canadian soldiers in the army of the United Kingdom

_____ **274. Canada's independence from the United Kingdom was granted after which event?**

A. World War I

B. the selection of a new monarch

C. a war with the United Kingdom

D. the monarchs of the United Kingdom and Canada divorced

QUEBEC'S INDEPENDENCE MOVEMENT

Quebec is an important part of Canada. A large part of Canadian industry is centered in Quebec. Many electronics and computer industries are based in the province. The people of Quebec and the rest of Canada share a history of cooperation and success. Most Canadians want to keep the French-speaking citizens as a part of Canada.

Some people in Quebec want Quebec to be independent. These people are called **separatists**. They believe that Quebec cannot keep its French language and culture in a country where most people have English as a first language. The people have voted on the issue. Both times, they decided to remain a part of Canada.

The government of Canada has passed several laws to help Quebec's citizens preserve their language and culture. First, they made Canada officially bilingual. That means that both the English and the French languages are used for government and business. Canadian law guarantees the right to preserve one's cultural heritage. Quebec has also been officially labeled a "distinct society" in Canada.

In Quebec, French is the only official language. English may be used in advertising, but it must be placed after the French words, and it must be in a smaller size. Some in Quebec are happy with these changes. Others are not satisfied. They still believe that Quebec should be independent.

_____ 275. **What is the term for a person who wants Quebec to become an independent country?**
A. Canadian
B. Separatist
C. Quebecois
D. Francophone

_____ 276. **The goal of the independence movement was for Quebec to**
A. have its own monarch.
B. be an independent country.
C. become a part of France again.
D. make the rest of Canada become French-speaking.

_____ 277. **Which is a way of protecting the language and culture of Quebec?**
A. Businesses must be bilingual in Quebec.
B. French is the official language of Quebec.
C. The Canadian government prints laws only in French.
D. Quebec's citizens have been ordered to learn English.

LATIN AMERICA AND CANADA

EUROPE

GEOGRAPHIC UNDERSTANDINGS

SS6G8 The student will locate selected features of Europe.

a. Locate on a world and regional political-physical map: Danube River, Rhine River, English Channel, Mediterranean Sea, European Plain, the Alps, Pyrenees, Ural Mountains, Iberian Peninsula, and Scandinavian Peninsula.

LOCATING PHYSICAL FEATURES OF EUROPE

To get to know Europe, you must understand its features, both land and water. Look at the map of Europe below and find the Atlantic Ocean. The Atlantic Ocean is on the eastern side of the United States, but it is on the western side of Europe. Put your finger on the large island off the northwest coast of Europe. The water that separates this island from the rest of the continent is the **English Channel**. Move your finger south along the coast of Europe until you reach another large body of water that joins the Atlantic Ocean. This is the **Mediterranean Sea**. It also touches the continent of Africa.

Europe has many peninsulas. The **Iberian Peninsula** is the landmass found where the Mediterranean Sea joins the Atlantic Ocean. Put your finger on the Iberian Peninsula. Moving north, your finger will cross the **Pyrenees Mountains**, a natural border between the Iberian Peninsula and the rest of Europe. The Pyrenees Mountains form the western border of the **European Plain**. This plain extends from France to Russia. It ranges from 50 to 1,500 miles wide. The eastern border of the plain is the Ural Mountains. Some of the world's best farmland is on this plain.

Now move your finger east from the Pyrenees. As your finger enters the European Plain, you will cross the **Rhine River**. The Rhine River begins in the **Alps**, the mountain range that forms the southern border of the European Plain. The European Plain contains another important river, the **Danube River**. The Danube and the Rhine rivers form natural political boundaries for many European countries. Locate the Danube River, the Rhine River, and the Alps. Continue north from the Alps to the **Scandinavian Peninsula**, the largest peninsula in Europe. Move your finger east to the **Ural Mountains**, the eastern boundary of the European Plain. The Ural Mountains, running in a north-south direction, also mark the northern border between the continents of Europe and Asia.

Physical Map of Europe

Use the following map to answer questions 278-281.

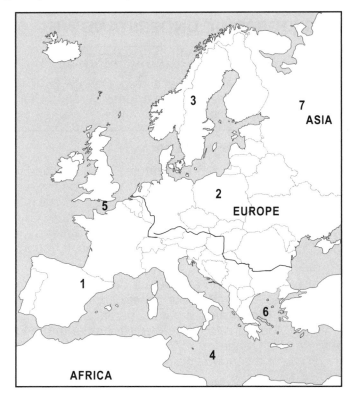

____ 278. Which physical feature is located near the "1" on the map?
A. Rhine River
B. Ural Mountains
C. Pyrenees Mountains
D. Scandinavian Peninsula

____ 279. Which physical feature is located near the "2" on the map?
A. Atlantic Ocean
B. European Plain
C. Ural Mountains
D. Iberian Peninsula

___ 280. Which number on the map marks the Mediterranean Sea?
A. 3
B. 4
C. 5
D. 6

____ 281. Which number on the map marks the English Channel?
A. 5
B. 6
C. 7
D. not shown

SS6G8 The student will locate selected features of Europe.

b. Locate on a world and regional political-physical map the countries of Belgium, France, Germany, Italy, Poland, Russia, Spain, Ukraine, and United Kingdom.

LOCATING COUNTRIES IN EUROPE

Many countries, both large and small, make up the continent of Europe. Put your finger on the **United Kingdom**. It is an island country off the northwestern coast of Europe. The United Kingdom contains the island of Great Britain, the northeastern part of the island of Ireland, and many other smaller islands. Move your finger to the south, across the English Channel to the country of **France**. France has many natural borders: the Pyrenees Mountains, the Alps, and the English Channel.

From France, move your finger to the southwest across the Pyrenees Mountains and enter the country of **Spain**. Spain is on the Iberian Peninsula. Spain is bordered by the Mediterranean Sea to the south and east. Move east across the Mediterranean with your finger, and you will find the boot-shaped peninsula of **Italy**. The country of Italy also includes two of the largest Mediterranean islands, Sardinia and Sicily.

Moving north from Italy, your finger will cross the Alps and enter the country of **Germany,** located in Central Europe. Germany is bordered on the west by the tiny country of **Belgium**. On Germany's eastern border is the country of **Poland**. Move your finger to the southeast to find **Ukraine**. One of the largest countries in Europe, Ukraine is mostly plateaus and fertile plains. The Danube River forms one of Ukraine's natural boundaries. Continue northeast into **Russia**, the largest country in the world. Russia covers all of northern Asia and almost half of Europe.

Political Map of Europe

EUROPE

111

Use the following map to answer question 282-287.

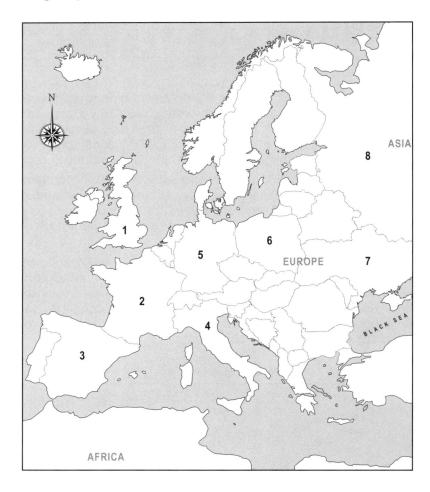

____ **282. Which country is located at the "3" on the map?**
   A. Spain
   B. France
   C. Belgium
   D. Germany

____ **283. Which country is located at the "4" on the map?**
   A. Italy
   B. Poland
   C. Russia
   D. Ukraine

____ **284. Which number on the map marks the country of Germany?**
   A. 3
   B. 5
   C. 6
   D. 8

____ **285. Which number on the map marks the United Kingdom?**
   A. 1
   B. 2
   C. 7
   D. 8

____ **286. Which of the numbered countries is northernmost on the map?**
   A. Italy
   B. Spain
   C. Russia
   D. United Kingdom

____ **287. Which countries share a border?**
   A. Italy and Russia
   B. Ukraine and Spain
   C. Poland and Germany
   D. United Kingdom and France

EUROPE

SS6G9 The student will discuss environmental issues in Europe.

a. Explain the major concerns of Europeans regarding the issues such as acid rain in Germany, the air pollution in the United Kingdom, and the nuclear disaster in Chernobyl, Ukraine.

ACID RAIN IN GERMANY

Germany is a country of old forests, beautiful rivers, and historic artwork and buildings. Over the past thirty years, ***acid rain*** has taken its toll on these landmarks. Acid rain has ruined nearly half of the Black Forest in southwestern Germany. It has damaged the soil and the trees growing in it. Many acres of diseased trees are at risk of dying. Sulfur and nitrogen found in acid rain eat holes in the surfaces of statues and buildings. Acid rain pollutes rivers, like the Danube and the Rhine, and kills the wildlife living there.

When it comes to the problem of acid rain, Germany is its own worst enemy. The main sources of acid rain are smoke from factories and power plants. These facilities burn fuels like natural gas, coal, and oil. Cars and buses that burn gasoline and diesel produce these gases too. Germany, however, depends on manufacturing. The country is one of the leading exporters of cars, steel, and chemical products. These industries have mostly coal-burning factories. Germans also own more cars than people of most other countries do. This adds to acid rain through auto emissions.

Nature plays a part in the acid rain problem. The toxic smoke from manufacturing plants is carried by air currents to other places before it falls to earth as acid rain. Germany shares its borders with many other countries. With other countries involved, it is also a more difficult problem to solve. For example, air currents bring the chemical-filled smoke from coal-burning factories in the United Kingdom to Germany. The chemicals fall to earth in Germany as acid rain.

Germany has been working on the problem of acid rain. In southern Germany, plants that use water power from streams and rivers in the region are replacing many coal-burning factories. The German government has passed laws to reduce emissions from automobiles and factories. Factories are switching to cleaner fuels. They are building taller smokestacks that scrub the smoke before it enters the air. In 2007, Germany, as a member of the European Union, promised to increase its use of cleaner, renewable energy by 20 percent. Germany's goal is to decrease the use of fossil fuels like coal and oil.

Germany is developing new types of energy. It is the leading producer of wind turbines and solar power technology in the world. It is home to the largest wind farm and the largest solar energy plant in the world. Because of these changes, the country's harmful emissions are falling. This is reducing the amount of acid rain.

_____ **288. How does nature play a role in Germany's acid rain problem?**

    A. The poisonous emissions from cars cause acid rain.

    B. Air currents carry toxic smoke from other countries' factories to Germany.

    C. The rivers of southwestern Germany are used to make electricity for other countries.

    D. Germany has many buildings that are being destroyed by the chemicals in the acid rain.

_____ **289. What are the main causes of acid rain?**

    A. farms and forests

    B. water power and electricity

    C. coal burning factories and automobile emissions

    D. solar power and wind turbines blowing the poison gases

290. Which situation is an effect of acid rain?

    A. cleaner rivers

    B. diseased forests

    C. buildings and statues that look new

    D. increased automobile manufacturing

291. Which solution to Germany's acid rain problem would be the most challenging?

    A. reducing automobile emissions

    B. increasing the use of wind and solar power

    C. getting other countries to stop using fossil fuels

    D. changing from coal-burning power plants to water-powered ones

AIR POLLUTION IN THE UNITED KINGDOM

London, the capital of the United Kingdom, is notorious for air pollution. In fact, the word *smog* was first used in 1905 to describe the air in London. Smog is air pollution caused by sunlight acting on the gases from automobile and factory exhausts. It sometimes hangs over cities in the United Kingdom. Thick London smog happens when water in the air mixes with smoke particles from a coal fire. In the *Great Smog* of 1952, the smog was so dense that, for four days, the people in London could not see what was in front of them. Transportation slowed, crime increased, and thousands of people died from the pollution. People around the world suddenly were frightened. They began to worry about the quality of the air they were breathing in.

The United Kingdom's major natural resources are oil, natural gas, and coal. Much of the United Kingdom's manufacturing uses these resources. The Industrial Revolution began around the coalfields where fuel was cheap and available. Many people in the United Kingdom work in these coalfields. Today, coal from these fields still fuels the country's power plants. It also burns in fireplaces and stoves in many homes. Use of coal is decreasing. However, that means fewer jobs for workers in coal mining.

In the past, the major source of air pollution was smoke and sulfur dioxide from burning coal or other fossil fuels. Today, exhaust from gasoline and diesel-powered vehicles is the major problem. Asthma and pneumonia are linked to vehicle emissions. This makes people concerned about air pollution and health. It burns the lungs, nose, and eyes and endangers human life. High air pollution keeps children and senior citizens indoors. Air pollution also blackens buildings and threatens wildlife.

As far back as the 1300s, King Edward I tried to solve the problem by banning coal fires. After the Great Smog, the government created *smokeless zones* in London where only smokeless fuels could be used. Cleaner coals, increased use of electricity, and use of gas have reduced air pollution. Today the government sets limits for industry. Laws have forced automakers to build vehicles that produce less harmful exhaust. The government regularly checks air quality. It asks citizens to drive less and use cleaner forms of energy.

Londoners no longer experience the blackout smog of the 1950s. Air quality has improved. However, the United Kingdom still ranks in the top ten in the world in harmful industrial emissions. Air pollution in the United Kingdom continues to cause acid rain in many countries in Western Europe.

292. What is the main cause of air pollution in the United Kingdom today?

    A. London smog

    B. factory smoke

    C. use of fossil fuels

    D. automobile exhaust emissions

EUROPE

____ **293. Which is one of the United Kingdom's solutions to the air pollution problem?**
   A. monitoring air quality
   B. restricting driving miles
   C. allowing factories to pollute without monitoring
   D. keeping drivers from using gasoline in their cars

____ **294. Which was created after the Great Smog of 1952?**
   A. a ban on coal fires
   B. an industrial revolution
   C. London's smokeless zones
   D. King Edward's ban on coal fires

____ **295. Which solution began to reduce air pollution in the United Kingdom?**
   A. the ban on coal fires
   B. acid rain in Western Europe
   C. the development of cleaner coal
   D. the link between asthma and vehicle exhaust

NUCLEAR DISASTER IN CHERNOBYL, UKRAINE

In 1986, in Ukraine, a country famous for its fertile plains and agriculture, the Chernobyl Nuclear Power Station experienced a disaster. This disaster exposed one-tenth of the Ukraine's 233,090 square miles and approximately one million of its people to unsafe levels of radiation. One of the nuclear reactors at the Chernobyl plant exploded. Tons of radioactive material surrounded the plant, poisoning the land and the water. Even more radioactive material entered the air, falling on northern Europe and Scandinavia. Drinking water was unsafe for months after the accident, and fish in the rivers of the Ukraine and neighboring countries were not safe to eat for years. Nearby pine forests turned brown and died. Many animals died or suffered thyroid damage. A thirty-mile area around the power station was abandoned by humans and became known as the "exclusion zone." The faulty reactor was quickly buried in concrete, but this structure requires major work and the radioactive material is still not safe.

It is difficult to determine the effects on human life. In the first months after the disaster, twenty-eight emergency workers died from acute radiation syndrome. Since the accident, doctors have noticed an increase in cases of cancer in people living in contaminated areas.

Because of Chernobyl, the Ukrainian government decided to become a nuclear-free country. However, due to a lack of power plants in the country and disagreements with Russia over how to get rid of nuclear waste, the three other reactors at Chernobyl continued to operate. The last reactor was finally shut down in 2000.

In the 1980s, many countries were using nuclear power. Nuclear power plants were producing cheaper energy without filling the air with pollution and without using up Earth's supply of fossil fuels. After Chernobyl, concerns about nuclear safety spread around the world. A mistake in one country could have devastating results in another country. Different countries also had different regulations about nuclear power. The reactors at Chernobyl were not housed in the same type of buildings required in other countries. Reactors were not always used for their intended purpose. The Chernobyl reactor was built for weapons material production, not for generating electricity. While regulations did not seem to cross borders, radiation did.

The debate continues. Is the cost savings of nuclear-generated electricity worth the risk of human life? How should nuclear waste be disposed of safely? How should it be regulated? Which is the bigger risk to the environment, nuclear energy or fossil fuel?

296. Which was an effect of the nuclear disaster at Chernobyl?
   A. People and animals did not get sick.
   B. Drinking water was unsafe for months.
   C. Forests got healthier than they had been.
   D. All the nuclear power plants in the world were closed.

297. What steps were taken by the government to make the reactor safe?
   A. The reactor was taken apart.
   B. The reactor was buried in concrete.
   C. The government quit using nuclear power.
   D. The reactor was moved to the exclusion zone.

298. Why were other countries concerned about the disaster?
   A. Chernobyl was immediately closed.
   B. The cost of nuclear power increased.
   C. Radioactive material fell on other countries.
   D. They did not have room for the sick people in their hospitals.

299. Which problem is associated with the debate about nuclear power?
   A. acid rain
   B. deforestation
   C. disposing of nuclear waste
   D. having enough oil to run nuclear power plants

EUROPE

LOCATION, CLIMATE, AND NATURAL RESOURCES OF THE UNITED KINGDOM

Location of the United Kingdom

The United Kingdom (U.K.) is a country of islands off the coast of mainland Europe. It is made up of Great Britain, Northern Ireland, Scotland, and Wales. The location of the U.K. makes it a hub for trade with other countries. Across the English Channel from the U.K. is France; west across the Irish Sea is the Republic of Ireland; east across the North Sea is the Scandinavian Peninsula. An island country with many ports and harbors, the United Kingdom at one time dominated world trade. Today, there are ten major ports along the coast. London's Heathrow Airport is the busiest airport in the world. Seven other airports can handle even the largest jets. There is so much air travel around the U.K., it ranks third in number of airports in Europe.

Location has helped the U.K. become an international banking and insurance center. Between London and Edinburgh, Scotland, the United Kingdom has more foreign bank branches than any country in the world. Businesses of all types, from clothing to computers, trade goods in the U.K. to be sold all over Europe. Its location on the Atlantic Ocean also helps it trade with the United States. The United States is the U.K.'s number one trading partner.

Climate of the United Kingdom

The United Kingdom has a mild climate with rainfall throughout the year. Almost no section goes without rain for longer than three weeks. The southeastern parts of Great Britain are protected by mountains from the wind blowing in from the Atlantic, so they are the driest areas. The rest of the country often has mild, wet weather. The highlands of Scotland are the wettest. The temperature changes with the seasons. Winters are mild and wet. Snowfalls are not very deep and usually occur in the mountains. Summers are warmest in the south. The mild climate keeps ports free of ice and open for trade all year.

Warm waters and winds from the Gulf of Mexico affect the climate of the U.K. The **Gulf Stream** moves warm water along the coast of North America. It crosses the Atlantic Ocean and warms Ireland and the western coasts of England, Scotland, and Wales. Other areas of the world along the same latitude as the U.K. have cold and harsh winters. The Gulf Stream makes the winters in the U.K. much milder.

The climate is good for farming. The land is good for farming too. Much of the land is used for grazing and agriculture because of the mild climate, but less than 2 percent of the people earn their living as farmers. Most people live in urban areas where jobs are more available.

Natural Resources of the United Kingdom

The United Kingdom has deposits of coal, petroleum, natural gas, and iron ore. These resources formed the backbone of the country's industry: auto production, steel manufacturing, and shipbuilding. Other resources include lead, zinc, gold, tin, limestone, salt, clay, chalk, gypsum, potash, sand, and slate. Today, manufacturing is declining because these natural resources are being used up and industry is changing to cleaner forms of energy. Competition with other countries has also increased. This has led to a loss of manufacturing jobs in the U.K.

Many people who once had jobs in mining and manufacturing are being retrained for jobs in service industries. In the United Kingdom, nearly 80 percent of the people work in service industries. These include tourism, health care, education, banking, and insurance. Often people must move to more urban areas to find new jobs and must work for a much lower wage.

EUROPE

Fishing is profitable along the shores of the U.K. Fishermen catch crabs and other shellfish, cod, herring, and mackerel. Nearly 25 percent of the country has **arable** land (land that is suitable for growing crops). Over half of the land in the U.K. is used for farms. A large amount of arable land means the country can produce about 60 percent of its own food. Farms with sheep, beef cattle, dairy cattle, and pigs use the land to keep their businesses going.

_____ **300. Which is a reason for the decline in manufacturing in the United Kingdom?**
A. trade competition
B. not enough workers
C. fuels are not as clean
D. natural resources are close by

_____ **301. Which accounts for most of the jobs in the United Kingdom?**
A. tourism
B. farming
C. manufacturing
D. service industry

_____ **302. Which makes the United Kingdom ideal for international banking?**
A. airports
B. climate
C. location
D. natural resources

_____ **303. Which condition helped the United Kingdom become a leader in world trade?**
A. It is an island with a mild climate located near many other countries.
B. Two percent of the people are farmers, and there is a lot of arable land.
C. It is home to the world's busiest airport and has seven other large airports.
D. Urban areas are heavily populated, and most jobs are found in the urban areas.

_____ **304. Why is it surprising that the U.K. has such a mild climate?**
A. It is very far north.
B. The ocean is always warm.
C. People in the U.K. like snowy winters.
D. It is warmer in northern parts of the world.

_____ **305. What causes the U.K. to have an unusually mild climate?**
A. the Gulf Stream
B. the Scottish highlands
C. snowfall that is not very deep
D. the mountains in the southeast

_____ **306. Which is an effect of a declining industry?**
A. Retraining is not needed.
B. Many people lose their jobs.
C. People earn more money at new jobs.
D. People have an easy time finding new jobs.

EUROPE

LOCATION, CLIMATE, AND NATURAL RESOURCES OF RUSSIA

Location of Russia

Russia spans two continents. It covers the eastern part of Europe, and it spans the northern part of Asia. It is so wide that a train trip from western Russia to eastern Russia would take a week. Russia shares a border with fifteen other countries including China, North Korea, Finland, Norway, Poland, and Ukraine. The eastern side of the country is bounded by the North Pacific Ocean. The northern side is bounded by the Arctic Ocean. At its closest point, Russia and the United States are only about three miles apart across the Bering Strait.

European Russia is almost landlocked. Most of the land is far from the sea or frozen over for most of the year. Murmansk and St. Petersburg are the exceptions. Murmansk is on the open ocean near Norway. The Gulf Stream keeps the port warm enough to stay open all year. Other ports on the Arctic Ocean must be cleared with icebreakers.

St. Petersburg is a port city on the Baltic Sea. St. Petersburg was home to the czars of Russia and the capital of Russia for over two hundred years. It has beautiful canals, gardens, and palaces. St. Petersburg is a major center for trade. A network of railroads surrounds St. Petersburg, bringing goods into the city for shipment around the world. It is home to over 5 million people. In the 1990s, tourism began to grow.

Climate of Russia

European Russia really only has two seasons, winter and summer. The hottest month is July and the coldest is January. The average yearly temperature of nearly all of Russia is below freezing. Many areas have soil that is permanently frozen. This ground is called *permafrost*. In the winter, railroad lines are changed to cross frozen lakes and rivers. Because of arctic winds, harsh winters are a part of Russian life. If you lived in the capital city, Moscow, you would expect to have snow on the ground in winter for four to five months. Winters are often dreary with gray skies. In summer, winds from the south bring warmer temperatures, but not much rain.

In Asian Russia, the climate is extreme. Siberia, the land furthest east, can have low temperatures of -40°F. during the long winters. Nights can be even colder. Three to four feet of snow are possible. Summers are usually mild. However, hot days in Siberia can reach over 90°F. Further north, a part of the ground stays frozen all year.

The distance from the sea influences the climate. The European Plain is the driest, but the lands bordering the Black Sea and the Baltic Sea are exceptions. They have more rainfall and warmer temperatures. The area around the Black Sea is considered subtropical, and it is a popular summer resort area. About 73 percent of the entire Russian population lives in European Russia, where the weather is harsh, but not as severe as the Asian Plains and Siberia. The climate, distance from the sea, and rugged terrain keep many of Russia's resources from being used.

Natural Resources of Russia

Russia is a land of many resources. Vast forests for lumber still are found there. However, on the European side of Russia, most of the deciduous and evergreen forests have been cleared away for cities and farms. Deposits of gold, aluminum ore, coal, and iron are found in the Ural Mountains, which border the European Plain. Russia is a leading producer and exporter of gold, minerals, metals, and machinery. Many factories that process iron and other metals are located in this region. The large cities in this area grew up around the mining industry. Today, machinery is produced in many of the factories.

The Volga River is the largest river in Europe. Over half of Russia's major cities are along the Volga. The Volga is a source of hydroelectric power for industry and a waterway to ship manufactured goods. Hydroelectric power is also a possibility on many of the rivers of Russia.

EUROPE

Russia's large size and cold climate make it difficult for Russians to use their resources. For example, oil and gas are natural resources of Russia. However, they are mostly in Siberia and in Asian Russia. That makes them difficult to reach.

_____ **307. Which area of Russia is a major center for trade?**
      A. Siberia
      B. Asian Russia
      C. St. Petersburg
      D. European Russia

_____ **308. Which condition keeps Russia's natural resources from being used?**
      A. harsh climate
      B. lack of workers
      C. no market for them
      D. no government funding

_____ **309. Which statement BEST describes the way the Volga River helps manufacturing?**
      A. It provides food and water for the workers.
      B. Workers' families ice skate and swim there.
      C. It is used to clean machinery before it is shipped overseas.
      D. It is used for hydroelectric power and transportation of goods.

_____ **310. With its long northern coastline, what makes shipping in Russia so difficult?**
      A. The northern ports are blocked by ice much of the year.
      B. Manufactured goods and people prefer to travel by train.
      C. The Volga River is used only for hydroelectric power, not for shipping.
      D. Cruise ships bringing tourists to St. Petersburg take up much of the harbor.

COMPARING THE UNITED KINGDOM AND RUSSIA

Russia and the United Kingdom are geographically very different. By area, Russia is the larger country, with a long coastline bordering the Arctic Ocean. Its port cities are locked by ice most of the year. The United Kingdom is an island country with a mild climate and many ports accessible all year round.

The natural resources of both countries include fossil fuels, like coal and oil. While the United Kingdom's are dwindling, much of Russia's coal and oil is untouched because of the climate and the geography of the country.

London, on the River Thames, is the capital of the United Kingdom. It is home to one of the largest financial centers in the world. International stocks are traded on the London Stock Exchange, and many foreign banks have branches there. Moscow, the capital of Russia, is its largest city. Moscow is the center for all transportation within Russia, but it is St. Petersburg, on the Baltic Sea, that is the Russian center for trade.

_____ **311. Which natural resources are found in both Russia and the United Kingdom?**
      A. coal
      B. gold
      C. forests
      D. hydroelectric power

EUROPE

____ **312.** **Which statement BEST describes the natural resources of the United Kingdom and Russia?**
  A. The United Kingdom and Russia both have gold, a valuable natural resource.
  B. The United Kingdom's coal resources are used as fuel for manufacturing, but Russia's are not.
  C. The United Kingdom and Russia both have large amounts of land and climates suitable for farming.
  D. The United Kingdom's fossil fuel resources are being used up, but much of Russia's are unused due to Russia's climate and geography.

____ **313.** **How do the ports of the United Kingdom and Russia differ?**
  A. The ports of the United Kingdom are open year round, and Russia's are not.
  B. Russia has no port cities, while the United Kingdom is an island with many.
  C. There is no difference in the year-round use of the ports in the United Kingdom and Russia.
  D. The ports of the United Kingdom are influenced by a mild climate, but Russia's ports are all subtropical.

____ **314.** **In what way are London and St. Petersburg alike?**
  A. Both are centers for trade.
  B. Both are ocean port cities.
  C. Both are capitals of their countries.
  D. Both are the largest city in the country.

> **SS6G10** **The student will explain the impact of location, climate, natural resources, and population distribution on Europe.**
> b. Compare how the location, climate, and natural resources of Germany and Italy affect where people live and how they trade.

LOCATION, CLIMATE, AND NATURAL RESOURCES OF GERMANY

Location of Germany

Germany is located in north-central Europe on the European Plain. Denmark, the Baltic Sea, and the North Sea lie to the north. Poland and the Czech Republic are to the east. On the southern side lies Austria and Switzerland. To the west are France, Luxembourg, Belgium, and the Netherlands. Germany is about the size of South Carolina, Georgia, and Alabama combined. However, five times more people live in Germany than in these three states. Germany is one of the most densely populated parts of Europe. About 85 percent of people live in urban areas. The land is generally in three zones: Alps Mountains in the south, hilly to mountainous in the middle, plains in the north.

The Rhine River, much of which lies in Germany, is very important for trade. This river is over eight hundred miles long. The Rhine begins in the Alps of Switzerland and flows north, through Germany, to the North Sea. Many German cities lie along the Rhine. This location gives those cities an excellent way to transport goods and people.

Germany's location in the center of Europe makes it a crossroads of travel and trade. The country's excellent highway system has helped Germany take advantage of its location. Countries from Eastern Europe and Western Europe transport goods to and across Germany. The relatively flat European Plain makes transportation easier in the northern part of the country. Toward the south, the Alps make transportation more difficult. Germany has built many highways, bridges, and tunnels to improve trade with countries to the south. Germany has eight major ports, which handle the country's exports and imports. Fourteen major airports transport goods and people all over the world.

Climate of Germany

Most of Germany has a marine climate. The waters of the Gulf Stream warm the region. That means that the warm waters of the ocean help to keep the land warm in winter. The sea also cools the land in summer. The ocean also brings moisture to the land. Precipitation provides enough moisture for the land to produce good crops. The Bavarian Alps have a climate that changes with their altitude. Some parts of the mountains are deep in snow all winter.

Eastern Germany is farther from the effects of the sea. This part of the country has longer, colder winters. Summers tend to be longer, hotter, and drier.

Natural Resources of Germany

Germany has many natural resources. Iron ore, coal, and potash are major products from mining. Uranium, which is used for nuclear fuel, is found in Germany. Nickel, natural gas, and copper are important too. Timber is a renewable resource. Much of the forests in the north has been cut to provide land for farms, villages, and towns, but there are still large amounts of timber in the south. About one-third of the land is arable (usable for crops).

Natural resources such as coal helped to build large industrial areas. These areas became large cities in Germany. Many of these are along the Rhine River. The Rhine River region is very densely populated.

_____ 315. **Which describes the climate of most of Germany?**
   A. very cold winters with hot and dry summers
   B. cool summers with land deep in snow most of the winter
   C. cool winters and mild summers with good precipitation for crops
   D. hot summers and cold winters with little precipitation except for winter snow

_____ 316. **Which is a natural resource of Germany?**
   A. coal
   B. gold
   C. diamonds
   D. rain forests

_____ 317. **Which has about the same area as Germany?**
   A. Florida and Georgia
   B. the continental United States
   C. the southeastern United States
   D. Alabama, Georgia, and South Carolina

LOCATION, CLIMATE, AND NATURAL RESOURCES OF ITALY

Location of Italy

Italy is a country in southern Europe. It is on a long, boot-shaped peninsula. The peninsula is surrounded on three sides by the Mediterranean Sea. The northern border of Italy is in the Alps. In this region, Italy shares a border with France, Switzerland, Austria, and Slovenia. Italy is about twice the size of the state of Georgia, but it has seven times as many people. Seven out of ten people in Italy live in urban areas. The largest urban areas are Rome, Naples, Milan, and Turin. About half of the people in Italy live in the most northern one-third of the country.

Islands and mountains affect life in Italy. The Apennine Mountains are like a backbone across Italy's length, stretching over six hundred miles. The mountains affect where people live and how they transport people and goods. Two large islands in the Mediterranean are a part of Italy. The island of Sicily is located a few miles west of the tip of "the boot" of Italy. The island of Sardinia is a bit further away. It lies about two hundred miles west of the main part of Italy.

Italy's location on the Mediterranean Sea affects trade with other countries. Italy has a long history of shipping goods to and from other countries in Europe and Asia. Merchants took advantage of Italy's location to trade goods from Africa, Asia, and Europe. Today, there are seven major airports and about one hundred smaller ones. Eight major seaports can handle the largest ships on the sea. Excellent highways, bridges, and tunnels connect Italy with their neighbors to the north.

Climate of Italy

Most of Italy has a Mediterranean climate. The Mediterranean Sea surrounding Italy keeps the temperature comfortable most of the year. Summer skies are generally clear, and rain is rare in summer. Dry summers are one of the main characteristics of this climate. Winters are usually cloudy and rainy. The sea helps keep the temperatures from getting too hot in summer and too cold in winter. The Alps block cold air moving from the north. The hot, dry air of the Sahara Desert plays a role in Italy's climate. It expands from the south sending warm dry air into Italy for much of the year.

Not all of Italy has the same kind of climate. The mountains have a climate that changes with altitude. The Alps and Apennines have snowy winters. Their temperature is usually cooler than the temperature in lower elevations. The south is drier than the north. Northern Italy has enough rain for growing crops. Southern Italy is much drier. It only gets about half as much rain as northern Italy.

Natural Resources of Italy

Italy has few mineral resources. Natural gas is the most valuable mineral resource found in Italy. It is used to help supply the country's energy needs. Marble and granite are available. These are used in the construction of buildings and artwork. Coal, mercury, zinc, and potash are other minerals found in Italy.

Arable land is important in Italy. Small farms cover much of the country. Grapes and olives are important crops. Italy is one of the world's top wine-making countries because of its excellent grape crop.

The sea is an important resource, too. The long coastline allows for more than eight hundred ports for fishing boats. About 50,000 Italians make their living as fishermen. Anchovies and sardines are two fish important to the economy. Italian fishermen also gather sponges and coral.

_____ 318. **What geographic feature makes it more difficult for Italian merchants to trade with countries north of Italy?**
A. Sardinia
B. Alps Mountains
C. Mediterranean Sea
D. Apennine Mountains

_____ 319. **What has helped Italian merchants become successful traders?**
A. the location of the Alps, which are a defense against other countries
B. the location on the Mediterranean Sea with access to Africa, Asia, and Europe
C. the islands of Sicily and Sardinia, which are not far from the coast of western Italy
D. the warm air from the Sahara Desert, which creates a warm, dry summer for most of Italy

320. Which condition is NOT a characteristic of Italy's Mediterranean climate?

A. dry summers

B. long, cold winters

C. clear, blue summer skies

D. mild temperatures all year

321. Which industry is MOST helped by Italy's arable land and good amounts of rainfall?

A. wine making

B. natural gas production

C. marble and granite mines

D. fishing fleets on the Mediterranean Sea

EUROPE

Use the following table to answer questions 322-325.

Comparing Italy and Germany

	Italy	Germany
Location	• long, boot-shaped peninsula surrounded on 3 sides by the Mediterranean Sea • the Alps form the northern boundary • Apennines Mountains run from the Alps to the sea • 2 islands, Sardinia and Sicily, are part of the country • about 26% arable land • mostly coastal lowlands and river valleys, with mountains like a spine through the peninsula	• in north-central Europe on European Plain • Poland to the east, France to the west, Baltic Sea to the north, Austria and Switzerland to the south • southern region, mountainous; central region, hilly and mountainous; northern region, flat plains • most important commercial waterway in Europe – Rhine River • about 34% arable land
Climate	• temperate climate with regional differences • coastal areas have mild winters and warm, dry summers • mountains have cold, wet, and snowy winters and humid subtropical summers	• in the west, winters are mild, summers are cool, with rainfall year round • in the east, winter are very cold, summers are very hot with long dry periods
Natural Resources	coal, mercury, zinc, potash, marble, barite, asbestos, pumice, fluorospar, feldspar, pyrite (sulfur), natural gas and crude oil reserves, fish, arable land	iron ore, coal, potash, timber, lignite, uranium, copper, natural gas, salt, nickel, arable land
Population	about 61,000,000	about 82,000,000
Area	about 116,000 square miles	about 138,000 square miles
Where People Live	• Urban: 68% • Rural: 32% • one-half of the population lives in one-third of the country – northern Italy • capital and largest city is Rome • most people live in urban areas around the major cities of Naples, Rome, Milan, and Turin	• Urban: 74% • Rural: 26% • Berlin is the largest city and the capital • most densely populated county in European Union • huge cluster of cities in the coal fields of Western Germany near Rhine
Trade	• 12+ major seaports • exports: chemicals, clothing, food, footwear, iron and steel, machinery, motor vehicles, petroleum products, textiles • major trading partners: Germany, France, U.K., and U.S. • tourism	• exports: chemicals, food, instruments, iron and steel, machinery, motor vehicles, potash, railway, textiles • major trading partners: European Union, Switzerland, Japan, and U.S. • tourism

EUROPE

_____ **322. Which trading partner is shared by both countries?**

    A. Japan

    B. Russia

    C. Norway

    D. United States

_____ **323. A similarity between Italy and Germany is that, in both countries, people tend to live in**

    A. rural areas.

    B. urban areas.

    C. the southern region.

    D. farming communities.

_____ **324. A difference between Italy and Germany is that Germany**

    A. has less arable land than Italy.

    B. is more densely populated than Italy.

    C. has a much smaller population than Italy.

    D. does not allow people to live near the Rhine River.

_____ **325. In which industries do Italy and Germany compete with each other for trade with other countries?**

    A. chemicals, machinery, food

    B. potash, clothing, instruments

    C. instruments, footwear, motor vehicles

    D. tourism, petroleum, produce, iron, and steel

SS6G11 The student will describe the cultural characteristics of Europe.

a. Explain the diversity of European languages as seen in a comparison of German, English, Russian, French, and Italian.

COMPARING THE LANGUAGES OF GERMAN, ENGLISH, RUSSIAN, FRENCH, AND ITALIAN

The continent of Europe is slightly larger than the United States in land area. However, Europe's population is more than double the population of the United States. In the United States, English is the dominant language. Other languages are spoken by immigrants and by Native Americans, but only in small numbers. Europe is much different. It is home to more than two hundred native languages. A few languages are dominant, but many more are spoken by large numbers of people.

Most European languages are in three main categories: *Germanic* languages, *Romance* languages, and *Slavic* languages. The Germanic language group has the most native speakers. European native speakers of this group live mostly in northwest and central Europe. About 20 percent of Europeans speak one of two languages—English and German—as their native language. Most Europeans learn English as a second language in their schools even if they don't speak English at home.

Another large group is the Romance languages, which includes French, Italian, and Spanish. These languages are found in the south and west of Europe. These languages come from Latin, the language of the ancient Roman Empire. The Roman alphabet is used to write both Romance and Germanic languages, although not every language has the exact same characters and punctuation. The words on this page are written using the Roman alphabet.

EUROPE

Slavic languages include Russian. Slavic languages are found in central and eastern Europe. These languages do not always use the Roman alphabet. Instead, they are written with a *Cyrillic alphabet*. Russian, for example, uses the Cyrillic alphabet.

Russian Alphabet

Аа Бб Вв Гг Дд Ее Ёё Жж Зз Ии Йй Кк Лл Мм Нн Оо Пп Рр Сс Тт Уу Фф Хх Цц Чч Шш Щщ Ъъ Ыы Ьь Ээ Юю Яя (Ii Ѳѳ Ѵѵ Ѣѣ)

Having so many languages can be a problem. It is difficult to live, work, and trade with people who cannot communicate with each other. Europeans have worked hard to solve this problem. Most schoolchildren learn one or two other languages besides their own. The European Union has twenty-three "official" languages to make sure that people can understand laws and decisions made by the government. There are special laws to protect languages too. Europeans want to keep alive the languages spoken by only a few people. At the same time, they are working to build a unified Europe.

_____ 326. **What have Europeans done to try to solve the problem of so many languages?**
   A. outlawed the use of languages spoken by only a few people
   B. decided not to trade with people who do not speak the same language
   C. made laws ensuring that English is the only official language of the European Union
   D. required schoolchildren to learn one or two other languages besides their native language

_____ 327. **Which languages come from the language of the ancient Roman Empire?**
   A. Latin
   B. Russian and Polish
   C. French, Italian, and Spanish
   D. English, German, and Dutch

_____ 328. **Besides differences in words, what other challenge do Europeans face in communicating with each other?**
   A. They use two different alphabets.
   B. People in the United States speak mostly English.
   C. Europe's population is double the size of the United States.
   D. Most of the people in Europe do not want to learn another language.

Use these statements to answer question 329.

- Schoolchildren in Europe learn more than one language.
- The European Union records all its business in twenty-three languages.
- Laws have been written to protect languages spoken by only a few people.

_____ 329. **What do these statements show about Europeans?**
   A. Europeans want to have one common language.
   B. Europeans respect the languages of other cultures.
   C. The people in Europe want English to be the main language.
   D. The European Union is working to get rid of languages that few people speak.

Use the table to answer questions 330-332.

Comparing Major Languages of Europe

Origin	Example Language	Official Language in	Approximate Number of European Native Speakers
West Germanic Languages • largest of the three language groups • derived from the Germanic tribes 750 BC-AD 1	German	Germany, Austria, Switzerland, Liechtenstein, Luxembourg, European Union	100 million people
	English	United Kingdom, Ireland, European Union	62 million people
Slavic Languages • Russian is the most widely spoke Slavic language • Russian is the largest native language in Europe	Russian	Russia, Belarus, Kazakhstan, Kyrgyzstan, United Nations, Commonwealth of Independent States	140 million people
Romance Languages • derived from Latin, the language of the Roman Empire • Latin is no longer spoken as a native language in any country	French	France, Belgium, Luxembourg, Monaco, Switzerland, United Nations, European Union	65-80 million people
	Italian	Italy, San Marino, Switzerland, Vatican, European Union	63 million people

____ 330. **In what way are the French and Italian languages alike?**
   A. The countries of France and Italy are close to each other.
   B. They are both Romance languages that derived from Latin.
   C. They are both the official language of the United Nations.
   D. French and Italian share the roots of the Germanic languages.

____ 331. **Which European language has the largest number of native speakers?**
   A. French
   B. Russian
   C. English
   D. German

____ 332. **Which describes a way that Russian is different from the other languages?**
   A. It is only spoken in Asia.
   B. It is not spoken by as many people.
   C. It is not an official language of the EU.
   D. It is not a native language for any country.

EUROPE

DIVERSITY IN EUROPEAN LANGUAGES TODAY

Many European countries have more than one official language. Notice in the earlier chart that Switzerland has three. There is actually a fourth official Swiss language not shown! Multiple official languages are a part of life in many countries in Europe due to the ethnic background of the people living there. Many countries share borders, and people move back and forth across borders easily. About 400 million people in the world speak English because it is often the choice for a second language. It is chosen because it is considered the worldwide language of business. Many more people in Europe speak English as a second language than are noted on the chart of native speakers. In European countries, students are often required to master another language. In France, almost 66 percent of the population speaks some English. Over half of all Europeans speak some English.

Immigration has created pockets of other language speakers in countries where their native language is not an official one. In Russia, a large community of German Russians moved there in 1871. As is often the case, the Russian government required the children of those immigrants to learn the Russian language in school. As a result, many older citizens use their native language, while the younger population change to the language of their new country.

Problems occur when many languages are spoken in one place. Communication is difficult. Documents are printed only in the official language. Government workers often only speak the official language. In France, the official language is only French, but when you look at the earlier chart and at the graph that follows, you will note how many other languages are used by the people of France.

_____ 333. **Which group is less likely to learn the language of a new country?**
   A. men
   B. women
   C. older citizens
   D. young students

_____ 334. **What is a problem caused by many languages spoken in the same country?**
   A. There are no problems.
   B. Children can't talk to their parents.
   C. Schoolchildren hate to learn other languages.
   D. It's difficult to read and understand official forms.

_____ 335. **What did children of German immigrants to Russia have to do in school?**
   A. learn the Russian language
   B. agree not to speak German at home
   C. attend classes away from Russian children
   D. move to a school where only German is spoken

Use the graph to answer questions 336-337.

Native Language of People in France

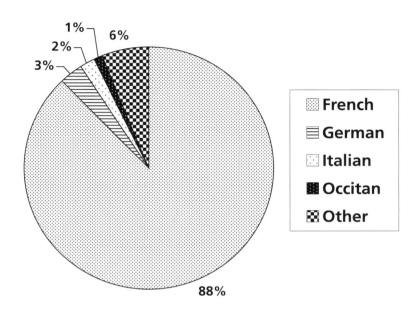

Legend:
- ▨ French
- ▤ German
- ▦ Italian
- ◼ Occitan
- ▩ Other

French: 88%
Other: 6%
Occitan: 1%
Italian: 2%
German: 3%

_____ 336. **Which question can be answered using the graph?**

    A. How many people in France speak Italian?

    B. How many people in France speak French?

    C. What part of the French population speaks English as a second language?

    D. What percentage of people in France have Italian as their native language?

_____ 337. **How many of the people in France speaks German as their native language?**

    A. 3 percent

    B. 6 percent

    C. 12 percent

    D. 88 percent

SS6G11 The student will describe the cultural characteristics of Europe.

b. Describe the major religions in Europe; include Judaism, Christianity, and Islam.

MAJOR RELIGIONS IN EUROPE: JUDAISM, CHRISTIANITY, AND ISLAM

Europe is home to many religions. There are three main religions, however. These are Judaism, Christianity, and Islam. These religions have some similarities and even a common history. They are also different in their beliefs about God and man. Sometimes these beliefs cause disagreements between people. Disagreements can even happen between people of the same religious group.

Religion has been very important in the history of Europe. Wars have been fought, and government leaders have been changed, because of religious issues. Today, most Europeans have the legal freedom to choose their religion. Most Europeans recognize and respect the rights of others to choose their own religion. Study the following table to learn about the three main religious groups of Europe.

Use the table to answer questions 338-341.

Comparing Judaism, Christianity, and Islam

	Judaism	Christianity	Islam
Founder	Abraham (about 2000 BC)	Jesus Christ (about 30 AD)	Muhammad (about 610 AD)
Holy book	Torah	Bible	Koran
Followers called	Jews ✡	Christians ✝	Muslims ☪
Number of followers	about 15 million	about 2.1 billion	about 1.3 billion
Additional facts	• Torah is the first five books of the writings of Moses, believed to be given to Moses by God at Mt. Sinai • Talmud is the written version of the Oral Law • belief is in the laws of one God and the words of his prophets • actions and following the laws are important • three main types of Judaism are: Orthodox (most traditional), Conservative, and Reform (least traditional) • Jews in Europe were nearly wiped out by Hitler and Nazi Germany	• the five books of Moses make up the first five books of the Bible • beliefs are based on the teachings of Jesus: love of God and neighbor, a regard for justice, a belief that Jesus is the Son of God • Christianity is divided into 3 major groups: Eastern Orthodox, Roman Catholic, and Protestant • Protestants include Anglicans, Baptists, Methodists, Presbyterians, Episcopalians and other non-Catholic, and non-Orthodox Christians • Christianity is in most parts of the world today	• Muslims believe that Muhammad was the last of the prophets, which included Abraham and Jesus • the main duties of Muslims (called the Five Pillars) are prayer, giving to charity, belief in and submission to one God (Allah), fasting during the month of Ramadan, and a trip to Mecca once in a lifetime • the two largest groups of Muslims are the Sunnis and the Shiites; the Sunnis account for 90% of the world's Muslims • it is the main religion of the Middle East, North Africa, and Asia • number of followers is rapidly growing

_____ **338. Which is the oldest of the three main religions of Europe?**
  A. Islam
  B. Judaism
  C. Christianity
  D. Roman Catholic

_____ **339. Which religion is growing at the fastest rate?**
  A. Islam
  B. Sunni
  C. Judaism
  D. Christianity

_____ **340. How are the three religions alike?**
  A. They each worship several gods.
  B. They each worship only one god.
  C. Each of the three religions is getting smaller.
  D. They each use a sacred text known as the five books of Moses.

_____ **341. Which pairing of sacred text and religion is correct?**
  A. Protestant – Bible
  B. Christianity - Talmud
  C. Shiite Muslim - Torah
  D. Orthodox Judaism - Koran

> **SS6G11   The student will describe the cultural characteristics of Europe.**
> c. Explain how the literacy rate affects the standard of living in Europe.

THE LITERACY RATE AND THE STANDARD OF LIVING IN EUROPE

Literacy is the ability to read and write. High rates of literacy are usually found in developed or **_industrialized countries_** like the United States and most of Europe. Industrialized countries depend more on manufacturing than farming for their wealth. Most people in industrialized countries work in manufacturing, communication, or service industries. The increased wealth of these countries allows them to provide education, health care, and access to technology to their citizens. The standard of living is high.

Developing countries are often called **_third world countries_**. Third world countries do not have much industry and depend on farming for most of their wealth. There are often fewer people in these countries that can read and write. Education, health care, and jobs are not easily available. When education is available, it may be restricted to allow only boys to attend school. People work in low-paying jobs and live in crowded cities. Without the skills of reading and writing, workers cannot get better jobs. Developing countries are poor, and their people are uneducated. It is difficult to pay for education when there is little money for food.

Russia is somewhat unusual in Europe. It has a high literacy rate, but a lower **_Gross Domestic Product (GDP) per capita_** (the total value of the final goods and services produced in a country in one year divided by the total population) than countries with the same percentage of people who can read and write. The government of Russia has always required education. Now the government is finding ways to bring more manufacturing and communication jobs to the country. Poverty is declining and Russia's economy is growing.

EUROPE

Literacy and Per Capita GDP

Country	Literacy Rate	Per Person Gross Domestic Product
United Kingdom	99%	$35,100
France	99%	$33,000
Russia	99%	$14,700
Germany	99%	$33,200
Italy	98%	$30,400

_____ **342. People in third world countries have**
  A. the best jobs.
  B. little education.
  C. a higher literacy rate.
  D. a greater standard of living.

_____ **343. Why does Russia have such a high literacy rate but such a low Gross Domestic Product?**
  A. Russians do not want a higher standard of living.
  B. Education is only required for boys, but girls may attend.
  C. There are too many jobs in manufacturing and not enough schools.
  D. The government has always required the children to be educated, but the economy is not as productive.

_____ **344. A literate person in a developed country is most likely to have all EXCEPT which item?**
  A. health care
  B. technology
  C. a high-paying job
  D. uneducated children

CIVICS/GOVERNMENT UNDERSTANDINGS

SS6CG4 The student will compare and contrast various forms of government.
a. Describe the ways government systems distribute power: unitary, confederation, and federal.

UNITARY, CONFEDERATION, AND FEDERAL GOVERNMENT SYSTEMS

Each country must decide how to set up its government. Countries must decide how to organize and how to distribute power. Governments can have all the power held by one central government, or they can spread out the power to lower levels of government. Governments may be unitary, confederation, or federal.

In a **unitary** government, the central government has all the power. This type of government has a constitution that outlines the duties, powers, and people of the central government. The central government can give power to or create lower levels of government, like states or communities. This power may be changed or taken back at any time. France has a unitary form of government.

EUROPE

A **confederation** is a group of states or communities that come together to support each other and to work on common problems. A confederation is usually formed by a treaty, which may be replaced later with a constitution. In a confederation, the participants are voluntary, equal members. They have to meet with each other before taking action on an issue. Confederations are usually just the first step toward creating a more powerful government. They can also replace central rule. The **British Commonwealth** was formed after the British Empire broke up. When the British Empire lost governing power over its colonies, the **Commonwealth of Nations** was formed. Membership is voluntary. Countries in the Commonwealth work together on common problems. The Commonwealth countries cannot force members to take actions they do not want to take, however.

Like the unitary system, the **federal** system has a constitution. This constitution explains the rights, responsibilities, and duties of the central government and the states. In this way, the power is divided between the central government and the lower levels of government. Unlike the unitary system, the central government cannot take back the power of the states, choose the state's leaders, or do away with these lower levels of government. The United States is an example of a federal government with its constitution and state and federal governments. Germany is an example of a European country that is a federal system. Germany has a federal central government. The country is divided into sixteen federal states. The document that divides and explains the powers of the central government and of the state governments in called the Basic Law.

_____ **345. Which phrase BEST describes a confederation?**
    A. partners
    B. divided power
    C. a strong federation
    D. a strong central government

_____ **346. What country in Europe has a federal government?**
    A. France
    B. Germany
    C. Great Britain
    D. United States

_____ **347. One reason that the British Commonwealth is called a confederation is that member countries**
    A. are voluntary members.
    B. must have a constitution.
    C. have strong central governments.
    D. must do what the majority of the members want to do.

CITIZEN PARTICIPATION IN AUTOCRATIC, OLIGARCHIC, AND DEMOCRATIC GOVERNMENTS

People have different rights when it comes to participating in government. In some countries, people hold the power and elect their leaders or rulers. They vote on their laws. Because many people are involved in making decisions, solving a problem or responding to a crisis often takes a long time.

In other countries, a small group of people holds power. Those that have wealth, own lots of land, or have military support may form this group. If needed, these groups select one of their own to be the leader.

There are also those countries that have only one ruler. This type of ruler may come to power through family bloodlines, like a king or queen, or may be a dictator in power because of military strength.

Citizens in countries with these last two types of government have no say in the laws or the government. Such rulers often do not do what is best for their country and its people.

Use the text and the following table to answer questions 348-351.

Comparison of Citizens' Rights in Different Governments

	Type of Rule	**Who Holds the Power**	**Who Can Be Elected**	**Who Can Vote**
Autocratic – Czarist Russia was an autocratic government.	Single ruler	Unlimited power for the ruler	No one – citizens have no choice in selecting a ruler	No citizen participation – no elections are held
Oligarchic – Many medieval governments were oligarchic.	Small group of people	Group answers only to each other	No one outside the ruling group – the rulers are selected by the group	No citizen participation – leaders are chosen from within the ruling group and by the group
Democratic – France is an example of a democratic country.	Citizens of the country	The voters	Any citizen (with some restrictions like age, not in jail, etc.)	Any citizen (with some restrictions like age, not in jail, etc.)

348. In which types of government do citizens have no voting rights?

    A. an autocracy and a democracy

    B. an oligarchy and a democracy

    C. an oligarchy and an autocracy

    D. any of the three types of government

349. An autocracy puts the power of the government into the hands of

    A. the citizens.

    B. a single person.

    C. the representatives.

    D. a small group of people.

350. How can autocratic rulers come to power?

    A. by voter election

    B. by legislative election

    C. through their bloodline

    D. by representative appointment

351. Which statement is TRUE about an oligarchy?

    A. Anyone can lead.

    B. Leaders are elected.

    C. Laws protect the citizens.

    D. A small group of people govern.

SS6CG4   **The student will compare and contrast various forms of government.**

b. Describe the two predominant forms of democratic governments: parliamentary and presidential.

PARLIAMENTARY AND PRESIDENTIAL FORMS OF GOVERNMENT

In Europe, there are two main types of democratic government. These are parliamentary government and presidential government. The **parliamentary system** is common in Europe. **Presidential democracies** are common in the Americas. Europe's presidential democracies are often organized differently than the U.S. model.

The head of state is different in these forms of government. The head of state is the chief representative of the country to other countries. This person has ceremonial duties and serves as a symbol for the country. The monarch of the United Kingdom is an example. She serves as the symbol for the United Kingdom and is officially "The Queen of the United Kingdom and other Commonwealth Realms." The U.K.'s **prime minister** is responsible for the day-to-day operations in the country. The prime minister serves as chief executive. In Germany, the person most like a prime minister is the **chancellor**. The members of the legislature choose the chancellor. Representatives of the legislature and representatives of the states choose the president of Germany. The president's role is to be the ceremonial head of state.

In the United States, the president serves as head of state and chief executive. The president is the symbol of the country and serves as a ceremonial leader in dealing with other countries. The president also has the job of running the U.S. government on a day-to-day basis. In France, the prime minister runs the government but is chosen by the president. The president is elected by the people to serve as head of state and has the power to deal with other countries.

EUROPE

Study the following Venn diagram to locate some of the key differences in the two forms of democratic government. Pay attention to the part of the diagram where the circles overlap. This shows the ways in which the two forms of democracy are *alike*.

Comparison of Parliamentary and Presidential Systems of Government

Parliamentary System

Presidential System

Prime Minister-leader–heads parliament, the lawmaking body

Parliament selects Prime Minister

Prime Minister can dissolve Parliament

MPs can vote to elect a new Prime Minister

May have a head of state with little power–king or queen

Citizens elect lawmakers

Leader heads the military & runs the government

Legislature-lawmaking body

President-leader

President is elected

Legislature and President serve a fixed amount of time

President does not make laws

The President is head of state and chief executive

_____ **352. In what way are the prime minister and the president alike?**
   A. The lawmaking body appoints them.
   B. They make the laws for their countries.
   C. They can dissolve the lawmaking body.
   D. They are in charge of the military and control the government.

_____ **353. Which statement about the executive is TRUE?**
   A. The president cannot make laws.
   B. The prime minister is the head of state.
   C. The president can dissolve the legislature.
   D. The members of the legislature choose the president.

_____ **354. Legislature is to parliament as a president is to**
   A. dictator.
   B. monarch.
   C. patriarch.
   D. prime minister.

355. **Who has the most government power in the parliamentary system?**
 A. a citizen
 B. the monarch
 C. the prime minister
 D. a member of parliament

356. **Why is the president of France more powerful than the prime minister?**
 A. The French monarch chooses the president.
 B. The president chooses who will be prime minister.
 C. The prime minister has no real power in the government.
 D. The citizens vote for the prime minister but not for the president.

> **SS6CG5** **The student will explain the structure of modern European governments.**
>
> a. Compare the parliamentary system of the United Kingdom of Great Britain and Northern Ireland (United Kingdom), the federal system of the Federal Republic of Germany (Germany), and the federation of the Russian Federation (Russia), distinguishing the form of leadership and the role of the citizen in terms of voting and personal freedoms.

PARLIAMENTARY SYSTEM OF THE UNITED KINGDOM

Parliament is the lawmaking body of the United Kingdom. It is composed of the ***House of Lords*** and the ***House of Commons***. The monarch is considered a part of Parliament too.

In the past, a seat in the House of Lords was passed down through aristocratic families. Today, Lords are elected by the House or are appointed to office by the monarch. The House of Lords has little power. Instead, it can make suggestions of ways to improve a bill that is on its way to becoming law.

The citizens of the United Kingdom elect the members of the House of Commons in a general election. There are 646 members: 529 from England, 40 from Wales, 59 from Scotland, and 18 from Northern Ireland. The power in the House of Commons comes from its control of the budget.

After the election, the leader of the political party with the most members in the House of Commons is asked by the queen to become prime minister. The prime minister is the head of the government, or chief executive, and runs the government on a day-to-day basis.

The monarch is the official head of state. The monarch is a symbol of the country. The monarch is sometimes referred to as "the crown." The monarch's duties are mostly ceremonial. The monarch's role is restricted by the constitution of the United Kingdom.

Citizens in the United Kingdom have personal freedoms like those in the United States. All citizens are treated equally and have the right to worship as they choose. British citizens have freedom of speech, the right to a fair trial, the right to own property, and the right to security.

357. **Which representative body of Parliament has the most power?**
 A. Monarch
 B. Prime Minister
 C. House of Lords
 D. House of Commons

EUROPE

____ **358. To be prime minister, a person must first be elected to which governing body?**
A. Congress
B. Privy Council
C. House of Lords
D. House of Commons

____ **359. Which part of government is responsible for making the laws for the United Kingdom?**
A. Congress
B. Monarchy
C. Parliament
D. High Court

FEDERAL SYSTEM OF GERMANY

The German parliament is made up of two houses: the **Bundestag** and the **Bundesrat**. The more powerful of the two is the lower house, called the Bundestag. The citizens of each German state elect its members. The Bundestag also selects the chancellor. The chancellor is the chief executive of the German government and head of the military. The president is the head of state. The president's role is mostly ceremonial and symbolic.

The **Bundesrat**, the upper house of parliament, represents the interests of the state governments. Each state government selects representatives for the Bundesrat. The sixteen states each have differing numbers of representatives, depending on their population. The Bundesrat is mainly concerned with law that affects the states, such as education and local government issues.

The constitution of Germany is called the **Basic Law**. Germany is a representative democracy and operates under the federal system. Power is divided between member states and the central government. Citizens have freedom of religion and expression. All are viewed as equal before the law. Germans have the same basic freedoms as citizens of the United Kingdom. They have equality, freedom of the press, and protection of the family. The Basic Law also states that Germany is a **welfare state**. This means that the government guarantees people certain benefits when they are unemployed, poor, disabled, old, or sick.

____ **360. The <u>United Kingdom</u> is to <u>House of Commons</u> as <u>Germany</u> is to the**
A. Basic Law
B. Bundesrat
C. Bundestag
D. Parliament

____ **361. How are members in the Bundestag selected?**
A. elected by the voters
B. elected by the Bundesrat
C. half through election and half appointed by the chancellor
D. half are selected by the president and half selected by the chancellor

____ **362. In the German welfare state, who receives guaranteed benefits?**
A. college students
B. unemployed citizens
C. government workers
D. Bundestag representatives

FEDERATION SYSTEM OF THE RUSSIAN FEDERATION

The Russian Federation is governed under a constitution. The head of state is the president, who is elected by the people. The president selects the prime minister. The president can also disband the legislature, or Federal Assembly. The Federal Assembly is divided into two parts: the **Federation Council** and the **State Duma**.

The Federation Council has two representatives from each of the states. The states appoint the council's members; they are not elected directly by the people. So, the Council represents the government of the states. One of the Council's important duties is to approve the president's choices of people to fill different government jobs.

The State Duma is larger than the Council. It has 450 members, who are elected by the people. This group controls the budget and makes the laws. They approve the president's choice for prime minister. The day-to-day running of the government is split between the prime minister and the president of Russia.

Russia's constitution guarantees human and civil rights for its citizens. All people are equal in the eyes of the law. Russians have the right to life and dignity, freedom of speech, and the right to privacy.

_____ **363. In the Russian Federation, which office do the people elect?**
   A. President
   B. Prime Minister
   C. Public Chamber
   D. Federation Council

_____ **364. Who is the Russian head of state?**
   A. President
   B. Prime Minister
   C. Deputy of the State Duma
   D. Federation Council Member

_____ **365. How is the Russian prime minister selected?**
   A. by a vote of the citizens
   B. by a vote of the State Duma
   C. by appointment of the Federal Assembly
   D. by appointment of the president with approval of the Duma

Use the statements in the box to answer question 366.

- The lawmaking bodies are divided into two houses.
- All have some part of their lawmaking body elected by the people.
- Each divides the jobs of head of state and head of government (chief executive).

_____ **366. Which statement BEST explains what these sentences are about?**
   A. They describe the governments of European countries.
   B. They tell how the countries of Europe choose their leaders.
   C. They explain how the EU countries must set up their parliaments.
   D. They are ways that governments of Germany, Russia, and the United Kingdom are alike.

EUROPE

_____ **367. Which BEST describes the rights of the citizens in Germany, Russia, and the United Kingdom?**

　　A. They are very similar.

　　B. They are nothing alike.

　　C. They only include religious freedom.

　　D. They make no mention of human rights.

SS6CG5 The student will explain the structure of modern European governments.
b. Describe the purpose of the European Union and the relationship between member nations.

THE PURPOSE OF THE EUROPEAN UNION AND THE RELATIONSHIP OF ITS MEMBERS

Twenty-seven countries are members of the ***European Union***, or ***EU***. The purpose of the EU is for its members to work together for advantages that would be out of their reach if each were working alone. The EU nations believe that when countries work together they are a more powerful force in the world because they involve more people, more money, and more land area. This helps make the smaller countries of Europe more competitive in the world market. Look at the table. Notice that together the EU has more people and a greater Gross Domestic Product than the United States. (The GDP is the combined value of the goods and services produced in a country each year.) The United States is much larger than the separate EU countries. When the EU countries combine, they have more people and a larger economy.

Comparing the EU and the United States

	EU	United States
Land area (approximate square miles)	1,500,000	3,700,000
Population (approximate)	500,000,000	305,000,000
Gross Domestic Product (total)	$14 trillion	$13.5 trillion
Gross Domestic Product per Capita (person)	$28,213	$43,444

One result of the EU is the creation of the ***euro***. Just as the United States has dollars ($), the European countries have their own currencies. The euro is the currency of most of the EU. Member countries can choose to give up their own currencies and exchange them for euros (€). France used to have French francs as currency. Germany used to have German marks. Today, both countries use the euro. This makes trade between the countries much easier and less expensive. The United Kingdom uses the ***British pound*** (£), however. Citizens in the U.K. have decided to keep their own currency even though they are in the EU. Twelve EU countries do not use the euro.

The EU does not handle all the government business for the member countries. Each country still makes its own laws, has its own military, and elects its own leaders. The EU works to improve trade, education, farming, and industry among the members. For example, there are no tariffs between countries in the EU. This makes a large **free-trade zone**. Citizens of one country can freely move to another country. They can live and work in any other EU nation. They can even vote in local elections even if they aren't citizens of the country.

_____ **368. The European Union was created to**
    A. practice reaching consensus.
    B. isolate Russia and make it work alone.
    C. promote the French franc as the money unit.
    D. make Europe more competitive in world markets.

_____ **369. Which problem is handled by individual EU member countries instead of the EU government?**
    A. training the country's army
    B. trade issues between two EU countries
    C. one country's farmers selling grapes at lower prices than another country's farmers
    D. making sure that gasoline sold in one country will work in cars from another country

_____ **370. What is the currency for MOST EU countries?**
    A. euro
    B. franc
    C. dollar
    D. pound

_____ **371. Which statement is a correct comparison between the EU and the United States?**
    A. The United States has fewer people and less land than the EU.
    B. The United States has more people and more land than the EU.
    C. The EU has more people and a higher total Gross Domestic Product than the United States.
    D. The EU has fewer people and a lower value on goods and services produced each year than the United States.

EUROPE

Use the following map to answer questions 372-374.

= Countries of the European Union
= Countries applying to the EU
= Non-EU Countries

____ **372. Which part of Europe has the most EU territory?**

    A. western

    B. eastern

    C. northern

    D. southern

_____ **373. Which is the largest country trying to gain membership in the EU?**
  A. Bosnia
  B. Russia
  C. Turkey
  D. Ukraine

_____ **374. How many countries have applied for EU membership and are waiting for approval?**
  A. 1
  B. 2
  C. 3
  D. 4

ECONOMIC UNDERSTANDINGS

SS6E5 The student will analyze different economic systems.
a. Compare how traditional, command, and market economies answer the economic questions of 1-what to produce, 2-how to produce, and 3-for whom to produce.

ANSWERING ECONOMIC QUESTIONS

Scarcity is the limited supply of something. Every country must deal with the problem of scarcity. No country has everything that its people want and need. As a result, every country develops an **economic system** to determine how to use its limited resources to answer the three basic economic questions: (1) **What** goods and services will be produced? (2) **How** will goods and services be produced? (3) **Who** will consume the goods and services? The way a society answers these questions determines its economic system.

Traditional Economy

In a **traditional economy**, the customs and habits of the past are used to decide what and how goods will be produced, distributed, and consumed. In this system, each member of the society knows early in life what his or her role in the larger group will be. Since jobs are handed down from generation to generation, there is very little change in the system over generations. In a traditional economy, people are depended upon to fulfill their traditional role. If some people are not there to do their part, the system can break down. Farming, hunting and gathering, and cattle herding are often a part of a traditional economy. There are no examples of a traditional economy in Europe.

Command Economy

In a centralized **command economy**, government planning groups make the basic economic decisions. They determine such things as which goods and services to produce, the prices, and wage rates. Individuals and corporations generally do not own businesses or farms; these are owned by the government. Workers at a business are told what to produce and how much to produce in a given time. The expectation is that everyone in the country will be able to have the goods they need when they need them. The former Soviet Union was an example of a command economy. After it collapsed in 1991, the new Russian Federation adopted a more mixed economy. However, the Russian economy is still less free than most other European countries. The government owns many of the large businesses and has many limits on private ownership.

EUROPE

Market Economy

In a decentralized *market economy*, decisions are guided by changes in prices that occur between individual buyers and sellers in the marketplace. Other names for market systems are *free enterprise*, *capitalism*, and *laissez-faire*. In a market economy, individuals or corporations generally own businesses and farms. Each business or farm decides what it wants to produce.

Most of Europe operates in a market economy. The United Kingdom has a market economy. It is considered one of the most *free economies* in Europe. "Free" means that businesses can operate without too many rules from the government. People are free to start a business and can do so quickly. Courts use the laws of the U.K. to protect the property rights of citizens.

____ **375. In the United Kingdom, who decides which goods will be produced and sold?**
   A. citizens
   B. the monarch
   C. business owners
   D. the prime minister

____ **376. Which country owns most of the large and important industries within its borders?**
   A. Germany
   B. Russia
   C. United Kingdom
   D. none of these

____ **377. Which is LEAST likely to be found in Europe?**
   A. capitalism
   B. market economy
   C. command economy
   D. traditional economy

MIXED ECONOMY

There are no pure command or market economies. All modern economies have characteristics of both systems and are **mixed economies**. However, most economies are closer to one type of economic system than another.

In a truly free market economy, for example, the government would not be involved at all. There would be no laws to protect workers from unfair bosses. There would be no rules to make sure that credit cards were properly protected. Many societies have chosen to have some rules to protect consumers, workers, and businesses. These rules reduce the freedoms that businesses have, but they also protect the workers and consumers.

The following diagram shows some world economies on a scale. The ones on the left are most restricted. The ones on the right are most free.

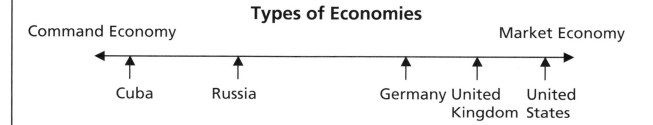

Types of Economies

Command Economy   Market Economy

Cuba   Russia   Germany United   United
                                          Kingdom States

_____ 378. **Which European country shown in the diagram has the LEAST free economy?**
   A. Cuba
   B. Russia
   C. Germany
   D. United Kingdom

_____ 379. **Because most economies have characteristics of both the command economy and the market economy, they are**
   A. free.
   B. closed.
   C. mixed.
   D. communist.

COMPARING THE BASIC ECONOMIC SYSTEMS IN THE UNITED KINGDOM, GERMANY, AND RUSSIA

Study the following table to compare and contrast the economies of the United Kingdom, Germany, and Russia.

EUROPE

Use information from the table to answer questions 380-382.

Comparing the Economies of the United Kingdom, Germany, and Russia

	United Kingdom	Germany	Russia
Who owns businesses and farms?	private citizens and corporations	private citizens and corporations	the government owns large industries such as shipping, oil and natural gas, and aerospace technology; private ownership is allowed in other areas
Who decides what to produce and how much to produce?	private citizens and corporations	private citizens and corporations; there is some regulation by the government in agriculture, energy, and telecommunications	private citizens and corporations for the most part; the government has many restrictions on businesses and controls many of the larger ones
Who decides how goods and services will be produced?	private citizens and corporations	private citizens and corporations; there is some regulation by the government in agriculture, energy, and telecommunications	private citizens and corporations for the most part; the government has many restrictions on businesses and controls many of the larger ones
Who decides distribution methods and prices for goods and services?	private citizens and corporations	private citizens and corporations; there is some regulation by the government in agriculture, energy, and telecommunications	private citizens and corporations for the most part; the government has many restrictions on businesses and controls many of the larger ones
Who decides the prices for goods and services?	buyers and sellers, based on supply and demand	private citizens and corporations; the government regulates prices of some products	private citizens and corporations; the government regulates prices of some products
How are property rights protected?	laws and a good court system protect people's property rights	laws and a good court system protect people's property rights	court system does not always protect the rights of property owners
How difficult is it to start your own business?	very easy (days)	very easy (days)	time-consuming (months)

EUROPE

380. In which country would it be most difficult for a person to start a business?

    A. Russia

    B. Germany

    C. United Kingdom

    D. about the same for each

381. In which countries do buyers and sellers usually come to agreement on prices in order to trade?

    A. Russia and Germany

    B. Russia and United Kingdom

    C. Germany and United Kingdom

    D. United Kingdom and United States

382. Which of these issues would make the United Kingdom a more desirable place to start a business than Russia?

    A. The government in Russia owns most industries.

    B. Russia's court system always protests the rights of property owners..

    C. It takes less time to start a business in Russia than the United Kingdom.

    D. Private citizens and corporations in the United Kingdom decide how goods will be produced.

EUROPE

SS6E6 The student will analyze the benefits of and barriers to voluntary trade in Europe.

a. Compare and contrast different types of trade barriers such as tariffs, quotas, and embargos.

TRADE BARRIERS: TARIFFS, QUOTAS, AND EMBARGOS

Trade is the voluntary exchange of goods and services among people and countries. Trade and voluntary exchange occur when buyers and sellers freely and willingly engage in market transactions. When trade is voluntary, both parties benefit and are better off after the trade than they were before the trade.

Countries sometimes try to limit trade with other countries by creating **trade barriers**. The most common types of trade barriers are **tariffs** and **quotas**. A tariff is a tax on imports. A quota is a limit placed on the number of imports that may enter a country. Another kind of trade barrier is an **embargo**. An embargo is a government order stopping trade with another country. An embargo might be put into place in order to put pressure on another country.

The European Union (EU) is a large **free-trade zone**. There are no tariffs between the countries in the zone. This means that goods can be bought for a lower price. In Russia, there are tariffs on many imports. The Russian government hopes that the tariffs help Russian workers and businesses. Food imported from Germany may have a high tariff placed on it. Therefore, Russian families might choose to buy food grown by Russian farmers.

Russia produces a lot of steel. Steelmakers in the EU may worry that if too much Russian steel comes into the EU, the price of steel will go down. If the price goes down, the EU companies would have trouble making enough money to stay in business. The EU might decide to put a quota on steel imports from Russia. A quota would stop the flow of steel into EU countries, which would keep the prices stable.

_____ **383. Which type of trade barrier involves a limit on goods brought into the country?**
A. quota
B. tariff
C. embargo
D. voluntary exchange

_____ **384. In order to help Russian farmers sell more food, some people want to put a tax on the food imported from other countries. This is an example of a(n)**
A. quota.
B. tariff.
C. embargo.
D. voluntary exchange.

_____ **385. Which might make an embargo against a country successful?**
A. Merchants are able to continue doing business.
B. People in the country are not affected by the embargo.
C. The country does not need to trade with other countries.
D. The citizens in the country suffer because of the embargo and demand a change from their government.

SS6E6 The student will analyze the benefits of and barriers to voluntary trade in Europe.

b. Explain why international trade requires a system for exchanging currencies between nations.

INTERNATIONAL TRADE AND THE EXCHANGING OF CURRENCIES

Currency is the money people use to make trade easier. In the United States, we use U.S. dollars (USD or $) to buy goods and services. When we Americans work at a job, we are paid in dollars. Most of the time, when you are in a different country, you cannot buy goods and services with currency from your own country. So what do you do? You trade it in, or exchange it! With each exchange, however, the bank charges a fee. A business that exchanges a lot of money will pay many fees.

Imagine an olive farm in Greece. The olive grower pays his workers in euros. He buys fertilizer and pesticide in euros. He pays for water and machinery in euros. When the olives are ripe, a store in Russia wants to buy them. The Russian storeowner has **rubles** (the Russian currency) to spend. In order to make the trade, the Russian storeowner exchanges his rubles for euros. The bank where he makes the trade charges a fee. The olive grower gets money for the olives in euros. The Russian gets the olives. Everyone is happy!

More than half of the EU countries use the euro today. This makes trade among the EU countries easier because they do not have to exchange currency. It also makes trade less expensive because people don't have to pay banks a fee to exchange their currency.

_____ 386. **What is the currency people use in much of the EU called?**
- A. euro
- B. ruble
- C. dollar
- D. pound

_____ 387. **What is the currency of Russia?**
- A. euro
- B. ruble
- C. dollar
- D. pound

_____ 388. **What is a problem with exchanging currency?**
- A. People make more money by trading currency.
- B. Most people want to use American dollars to trade.
- C. Banks do not like to exchange their money for other currencies.
- D. It costs more to do business because banks charge fees for exchanges.

HUMAN CAPITAL AND THE GROSS DOMESTIC PRODUCT

The **Gross Domestic Product (GDP)** of a country is the total value of all the final goods and services produced in a country in one year. The GDP is one way to tell how rich or how poor a country is. The GDP can be used to tell if the economy of a country is getting better or getting worse. Raising the GDP of the country can mean a higher **standard of living** (economic level) for the people in the country. To increase the GDP, countries must invest in **human capital**. This resource includes the education, training, skills, and health of the workers in a business or country.

Russia, Germany, and the United Kingdom have made large investments in human capital. The **literacy rate** of each country is nearly 100 percent. The workforce is very well trained and educated. This has helped the standard of living in these countries improve over time.

Russia has the most poverty of the three countries. The Russian government is spending large amounts of money to train workers and to educate youth so that they will have more opportunities to be successful in the economy. In the former Soviet Union, everyone was assigned a job. Today, in Russia, workers must show they are skilled and valuable to the business in order to keep their jobs.

_____ **389. Which is an example of investing in human capital?**

A. cash

B. factories

C. highways

D. education

_____ **390. A country that does not invest in human capital will have problems because**

A. there will be no money to pay its workers.

B. workers will learn on their own the skills they need.

C. businesses will not pay the taxes to pay for good schools.

D. workers who are not educated, skilled, and healthy are less productive.

_____ **391. What is human capital?**

A. a country's standard of living

B. the cash a business has to spend

C. investment in the workers of a business or country

D. the buildings, equipment, and property owned by a business

EUROPE

CAPITAL INVESTMENTS AND THE GROSS DOMESTIC PRODUCT

To raise the Gross Domestic Produce (GDP), countries must invest in **capital goods**. Physical capital is the factories, machines, technologies, buildings, and property needed by businesses to operate. If a business is to be successful, it cannot let its equipment break down or have its buildings fall apart. New technology can help a business produce more goods for a lower price.

The former Soviet Union did not do a good job of investing in capital goods. Highways and buildings are in need of repair. Factory equipment and technology are out of date. These conditions are keeping workers from being as productive as workers in the EU. Today, the Russian Federation has the job of helping companies overcome this problem. To solve the problem, the government has a plan to invest $1 trillion over the next few years in capital improvements.

_____ 392. **Which is an example of investing in capital goods by a company?**

A. constructing a new factory

B. keeping old delivery trucks

C. training workers to do their jobs better

D. keeping old computers in order to save money

_____ 393. **The Soviet Union did not invest in capital improvements, so Russian workers today**

A. do not want to increase their standard of living.

B. are not as productive as workers in other countries.

C. work in brand new factories and are very productive.

D. have shut down their factories until new ones are built.

EUROPE

> **SS6E7 The student will describe factors that influence economic growth and examine their presence or absence in Europe.**
>
> c. Describe the role of natural resources in a country's economy.

THE ROLE OF NATURAL RESOURCES IN A COUNTRY'S ECONOMY

A country has different kinds of resources that can help its people produce goods and services. Human resources are the education and skills that people have to produce goods and services. Capital resources are the things like machines and equipment that people need to produce goods and services. Natural resources, "gifts of nature," include forests such as those in southern Germany. They include fertile soil, such as the farms of the United Kingdom. Water is another natural resource. Russians use their water resources by damming rivers and creating hydroelectric power.

Natural resources are important to countries. Without natural resources of their own, countries must import the natural resources that they need. This adds to the cost of goods and services. A country is better off if it can use its own natural resources to supply the needs of its people. It can also use the natural resources to create goods that can be traded to other countries. If a country has many natural resources, it can trade these to other countries for goods and services it needs.

In Europe, many countries have used up much of their nonrenewable natural resources. They have had to find other ways to make their economies work. For example, coal was once a plentiful resource in the United Kingdom. Today, most of the supply has been used. Russia is a major exporter of oil and natural gas. Money from these resources has helped many Russians become wealthy. However, these resources will not last forever. Russia must find ways to not only use these resources but also develop other ones.

____ **394. Which is an example of a natural resource?**

    A. forests

    B. highways

    C. education

    D. automobiles

____ **395. Which natural resources have helped the Russian economy in the twenty-first century?**

    A. oil and natural gas

    B. highways and factories

    C. machines and equipment

    D. education and health care

____ **396. Why is a country better off if it does not have to import natural resources?**

    A. Other countries may need the resources.

    B. Buying from other countries costs more money.

    C. People in other countries don't want to sell their natural resources.

    D. Businesses have a hard time using the natural resources that are located nearby.

THE ROLE OF ENTREPRENEURSHIP

The person who provides the money to start and own a business is called an ***entrepreneur***. Entrepreneurs risk their own money and time because they believe their business ideas will make a profit. They must organize their businesses well for those businesses to be successful. Entrepreneurs bring together natural, human, and capital resources to produce goods or services to be provided by their businesses.

In Europe, Russia is a country that has many entrepreneurs. Laws have made it easier than it used to be to own a business. Russia's natural resources and skilled labor make it a good place to have a business. In the twenty-first century, many entrepreneurs in Russia are getting rich. Russia is one of the top five countries in the number of billionaires. Still, doing business in Russia is difficult. Entrepreneurs say that the government needs to do a better job of protecting private property. The courts need to be stronger to protect businesses. It can take months for an entrepreneur to get the proper permissions to start a business.

Entrepreneurs play an important role in the economy of a country. As they work to make their businesses profitable, entrepreneurs hire more workers, giving more people jobs. The tax money that comes from their businesses helps the government. Goods and services entrepreneurs produce encourage trade within a country. This provides more jobs and more money for the economy. Entrepreneurs trading with other countries bring in goods and services that are not already available.

_____ 397. **Which is an example of an entrepreneur?**

    A. people who operate a hospital

    B. a person who runs a government-owned coal mine

    C. roofers who work for a business owned by an individual

    D. a person who uses her money to start a business selling cell phones

_____ 398. **What is a problem faced by entrepreneurs in Russia?**

    A. No one has money.

    B. There are no skilled workers.

    C. Courts don't protect property rights.

    D. There is a lack of natural resources, such as gas and oil.

_____ 399. **Which is a way that entrepreneurs help increase a country's GDP?**

    A. writing laws to protect personal property

    B. creating businesses that give people jobs

    C. providing the ideas to start and expand businesses

    D. working to increase the amount of goods and services bought by a country

EUROPE

HISTORICAL UNDERSTANDINGS

> **SS6H6 The student will analyze the impact of European exploration and colonization on various world regions.**
>
> a. Identify the causes of European exploration and colonization; include religion, natural resources, a market for goods, and the contributions of Prince Henry the Navigator.

THE CAUSES OF EUROPEAN EXPLORATION AND COLONIZATION

Portugal is a small country on the Atlantic coast in southern Europe. During the fifteenth century, Portugal led the world in sea exploration. Beginning in 1415, and for nearly one hundred years, Portugal explored the western coast of Africa.

The Portuguese wanted to find a route around Africa into the Indian Ocean. Goods brought over land from China and India were expensive. Europeans wanted Asian silks and spices, but they wanted to find a way to get them at a lower cost. The Portuguese believed that they could make a lot of money as traders if they could get Asian goods for a cheaper price. There were religious reasons to explore too. The Portuguese wanted to spread Christianity along Africa's west coast.

Prince Henry the Navigator was the son of the Portuguese king. He fought in a battle that helped capture Ceuta, a city on the coast of North Africa. The Moors had controlled Ceuta for hundreds of years. This gave Portugal an important outpost from which to explore Africa. Prince Henry became governor of Portugal's southernmost coasts. He sent more than fifty expeditions down the west coast of Africa. Henry wanted to establish colonies and break the Muslim hold on trade routes.

Henry studied navigation and mapmaking. He established a naval observatory. Students there learned navigation, astronomy, and **cartography** (mapmaking). Henry's efforts advanced what Europeans knew about these sciences.

Henry was unable to make money trading in gold, so he tried creating sugar cane plantations. One of his expeditions discovered the island of Madeira. The climate there was good for growing sugar cane, and he knew that it was a very profitable crop. It also required lots of labor. Henry imported slaves from Africa to work the fields. This plan became successful and was later copied in the New World. In fact, the expansion of the sugar cane economy encouraged a slave trade that lasted another four hundred years.

The Portuguese also gained access to the Spice Islands. By 1513, Portuguese trade extended to China and Japan.

_____ **400. Why did Prince Henry the Navigator want to send ships south to Africa?**
   A. He hoped to learn more about marine life.
   B. He wanted to prove the world was not flat.
   C. He felt his father, the king, would be proud.
   D. He wanted a route around Africa to the Asian markets.

_____ **401. Which religion did Prince Henry the Navigator hope to spread?**
   A. Islam
   B. Hinduism
   C. Buddhism
   D. Christianity

THE EMPIRES OF PORTUGAL, SPAIN, ENGLAND, AND FRANCE IN ASIA, AFRICA, AND THE AMERICAS

The **Crusades** (1096 to 1272) were military expeditions sent by different **Popes** (leaders of the Roman Catholic Church) to capture the Holy Land from the Muslim Turks. Though the Crusades were not successful, one positive result was that the people of Western Europe learned how to draw better maps and build better ships. The Crusades also exposed the European Crusaders to desirable products of the East. Europeans and Asians created trade routes to bring products from the East to Europe. These benefits of the Crusades later contributed to the expansion of Portugal, Spain, England, and France.

By the fifteenth century, the major trade routes from the East to Europe went to two Italian cities, Venice and Genoa. The Italian merchants marked up the prices on spices, precious jewels, fragrances, woods, and finished goods and sold them throughout Europe.

Portugal, Spain, France, and England resented the huge profits made by Venice and Genoa. Since Venice and Genoa controlled the trade routes through the Mediterranean Sea, the jealous European countries looked for another way to India, China, and the Spice Islands.

The Empire of Portugal

Portugal established the earliest of the modern European colonial empires. The Portuguese empire lasted for centuries. It started with Prince Henry, the son of the king of Portugal. Henry sent Portuguese ships down the west coast of Africa. He wanted to find a route around the continent to India and China.

Bartolomeu Dias reached the southern tip of Africa and discovered the Cape of Good Hope and the Indian Ocean. Vasco da Gama, another Portuguese explorer, later sailed around the cape. He continued on to India.

Over the following decades, Portuguese sailors continued to explore the coasts and islands of East Asia, establishing forts and trading posts. By 1571, a string of outposts connected Portugal with Africa, India, the south Pacific islands, and Japan.

Portugal grew wealthy from its trade route around Africa to Asia. Its most profitable **colony** was Brazil in South America. Brazil was a Portuguese colony until 1822.

The Empire of Spain

Other explorers from Spain, France, and England searched for a route through or around North America and South America. They hoped to find a route that would lead them to the riches of the East. In the late 1490s, Christopher Columbus, an Italian, was given ships and men to try to find a passage across the Atlantic Ocean to Asia. His first discoveries were the islands of the Bahamas, although he thought he was in Asia. It was later learned that Columbus had found entire continents that were unknown to the Europeans. Exploration and colonization of this "New World" gave Spain enormous wealth.

The Spanish empire was one of the largest empires in history. Spanish conquistadors conquered the Inca and Aztec civilizations in the 1500s and brought home the wealth of these people. Spain claimed huge areas of North and South America and ruled parts of them for over three hundred years. Their empire stretched to Asia, where they controlled the Philippines until almost the twentieth century.

EUROPE

The Empire of England

At one time, England was one of three countries (England, Scotland, and Wales) that shared an island. By the early 1700s, the three united as **Great Britain**. The British empire was the largest in history. At its peak, Great Britain controlled Canada, Australia, India, much of eastern Africa, and numerous islands across the world.

North America came under the control of England and France during the eighteenth century. Great Britain won out over its European rivals—the Dutch, France, and Spain—in gaining control of North America. However, Great Britain lost its American colonies. The United States became an independent country after a war that began in 1776. Great Britain maintained control over Canada, however, until the twentieth century.

Great Britain colonized the continent of Australia, including many islands along the trading routes. During the nineteenth century and into the early twentieth century, Great Britain's influence increased.

By the 1920s, one-fourth of the world's population was under British control. It was said that "the sun never sets on the British empire." This was because it was always daylight at some location in the British empire. After World War II, most of Great Britain's territories and colonies became independent.

The Empire of France

From the 1600s to the 1900s, France was one of the world's dominant empires. The French possessed colonies around the world. During the reign of Napoleon I, France dominated much of the European continent. By 1812, France controlled much of Germany, Italy, and Spain.

Other parts of the French empire were originally established during the sixteenth and seventeenth centuries. This included islands in the Caribbean, the Indian Ocean, the South Pacific, the North Pacific, and the North Atlantic. France maintained influence in parts of Canada, South America, Southeast Asia, and Northwest Africa. In the nineteenth and twentieth centuries, only the British empire was larger than the empire of France.

_____ 402. **Which Italian cities dominated the trade routes from Asia to Europe for a long time?**
A. Rome and Turin
B. Florence and Bari
C. Genoa and Venice
D. Milan and Palermo

_____ 403. **Which result of the Crusades to the Holy Land helped Europeans become explorers?**
A. Europeans' mapmaking skills improved.
B. Shipbuilding skills were lost when the crusaders were killed.
C. The Pope was not able to free the Holy Land from Muslim control.
D. Europeans learned of markets and trade routes into southern Africa.

_____ 404. **Which islands in the Americas did Christopher Columbus believe were part of Asia?**
A. Cayman
B. Bahamas
C. Turks and Caicos
D. Trinidad and Tobago

405. Put the following events in the order in which they occurred.

> 1. The Spanish conquered the Aztecs and the Incas.
> 2. The Pope sent Europeans to remove Muslims from the Holy Land.
> 3. Christopher Columbus explored the Bahamas.
> 4. Spain controlled the Philippines.

A. 1, 2, 3, 4
B. 2, 3, 4, 1
C. 2, 3, 1, 4
D. 4, 1, 3, 2

SS6H6 The student will analyze the impact of European exploration and colonization on various world regions.
c. Trace the colonization of Australia by the United Kingdom.

THE COLONIZATION OF AUSTRALIA BY THE UNITED KINGDOM

The first Europeans to sail into Australian waters arrived in 1606. To reach Australia from Europe, ships sailed south along the west African coast to the Cape of Good Hope and then turned east across the Indian Ocean. For nearly two hundred years, ships from several European nations sailed to the continent.

In 1770, Captain James Cook charted the eastern Australian coast in his ship *Endeavour*. Following orders from British King George III, Cook claimed the east coast for Great Britain. Cook named eastern Australia "New South Wales." The British mapped the coast of Australia, including the island of Tasmania.

The independence of the thirteen American colonies led the British to colonize Australia in 1788. Britain created a new *penal* (prison) colony by shipping prisoners from Great Britain to Australia.

There were four main reasons for the British to colonize Australia. First, the British wanted to colonize Australia to relieve overcrowding in Great Britain's jails. Second, the British government recognized the importance of having its navy stationed in Australia in the southern hemisphere. The British viewed Australia as an economic base to expand trade. Finally, the British government did not want its rivals, especially the French, to start a colony on the Australian continent.

406. Who claimed Australia for Great Britain?
A. George III
B. the Prince of Wales
C. Captain James Cook
D. Christopher Columbus

407. Which coast of Australia did Captain James Cook claim for England in 1770?
A. east
B. west
C. north
D. south

___ **408.** **What type of people were the first British colonists in Australia?**
   A. sailors
   B. captains
   C. prisoners
   D. conquistadors

___ **409.** **What was the common route used by ships sailing from England to Australia in the eighteenth century?**
   A. due south to Antarctica then north to Australia
   B. across the Atlantic Ocean and then around Cape Horn
   C. south along the west African coast to the Cape of Good Hope, then east into the Indian Ocean
   D. west to Central America, through the Panama Canal, then south into the South Pacific Ocean

___ **410.** **Which was NOT a reason that Great Britain colonized Australia?**
   A. to keep it out of French control
   B. to have a naval base in the area
   C. to find gold and spread Christianity
   D. to relieve overcrowded prisons in Great Britain

> **SS6H6 The student will analyze the impact of European exploration and colonization on various world regions.**
> d. Explain the impact of European empire building in Africa and Asia on the outbreak of WWI.

THE IMPACT OF EUROPEAN EMPIRE BUILDING IN AFRICA AND ASIA ON THE OUTBREAK OF WORLD WAR I

During the late nineteenth century, several European countries wanted more overseas land. These countries were Great Britain, France, Portugal, Spain, Denmark, Germany, Italy, and the Netherlands. The result was a "**Scramble for Africa**" between 1885 and 1910. During this period, several European countries divided the continent of Africa among themselves.

Economic development played a large role in the colonization of Africa. During the nineteenth century, factories in Europe required raw materials to manufacture finished products. The Europeans looked for new sources of raw materials and markets for their goods. Gold, diamonds, and oil were some of the resources the Europeans wanted. Asia and Africa had those resources.

Politics also led to the colonization of Africa. Some European nations showed national pride by competing for colonies in Africa. No major nation—including Great Britain, France, and Germany—wanted to be without colonies. Colonies in Africa and Asia made the Europeans feel pride in their country.

Another reason for colonizing was the European worldview. Many nineteenth-century Europeans viewed themselves as the world's most advanced civilization. Some felt it necessary to "civilize" people in the rest of the world. Increased activity by African missionaries helped make colonization seem less offensive to citizens in Europe.

This scramble for land also reached farther into Asia. Many Asian territories saw a change from Europe as trading partner to Europe as conqueror. Great Britain, for instance, took control of India. France controlled lands in Southeast Asia, including Vietnam. The British fought for control of other lands like Burma, Laos, Siam, and Cambodia.

Nationalism (the love of one's country) and **militarism** (using strong armies and threats of war) were on the rise in Europe. European countries signed treaties agreeing to help one another in case of attack. In 1914, a series of events caused Germany to declare war on Russia and France. On the other side, the British joined France and Russia and formed the **Allied Powers**. Austria-Hungary, the **Ottoman Empire** (Turkey and its colonies), and Bulgaria joined the Germans as the **Central Powers**.

Because these countries were large and controlled lands around the world, the war was called the **Great War**. Later, the United States became involved on the side of the Allied Powers. The war lasted until 1918, and an estimated 10 million people died. Some believed it was "the war to end all wars." Unfortunately, just twenty years later, Europe would be at the center of an even bigger conflict. The Great War became known as **World War I**. The later, larger conflict was called **World War II**.

_____ 411. **Which statement best describes how economics played a role in European colonies in the nineteenth century?**
   A. The desire for international tourism increased.
   B. Europe felt Asia's growing population was a threat to expansion.
   C. Trade routes to Asia from Europe were less important than before.
   D. Europe wanted more sources of raw materials needed for manufacturing.

_____ 412. **How did nationalism play a part in Europe's competition to colonize Africa and Asia?**
   A. European missionaries were trying to spread their religion.
   B. Europeans felt a need to "civilize" other parts of the world.
   C. Smaller countries wanted more land to accommodate growing populations.
   D. Having colonies made countries feel more important and successful than other countries.

_____ 413. **What war was a result of militarism and nationalism in the late nineteenth and early twentieth centuries?**
   A. Civil War
   B. World War I
   C. World War II
   D. Vietnam War

_____ 414. **Which group of nations formed the Central Powers?**
   A. Japan, Germany, Italy
   B. United States, France, Great Britain
   C. Ottoman Empire, Germany, United States
   D. Germany, Austria-Hungary, Ottoman Empire

EUROPE

Use the following maps to answer questions 415-418.

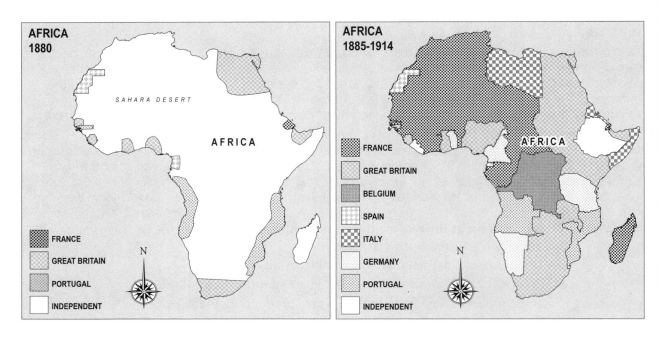

____ 415. **During the Scramble for Africa during the late nineteenth and early twentieth centuries, which two European powers controlled the most African land?**
A. Spain and Italy
B. Germany and Portugal
C. Great Britain and France
D. Belgium and the Netherlands

____ 416. **What physical feature covered most of French West Africa?**
A. desert
B. rain forest
C. mountains
D. swamplands

____ 417. **Which European power controlled most of northwest Africa during the colonial era?**
A. France
B. Belgium
C. England
D. Germany

____ 418. **Which statement summarizes the information on the maps?**
A. Europe's claims in Africa declined from 1880 to 1914.
B. Europe's claims in Africa increased from 1880 to 1914.
C. Between 1880 and 1914, European countries did not expand much in Africa.
D. Between 1880 and 1914, African countries gained independence from Europe.

EUROPE

SS6H7 The student will explain conflict and change in Europe to the 21st century.

a. Describe major developments following World War I: the Russian Revolution, the Treaty of Versailles, worldwide depression, and the rise of Nazism.

THE RUSSIAN REVOLUTION

Before 1917, Russia was an autocracy. The **czar** was the absolute ruler. The last of the czars was Nicholas II.

During World War I, Russia did not do well. Millions of people were killed, wounded, or missing. Citizens did not have enough food. Soldiers did not have enough clothes, shoes, or weapons. Germany seemed to be winning the war. The czar ignored the signs that people were unhappy. He did not see that changes were needed in the way that his country was run.

In early 1917, there were riots in the streets. Women, factory workers, and farmers shouting for change outnumbered police. The military could not keep the peace. Many in the czar's army turned against the rulers. The czar and his family were captured. A government was set up to try to run the country. However, there were too many problems. Later in the year, there was another revolution. Communists led by Vladimir Lenin took control. The czar and his family were executed. Lenin reorganized the country and renamed it the Soviet Union.

The new Soviet Union signed a peace treaty with Germany. The Soviets gave up a large amount of land to Germany. This land was good for farming and had many natural resources. The Soviets had little choice. Their country was falling apart around them.

_____ **419. What type of government did Czar Nicholas II have in Russia?**

A. republic

B. autocracy

C. oligarchy

D. democracy

_____ **420. Which was a cause of the Russian Revolution?**

A. The czar was executed.

B. There were food shortages in Russia.

C. The Germans showed signs of surrender.

D. Soldiers did not know how to use their weapons.

Use the statements in the box to answer question 421.

> - did not protect the Russian royal family
> - changed Russia's name to the Soviet Union
> - made a treaty with Germany to end the war
> - gave up large amounts of Russian land to Germany

_____ **421. Which person did the actions listed in the box?**

A. Vladimir Lenin

B. Czar Nicholas II

C. Woodrow Wilson

D. Emperor Wilhelm I

EUROPE

TREATY OF VERSAILLES

Versailles is a grand palace outside the city of Paris, France. At the end of World War I, leaders from the countries involved in the war met there to write a treaty. The Treaty of Versailles explained what the winners would gain and what the losers would lose.

Many of the leaders of the winning countries blamed Germany for the war. They wanted the Germans punished severely. Germany lost important territory, including lands rich in natural resources. It also lost all of its colonies. German Emperor Wilhelm II was to be put on trial for war crimes. France and Great Britain wanted to make sure that Germany could not attack them again. Their goal was to make Germany a weak country. Germany had to reduce the size of its army and navy.

France lost a lot in the war. Over 2 million French people lost their lives. A large part of the war was fought in France. Farms, homes, cities, and industries were destroyed. Highways, bridges, and railroads had to be rebuilt. The Allies added a part to the treaty that said Germany had to pay the Allies a very large amount of money. This money was to be used to repay civilians who lost property because of the war.

_____ 422. **What was the goal of France in the Treaty of Versailles?**
A. to help Germany rebuild its industry
B. to build better roads and factories in Germany
C. to make sure Germany did not invade France in the future
D. to give Great Britain and the United States credit for their help in the war

_____ 423. **Which part of the Treaty of Versailles was most damaging to the German economy?**
A. Germany lost its colonies.
B. The German emperor was to be put on trial.
C. Germany had to pay the Allies large sums of money.
D. Germans were not allowed to have a large army and navy.

_____ 424. **How did the Allies hope to keep Germany from becoming too powerful again?**
A. France took over the German bases.
B. Great Britain sent troops into Germany for ten years.
C. The Germans were not allowed to have a large army or navy.
D. Germany was divided into four parts and controlled by four different countries.

WORLDWIDE DEPRESSION

After World War I, most countries in the world began to prosper. Americans enjoyed a time called "the Roaring Twenties." People felt good about the economy. They believed that they had a chance to do well. In 1929, the good times ended.

In the fall of 1929, the United States experienced a **_stock market crash_**. The value of stocks (shares of ownership) people held in companies began a steep and quick drop. Stockholders realized that they were in danger of losing everything they owned. They began to sell their stocks as fast as they could. Because there were more sellers than buyers, the prices continued to fall.

Businesses found they could no longer sell their goods because people had less money to spend. The businesses could not pay their debts. When businesses could not pay their debts, they had to close. This meant workers lost their jobs. These events happened so quickly that a panic occurred. People tried to get to their banks to get their money, and they tried to sell their stocks for any amount they could get. Panic selling and a "run on the banks" caused the economy of the United States to come to a halt. Farmers who could not get money to pay their loans lost their farms.

Businesses around the world traded with America. When the United States stopped buying goods, it hurt businesses in other countries. When U.S. banks closed, banks in other countries were hurt too. Stockholders in other countries began to sell their stocks for low prices. They could not sell their stocks in American companies for any price.

What followed was called a worldwide *economic depression*. As businesses and factories closed one by one, buying and selling almost stopped. Here's one example.

> *Mr. Jones managed a shirt factory. Because his customers were losing money in the stock market and in the banks, they did not buy shirts. They just kept the old shirts they already had. Mr. Jones kept the factory going for a while. New shirts began to fill his warehouse. Only a few shirts were sold each day.*
>
> *Because the company had few sales, Mr. Jones had no money to pay his workers. He told them to go home, but he promised to call them back to work when he had sold the shirts in the warehouse.*
>
> *Days went by. Now he was selling no shirts. Mr. Jones had no money to pay himself or the guards at the warehouse. The owner of the factory locked its doors. He put a "For Sale" sign out front. He hoped that someone would buy the factory, the warehouse, and the shirts.*
>
> *Mr. Jones went home. He had no job and no money. His wife wanted to get some new shoes. Mr. Jones told her that was impossible. She would just have to keep the old shoes that she already had.*
>
> *Meanwhile, at the nearby shoe factory, the manager looked at his warehouse full of shoes and shook his head.*

_____ **425. In the story, why was the manager of the shoe factory shaking his head?**
    A. He had a headache from counting shoes.
    B. He was excited to have so many shoes in his warehouse.
    C. He wanted Mr. Jackson to come and work for his shoe factory.
    D. He did not know what to do with all the shoes that no one bought.

_____ **426. Which were effects of the depression?**
    A. Employment rose and wages fell.
    B. Farmers gained land and business grew.
    C. People had more money and better jobs.
    D. Farmers lost their land and banks closed.

_____ **427. Why did business come to a halt after the stock market crash?**
    A. Everyone was waiting for prices to come down.
    B. Businesses were moving their factories to Europe.
    C. People thought they could get a good deal on goods from Europe.
    D. People did not have money to spend, or they were afraid to spend what money they did have.

RISE OF NAZISM

Germany faced many problems after World War I. It had lost lands that contained valuable natural resources. About 2½ million Germans had lost their lives. About 4 million were wounded. The industry and farms in the country had been destroyed. Highways, bridges, and railroads had to be rebuilt.

The German government worked to solve the country's problems. However, the country had another obstacle. It had to pay back the Allied countries for the war. Millions of dollars were leaving Germany for France and Great Britain. Germany was forbidden to have a large army or navy, so many military people lost their jobs.

Prices went up as goods became scarce. Basic items such as food and clothing were not always available. Men had trouble finding jobs to support their families. As things got worse, people blamed the government. They wanted their leaders to find solutions to their problems. Then, the stock market crashed in the United States. This made conditions even worse for Germans. Businesses and people around the world stopped buying as much. They were worried about losing their money.

Adolf Hitler came on the scene with a big plan. He and his followers, called the National Socialist or **Nazi Party**, said they could fix the problems in Germany. They blamed the Treaty of Versailles for many of the problems. They also said that Jews in the country were controlling the banks and money. They blamed Jews for the fact that many Germans were not able to make a good living.

Hitler was named chancellor of Germany in 1933. He made sure that laws were quickly passed to give him more power. Soon he had complete control of the government. He had the powers of a dictator. He and the Nazis began the work to rebuild Germany's military. He opened factories to build weapons. He put unemployed people to work building a superior highway system. The economy improved for a time, but people lost many of their civil rights. However, many decided that it was better to lose rights than to go without food.

The Nazis continued to build their military power. Germans who spoke against them were put in prison or murdered. As Hitler's strength grew, he made plans to go to war. In 1936, Hitler sent troops into some of Germany's former territory. By 1938, German troops controlled Austria and Czechoslovakia. Other European countries protested, but did nothing to stop Hitler. In 1939, Germany invaded Poland. With that, France and Great Britain decided something must be done. They declared war on Germany, and World War II began.

_____ **428. Who was the leader of the Nazi Party in Germany?**
   A. Wilhelm II
   B. Adolf Hitler
   C. Vladimir Lenin
   D. Woodrow Wilson

_____ **429. What happened to people who spoke out against Hitler in Germany?**
   A. They were sent to Siberia.
   B. They were put under house arrest.
   C. Some were put in prison; others were murdered.
   D. Some were allowed to leave Germany; others were arrested.

____ **430. Put the following events in the order in which they happened.**

> 1. Hitler was named chancellor of Germany.
> 2. Germany invaded Poland.
> 3. Germans were unhappy because of high unemployment and poverty.
> 4. France and Great Britain declared war on Germany.

    A. 1, 2, 4, 3
    B. 2, 4, 3, 1
    C. 3, 1, 2, 4
    D 4, 3, 1, 2

Use the statements in the box to answer question 431.

> • Hitler promised to rebuild Germany's military.
> • The Treaty of Versailles angered Germans.
> • Hitler said he would get back Germany's lost land.

____ **431. Which statement explains what these sentences are about?**
    A. events that led to World War I
    B. feelings Germans had about other countries
    C. ways that German leaders tried to rebuild their country
    D. reasons why Hitler and the Nazis came to power in Germany

EUROPE

Use the following timeline to answer questions 432-434.

Major Developments in Europe after World War I

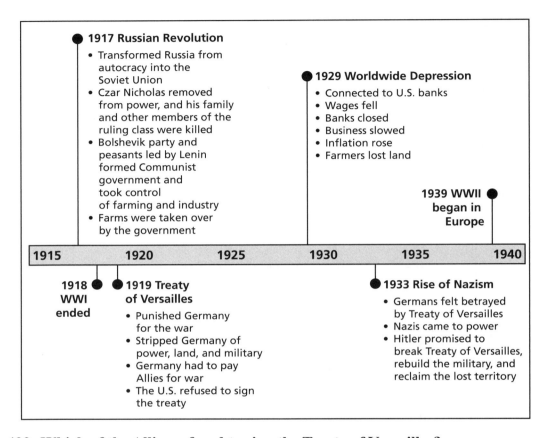

1917 Russian Revolution
- Transformed Russia from autocracy into the Soviet Union
- Czar Nicholas removed from power, and his family and other members of the ruling class were killed
- Bolshevik party and peasants led by Lenin formed Communist government and took control of farming and industry
- Farms were taken over by the government

1929 Worldwide Depression
- Connected to U.S. banks
- Wages fell
- Banks closed
- Business slowed
- Inflation rose
- Farmers lost land

1939 WWII began in Europe

| 1915 | 1920 | 1925 | 1930 | 1935 | 1940 |

1918 WWI ended

1919 Treaty of Versailles
- Punished Germany for the war
- Stripped Germany of power, land, and military
- Germany had to pay Allies for war
- The U.S. refused to sign the treaty

1933 Rise of Nazism
- Germans felt betrayed by Treaty of Versailles
- Nazis came to power
- Hitler promised to break Treaty of Versailles, rebuild the military, and reclaim the lost territory

432. Which of the Allies refused to sign the Treaty of Versailles?
A. Italy
B. France
C. Russia
D. United States

433. About how many years passed between the end of World War I and the start of World War II?
A. 18
B. 21
C. 33
D. 45

434. What major event happened in 1917?
A. World War I ended
B. the Treaty of Versailles
C. the Russian Revolution
D. worldwide economic depression

EUROPE

THE HOLOCAUST

As part of Hitler's plan to conquer the world, he began the systematic killing of every Jew– man, woman, or child–under Nazi rule. The Nazis imprisoned Jews in certain sections of cities, made them wear special identifying armbands, and separated them from their families. This was only the beginning. The Nazis built concentration camps and sent Jews from the cities by railcar to these camps. When the Jews arrived, their heads were shaved and a number was tattooed onto their arms. Many were immediately herded into showers, which were nothing more than gas chambers. In such places, as many as 2,000 people could be killed at one time. Thousands died from forced labor, little food, and exposure to the summer heat and winter cold. By the time World War II was over, as many as 6 million Jews were dead. Other groups were Hitler's victims as well. He targeted anyone he felt was inferior: political prisoners, the mentally ill, and the disabled. ***Genocide,*** the planned killing of a race of people, became a crime when the United Nations passed the Genocide Convention in 1948.

At the end of World War II, when the Allies gained control of the camps, the survivors of the ***Holocaust*** had no place to go. Many had no living family members. They were trapped in the country of their oppressors. The Jews wanted a state in Palestine, their ancient homeland in the Middle East. In 1947, the United Nations divided Palestine into an Arab state and a Jewish state, Israel. Israel officially opened its borders to Jews in 1948.

_____ **435. What is genocide?**

A. forced labor or slavery

B. the planned killing of a race of people

C. the division of Palestine into Arab and Jewish states

D. not shown

_____ **436. Who created the country of Israel?**

A. Allies

B. Arabs

C. Nazi Germany

D. United Nations

_____ **437. Who was spared in the Holocaust?**

A. men

B. women

C. children

D. none of the above

_____ **438. What actions did the United Nations take as result of the Holocaust?**

A. divided Palestine and Germany

B. defeated Hitler and freed the Jews

C. helped the Jews find jobs and shelter

D. created a Jewish state and made genocide a crime

EUROPE

THE COLD WAR

Beginning in 1945, the **Cold War** was a period of distrust and misunderstanding between the Soviet Union and its former allies in the West, particularly the United States. The Soviet Union was a communist country that believed a powerful central government should control the economy as well as the government. This idea was very different from the democracy and capitalism found in the United States. The United States believed that business should be privately owned. After World War II, Soviet dictator Joseph Stalin placed most of the Eastern European countries under communist control. These countries became known as the Eastern Bloc. The United States led the Western Bloc countries of Western Europe. The line separating the two was called the "Iron Curtain."

Another problem of the Cold War was the division of Germany. At the end of the war, the Allies divided Germany into four sections to keep it from regaining power. The United States, Great Britain, France, and the Soviet Union each controlled a section. In 1948, the Western Allies wanted to reunite Germany, but the Soviets disagreed. The Soviets declared their section of the country "East Germany;" the reunited sections became West Germany. Even the capital of Berlin in East Germany was divided into East and West. Tensions grew. In 1961, communist leaders built the Berlin Wall. It separated the communist part of the city from the free sections.

Some countries under communist rule tried to break away from the Soviet Union, but the Soviets sent the military into these countries to keep them in line.

Each side in this Cold War thought the other was trying to rule the world. Neither side gave up, and people lived in fear that another world war might erupt. People worried that if such a war happened, it would be a nuclear war. Such a war would be a disaster for everyone on the earth. Countries formed new alliances to protect themselves. In 1949, the western European countries plus the United States and Canada formed the **North Atlantic Treaty Organization (NATO).** The eastern countries signed the **Warsaw Pact**.

_____ 439. **Which country was the leader of the Eastern Bloc?**
   A. Germany
   B. Soviet Union
   C. United States
   D. United Kingdom

_____ 440. **What are the two terms used to describe the dividing line between eastern and western, communist and noncommunist areas?**
   A. NATO and Warsaw Pact
   B. Berlin Wall and Iron Curtain
   C. Allied Powers and Axis Powers
   D. Nazi Germany and Free Germany

_____ 441. **Which was one of the areas of disagreement between the Soviet Union and the United States during the Cold War?**
   A. defeat of Hitler
   B. best type of economic system
   C. the danger of nuclear weapons
   D. the need to work with other countries

EUROPE

____ **442. When was the Cold War?**
   A. after World War II
   B. before World War I
   C. between World War I and World War II
   D. before the worldwide economic depression

____ **443. The <u>Warsaw Pact</u> was to the <u>Soviet Union</u> as <u>NATO</u> was to the**
   A. Eastern Bloc
   B. United States
   C. West Germany
   D. European Union

RISE OF THE SUPERPOWERS

As the Cold War continued, the United States and the Soviet Union increased their area of influence. More countries allied with each. The United States and the Soviet Union had the ability to influence world events and project worldwide power. The countries were evenly matched. The world took sides, communist or democracy, socialist or free market.

The Soviets had a permanent seat on the UN Security Council. They influenced other communist countries and dictatorships around the world. The Soviets occupied the largest country in the world. The Soviet Union had the third-largest population in the world and the second-largest economy. The Soviets had military and space technology, a worldwide spy network (the KGB), and one of the largest stockpiles of nuclear weapons in the world.

The third-largest country in the world, the United States also had a permanent seat on the UN Security Council and strong ties with Western Europe and Latin America. The fourth most populated country, the United States supported undeveloped countries and developing democratic ones. The United States had powerful military support from NATO, the largest navy in the world, and bases all over the world, even bordering the Warsaw Pact countries. The Central Intelligence Agency (CIA) spent money to spy on the Soviet Union. The United States had a large reserve of nuclear weapons.

____ **444. As a world superpower, the Soviet Union had**
   A. support from NATO.
   B. the largest navy in the world.
   C. strong ties with Latin America.
   D. a seat on the UN Security Council.

____ **445. As a world superpower, the United States had**
   A. the KGB, a spy network.
   B. military bases all over the world.
   C. influence over communist dictatorships.
   D. the second-largest economy in the world.

____ **446. Which condition is required to be considered a superpower?**
   A. a space program
   B. membership in NATO
   C. democratic government
   D. influence over world events

EUROPE

THE COLLAPSE OF THE SOVIET UNION AND GERMAN REUNIFICATION

The Soviet Union was spending more and more of its money putting down revolts within its country, protecting its borders, and keeping up with the United States in the arms race. By 1985, the economy was so unstable that Mikhail Gorbachev, the head of the Soviet Union, reduced government control of business and increased freedoms for Soviet citizens. These actions helped to improve relations with the United States and inspired people in other Eastern Bloc countries to demand freedom from communist rule.

In November 1989, the Berlin Wall was torn down, and Germany began the process of unifying. People around the world celebrated. East and West Germany were made one country in 1990. The Cold War was over. The Soviet republics that had once been separate countries began seeking their independence too. The Soviet Union was no more. Many countries were created from the former Soviet Union. Russia was the largest.

_____ **447. Why did Gorbachev reduce government control of the economy?**
   A. citizens demanded more personal freedom
   B. other Eastern Bloc countries were reducing control
   C. an unstable economy due to increased military spending
   D. not shown

_____ **448. What marked the end of the Cold War?**
   A. the rule of Gorbachev
   B. the creation of Russia
   C. the break-up of the Soviet Union
   D. the destruction of the Berlin Wall

_____ **449. What was the largest country created from the former Soviet Union?**
   A. Belarus
   B. Germany
   C. Russia
   D. Ukraine

AUSTRALIA

GEOGRAPHIC UNDERSTANDINGS

SS6G12 The student will be able to locate selected features of Australia.

a. Locate on a world and regional political-physical map: the Great Barrier Reef, Coral Sea, Ayers Rock, and Great Victoria Desert.

LOCATING PHYSICAL FEATURES OF AUSTRALIA

The best way to visualize **Australia** is to think of huge desert plains stretching across the country's middle. Think of milder climates along the southeastern and southwestern coasts. Most Australians live in these southern coastal regions, especially on the east coast.

The largest part of Australia consists of semi-arid or dry lands known as the ***outback***. The climate of the north is more varied. Northern Australia has a tropical climate. In the north, you will also find rain forest, mangrove swamps, grassland, and even more desert.

Australia is unique. Australia is the only country on the world's smallest and flattest continent. It has our Earth's oldest and least fertile soils. Only the continent of Antarctica, located more than 4,000 miles south of Australia, receives less annual rainfall. Most of the Commonwealth of Australia is located on the continent's mainland. The Commonwealth of Australia also includes Tasmania, a large island south of the mainland, and several other islands in the Indian and Pacific Oceans. These two major oceans surround Australia, along with some seas.

Four important physical regions of Australia can be located on a political-physical map. These are the **Great Barrier Reef**, the **Coral Sea**, **Ayers Rock**, and the **Great Victoria Desert**.

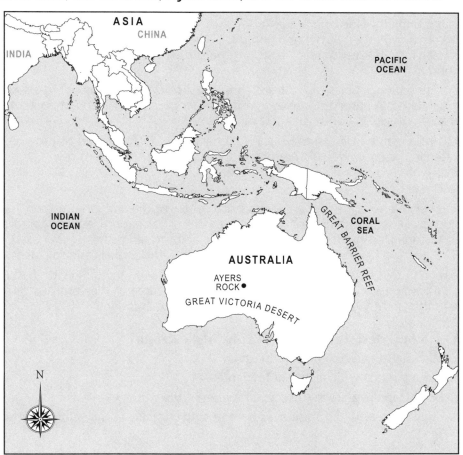

AUSTRALIA

Great Barrier Reef

The Great Barrier Reef is the world's largest coral reef. The reef lies a short distance off the northeast coast of Queensland. Queensland is one of Australia's states. The reef extends along Queensland's coast for more than 1,200 miles. The reef is in waters known as the Coral Sea. Locate Queensland on the northeastern coast of Australia's mainland.

As you move south along the coastal waters, you will find an amazing variety of marine life. The reef contains the world's largest collection of coral. There are 400 types of coral, more than 1,500 species of fish, and 4,000 types of mollusks (animals like snails, clams, octopi, and squid). Some species are rare. The reef's rare species include the "sea cow" or dugong, and the large green turtle. They depend on the Great Barrier Reef as their habitat.

The Coral Sea

The Coral Sea, an important source of coral for the Great Barrier Reef, is actually part of the Pacific Ocean. The sea is off the northeast coast of Australia. When Earth's crust moved millions of years ago, the movement created the Coral Sea and the Great Dividing Range. The Great Dividing Range is the largest mountain range in Australia.

Coral Sea islands are scattered over thousands of square miles of ocean. Australia claimed these islands as a territory of Australia in 1969. No one lives on these islands except for a small group of weather specialists based on the Willis Islets. Many other Coral Sea islands and reefs house automated weather stations and light beacons.

Ayers Rock

If you leave the eastern coast of Australia and travel into the continent's center, you could find a huge, reddish rock towering out of the flatlands. This rock is a **monolith** called Ayers Rock. A monolith is what you can see of a single, large rock sticking out of the earth. Stone Mountain, near Atlanta, is a monolith made of granite. Ayers Rock is the visible tip of a massive underground sandstone rock cemented together by sand and mud. Ayers Rock is gray-colored before it rusts. It appears reddish because its iron content "rusts" at the surface. It is nearly 12 stories tall and almost six miles wide around its base!

The Anangu are native peoples of Australia. They are **Aborigines**. They call Ayers Rock "Uluru," which is its official name. A European surveyor visited the rock in 1873 and named it after Sir Henry Ayers, a government official in South Australia at the time.

In 1950, Australia created Uluru-Kata Tjuta National Park, which you can visit to view Ayers Rock. The park is located in the southwest corner of the state called Northern Territory.

Great Victoria Desert

Ayers Rock is very close to the actual geographical center of the continent. When you leave Ayers Rock, you could travel southwest into the states of South Australia and Western Australia. There you enter the Great Victoria Desert. This desert receives only eight to ten inches of rain each year, and it never snows. There are some grasslands in the desert along with sandhills and salt lakes.

The first European to cross the desert named after British Queen Victoria in 1875. It is a large area–more than 160,000 square miles–and is a protected wilderness area of Western Australia. Very few Australians live in the Great Victoria Desert because it is too hot and dry.

_____ **450. Which best describes the geography of Australia?**
   A. lake district across the southwest
   B. mountainous with scattered lowlands
   C. large tropical zone in the central region of the country
   D. large semi-arid, dry region with temperate climates in the southeastern coastal areas

_____ **451. Which statement describes a monolith?**
   A. giant salt lake
   B. massive sand-filled pit
   C. inactive volcanic crater
   D. visible tip of a massive underground rock

_____ **452. What is the main reason few people live in the Great Victoria Desert?**
   A. It is too hot and dry.
   B. There are winter floods.
   C. Australians prefer city life.
   D. The area has not been explored.

_____ **453. Where is the Great Barrier Reef?**
   A. Coral Sea
   B. Shark Bay
   C. Arafura Sea
   D. Tasman Sea

_____ **454. What climate conditions are found in central Australia?**
   A. hot and dry
   B. mild temperatures
   C. rainy with high humidity
   D. cold with likely snowfall

AUSTRALIA

Use the following map to answer questions 455-456.

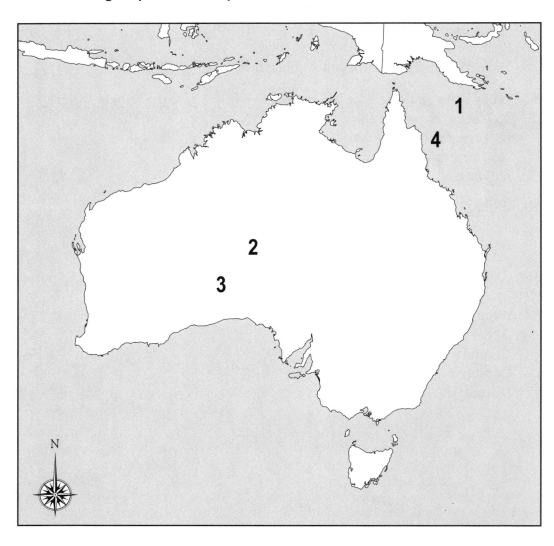

_____ **455. Which feature is marked with a "1" on the map?**
A. Coral Sea
B. Ayers Rock
C. Great Barrier Reef
D. Great Victoria Desert

_____ **456. Where is the Great Barrier Reef located in relation to Ayers Rock?**
A. southeast
B. northeast
C. southwest
D. northwest

HOW AUSTRALIA'S LOCATION, CLIMATE, AND NATURAL RESOURCES HAVE AFFECTED WHERE PEOPLE LIVE

Location of Australia

Australia is both a continent and a country. The continent lies about 2,000 miles southeast of Asia. It is surrounded by the Pacific Ocean on the east and the Indian Ocean on the west. The country lies in the southern hemisphere. Australians say they come from a land "down under" because their country is on the lower part of the globe.

The coastal areas of Australia are the most highly populated. Most people live along the eastern coast. The most populated city is Sydney, the capital of the state of New South Wales. Queensland is another state. It is seven times the size of England. More than half of Queensland's population lives near its capital city of Brisbane.

Nearly 80 percent of Australians live in urban areas. That makes Australia one of the world's most urbanized countries. About 70 percent of all Australians live in cities of more than 100,000 people. Sydney has about 3½ million people, and about 3 million people live in Melbourne.

Climate of Australia

The climate of Australia varies across the continent. Australia is south of the equator, so the seasons are opposite of those in North America. Its summers are December to March, and winters are June to September.

The northern part of Australia is closest to the equator. It has a tropical climate, and it is warm-to-hot all year long. This area also gets more rain than other parts of the country. There are seasons in this region, wet and dry. Winter is wetter and cooler than the hot and dry summer.

Desert is the largest part of Australia. Little rain falls in the central part of the country. Most of the central part of the country gets less than 10 inches of rain a year.

Only the southeast and southwest corners have a temperate climate. They have summers that are not too hot and winters that are not too cold. The climate in these regions is the one that Australians like most. In fact, most Australians live along the southeastern coast.

Natural Resources of Australia

Australians call the remote countryside the ***bush***. The term ***outback*** refers specifically to the continent's dry interior. The outback is mainly open countryside, including vast expanses of grazing land. There are a few widely scattered settlements in the outback. Many of these outback settlements grew up around mining operations.

Mining takes advantage of the natural resources in the ground. Australians mine for coal, iron ore, copper, tin, gold, silver, uranium, nickel, tungsten, mineral sands, zinc, oil, and natural gas. Australians lead the world in the production of diamonds and lead. They also lead in the mining of bauxite, an ore from which we get aluminum.

Australia's minerals are often found in areas that are difficult to reach. Highways and railroads are expensive to build, but they are needed to get workers and machinery to remote locations. Once these resources have been mined, expensive equipment is needed to move the minerals to populated areas for trade.

AUSTRALIA

Another of Australia's natural resources is arable land. There are enough areas with good land and rainfall to make farming an important business. Farmers in Australia produce more than Australians can consume. The food from Australia's farms is sold around the world.

____ **457. Which BEST describes where people live in Australia?**
   A. Most live in larger cities.
   B. Most live in rural areas on farms.
   C. Most live in the interior of the country.
   D. Most live on islands surrounding the mainland.

____ **458. What important business is done in the outback?**
   A. fishing
   B. mining
   C. farming
   D. shipping

____ **459. Why is southeastern Australia a popular place for Australians to live?**
   A. It is near Ayers Rock.
   B. Australians enjoy living near the ocean.
   C. The government tells people to move to this area.
   D. The climate in this region is not too hot or too cold.

Use the following maps to answer questions 460-462.

Population of Australia

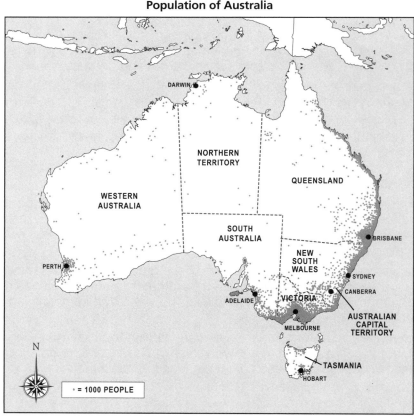

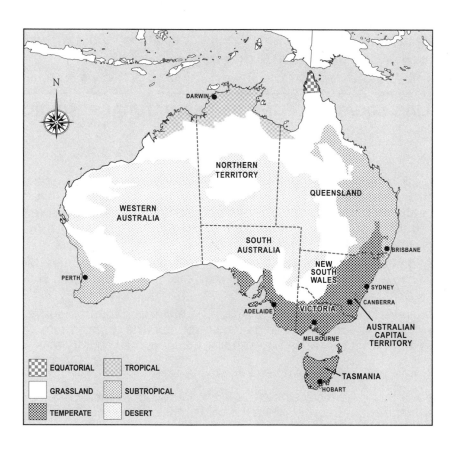

____ 460. **Where is the largest concentration of people in Australia?**
  A. in the bush
  B. near Darwin in the north
  C. in central western Australia
  D. in the state of New South Wales

____ 461. **Where is the coolest climate in Australia?**
  A. in the outback
  B. in western Australia
  C. in the Northern Territory
  D. in Tasmania and the southeastern coast

____ 462. **Which city has the warmest climate?**
  A. Darwin
  B. Sydney
  C. Canberra
  D. Melbourne

AUSTRALIA

SS6G13 The student will explain the impact of location, climate, distribution of natural resources, and population distribution on Australia.

b. Describe how Australia's location, climate, and natural resources impact trade.

HOW AUSTRALIA'S LOCATION, CLIMATE, AND NATURAL RESOURCES IMPACT TRADE

Location

China is Australia's large neighbor to the north. Its economic growth has a direct impact on the Australian economy. Australia is the major supplier of natural resources to China. China needs Australian minerals and metals for its industries. About half of all Australian iron ore goes to China. In return, China provides Australia with affordable finished goods, from cars to dishwashers. Chinese investors are buying into Australian mining companies.

Australia's location makes it expensive for people to visit from other countries. Most international tourists to Australia come from New Zealand. After that, they mostly come from England, the United States, and China.

Foreign tourists create about one-fourth of Australia's $81 billion tourist industry. Australians themselves do the majority of tourism within their own country. The country's remote location in the Southern Hemisphere makes it expensive for Australians to leave their country to visit another one.

Climate

The Australian summer is from December to March. Tourists from the Northern Hemisphere often visit Australia's warm and sunny beaches when it is cold in their homeland. Summer is the rainy season in the tropical regions of the north.

Tourists usually wait until spring or fall to visit the rural areas outside the cities (the bush) and the outback (wilderness areas in the country's interior). That is because the weather is milder in spring and fall. The winter months of June through September are generally mild, but there are snowfields in the southern mountain regions.

In the nondesert regions, Australians grow many grains. Grain is grown in inland regions of Australia's coastal states. Farmers grow grains in central inland Queensland, central New South Wales, inland Victoria, southeast Australia, and southwest Western Australia. Australia is developing its cotton industry, and it has a large beef cattle industry.

The Australian grains industry includes a range of different crops. The most common field grains are wheat, barley, sorghum, and cereal rye. Australians also export rice, chickpeas, lentils, and oilseeds, such as sesame seeds, canola, soybeans, and sunflowers.

Natural Resources

In the outback and across much of Australia, the ground is barren. This is not ideal for farming. However, many important natural resources lie below the continent's surface. These resources include precious metals (gold and silver), uranium, coal, copper, and iron ore.

Australia exports more coal and iron ore than any other country. Many industries use coal and iron ore. Australia leads in mining bauxite, titanium, and industrial diamonds. No country has more reserves of lead, cadmium, or nickel.

Australia has exported nearly $400 billion worth of metals, minerals, and fuels in the past twenty years. Natural resources account for one-third of the country's economy.

Natural resources have always been important to Australian trade. In the mid-nineteenth century, Australia experienced a gold rush in its southern region. Hundreds of thousands of speculators moved to Australia in search of gold. Most of these immigrants arrived from England, Ireland, Germany, and China.

AUSTRALIA

Uranium is a metal needed to make nuclear fuel. China and the United States are very interested in buying uranium from Australia.

_____ **463. Which nation's citizens visit Australia more than any other?**
  A. China
  B. Great Britain
  C. New Zealand
  D. United States

_____ **464. Which resource attracted thousands of immigrants to South Australia in the nineteenth century?**
  A. coal
  B. gold
  C. uranium
  D. iron ore

_____ **465. Which month is best for beachgoers in Sydney?**
  A. June
  B. March
  C. December
  D. September

_____ **466. Which nearby country is most important to Australia for trade?**
  A. China
  B. United States
  C. New Zealand
  D. United Kingdom

AUSTRALIA

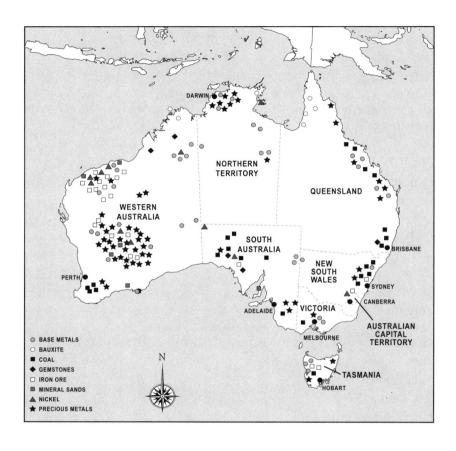

467. Which Australian state has the highest concentration of precious metals?
A. South Australia
B. Western Australia
C. New South Wales
D. Northern Territory

468. What part of Australia has the least amount of mineral resources?
A. central
B. eastern
C. western
D. They are all about the same.

Use the following graph to answer questions 469-471.

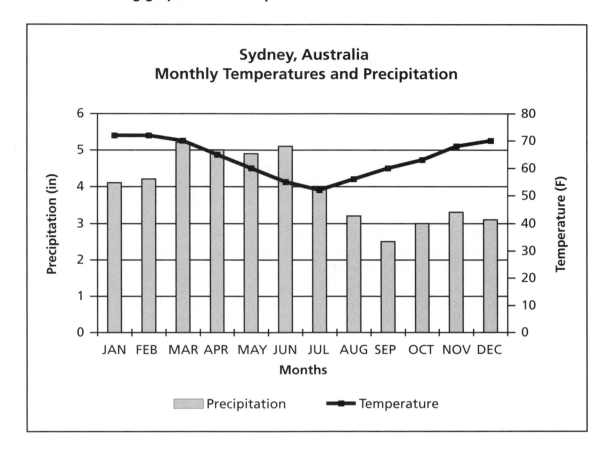

Sydney, Australia
Monthly Temperatures and Precipitation

_____ **469. Which is the warmest month?**
    A. June
    B. April
    C. August
    D. January

_____ **470. In which month does Sydney get less than 2 inches of rain?**
    A. June
    B. April
    C. August
    D. none of these

_____ **471. Which statement is true about Sydney?**
    A. June is usually one of Sydney's hottest and driest months.
    B. June is usually one of Sydney's coolest and wettest months.
    C. The temperature and precipitation do not change much from month to month.
    D. The temperature and precipitation both increase in the second half of the year.

AUSTRALIA

SS6G14 The student will describe the cultural characteristics of people who live in Australia.

a. Explain the impact of English colonization on the language and religion of Australia.

THE IMPACT OF ENGLISH COLONIZATION ON THE LANGUAGE AND RELIGION OF AUSTRALIA

Language of Australia

The story of Australia's official language is a result of British colonization and expansion. Australia was the final continent discovered by the Europeans. Native Aborigines had inhabited the continent for centuries, however. Dutch explorers had discovered and mapped parts of Australia but did not send colonists to the continent.

Captain James Cook left England in 1768 to explore the South Seas. Cook explored and mapped parts of eastern Australia. He claimed the land for England and named it New South Wales. England did not immediately colonize Australia, however.

In 1788, England sent a crew to Australia to begin building prisons to house convicts. From 1788 to 1823, the colony of New South Wales was a penal (prison) colony housing mainly convicts, marines, and wives of marines. In 1823, the British government established Australia's first parliament. Parliament established criminal and civil courts. By 1868, more than 170,000 convicts had arrived in Australia from England. The language of the prisoners, the guards, the courts, and businesses was English.

The French government became interested in Australia's west. To keep the French out, English settlers built new villages and cities as fast as possible. This spread the English language to the western part of Australia.

More British immigrants entered Australia during the mid-nineteenth century. Gold in southern Australia attracted thousands from England and Ireland. Thousands of Chinese immigrants arrived as well. Chinese did not become an important language; the English-speakers were too plentiful. When Australia gained independence from Great Britain, the government wanted to make sure the country did not get too many immigrants. It allowed people from England or the United States to move to the country. The government made rules to stop immigrants from Africa and Asia. This encouraged even more English-speakers to come to Australia.

Today, more than 20 percent of Australians were born in another country. Over half came to Australia from non-English speaking countries in Europe, Asia, the Middle East, and South America. Because of Australia's history, though, English is the official language, and it is the most common language for people and business.

Religion in Australia

Europeans introduced Christianity to Australia in 1788. Irish convicts were mostly Roman Catholic. Other convicts and those who managed them were Anglicans and Methodists.

During the 1800s, European settlers brought their traditional churches to Australia. Faiths included the Church of England (now the Anglican Church), Methodist, Catholic, Presbyterian, Congregationalist, and Baptist.

Today, most Australians are Christians. The Roman Catholic Church and the Anglican Church claim the most members. Muslims, Buddhists, Jews, and Hindus combined make up less than 5 percent of the population.

AUSTRALIA

_____ **472. What religion did most of the Australia's Irish prisoners practice?**
   A. Baptist
   B. Anglican
   C. Presbyterian
   D. Roman Catholic

_____ **473. Why did the Australian government restrict immigration after it became independent from Great Britain in 1901?**
   A. The ports were blockaded.
   B. It felt the country had enough citizens.
   C. There wasn't enough housing for immigrants.
   D. It only wanted immigrants that were of European ancestry.

_____ **474. What did English Captain James Cook name the first colony of Australia?**
   A. New Britain
   B. New Tasmania
   C. South Cockney
   D. New South Wales

_____ **475. What language did the first European settlers speak in Australia?**
   A. Dutch
   B. French
   C. English
   D. Aboriginal

AUSTRALIA

SS6G14 The student will describe the cultural characteristics of people who live in Australia.

b. Evaluate how the literacy rate affects the standard of living.

HOW THE LITERACY RATE AFFECTS THE STANDARD OF LIVING

Literacy is the ability to read and write. It means you can use language to read, write, listen, and follow directions. The *literacy rate* is the percentage of a population's adults that can read and write. Australia has a very high literacy rate. About 99 percent of adult Australians are considered literate, according to census surveys.

Having a high literacy rate is important to the success of the people in a country. When parents are illiterate (not able to read or write), their children are likely to be unable to read or write. When adults cannot read or write, they often must take lower-paying jobs. That means they earn less money.

Countries with high literacy rates are generally wealthier. These countries compete better in the world economy. People who read often get better jobs, earn more, and can afford to buy more and better things. They can afford better housing and food for their families. They can afford better clothing and health care.

The *standard of living* measures how well off people in a country are. When thinking about the standard of living, think about what it costs a family to live. Housing, food, health care, educational opportunities, and income can all be a part of the standard of living.

In Australia, the literacy rate and the standard of living are both high. In fact, Australians enjoy one of the highest standards of living in the world. There is poverty, however. The worst conditions are among the Aborigines. The *life expectancy* of Aborigines is much lower than for other Australians. Life expectancy is the average number of years a person in a country may be expected to live. Aborigines also tend to earn less income. They often do not have good health care.

_____ **476. Which is an effect of a low literacy rate?**

    A. The population is generally wealthier.

    B. The population can expect to live longer.

    C. The population has a lower standard of living.

    D. The population competes better in the world economy.

_____ **477. Which is TRUE of the literacy rate in Australia?**

    A. About one-third of Australians are literate.

    B. Nearly two-thirds of Australians are illiterate.

    C. Nearly all adult Australians can read and write.

    D. Only about half of the population can read and write.

_____ **478. Which is TRUE about Australia's standard of living?**

    A. There is no poverty in Australia.

    B. It is not very high compared to other countries.

    C. Australia has one of the highest standards of living in the world.

    D. Few Australians can afford good food, shelter, education, and health care.

AUSTRALIA

CIVICS/GOVERNMENT UNDERSTANDINGS

> **SS6CG6 The student will compare and contrast various forms of government.**
> a. Describe the ways government systems distribute power: unitary, confederation, and federal.

WAYS GOVERNMENT SYSTEMS DISTRIBUTE POWER

Governments can be set up in different ways. One of the ways to compare governments is to think about how power is distributed.

Unitary Governments

The central government possesses most of the decision-making power and authority in a unitary government. The central government is the controlling body. Local governing bodies act as administrative assistants to the central government.

The United Kingdom is a country that uses a unitary style government. In the UK, individual counties do not have much power. The power rests with the central government. Local governments follow the direction of the central government. Even though people from the United Kingdom settled Australia, Australians did not organize their government in this style.

Confederate Governments

In a confederate government, local governments protect and operate under their own authority. The states or local governments control the primary governing power. This weakens the power of the central government. The central government has less control than a unitary style central government.

The United States originally tried a confederate government. The Articles of Confederation (the country's first constitution) in the early years of the United States had weaknesses. One of them was that states did not have to follow laws made by the central government. Australia does have six states and two territories. The states, however, do not have the power to ignore laws passed by the Australian Parliament.

Australia is a member of the ***Commonwealth of Nations***. The Commonwealth is a very weak association of member countries that were once part of the British empire. Some of them recognize the Queen as the head of state; others do not. The Commonwealth has no power to force any member to take an action that it does not want to take. Instead, the Commonwealth works to promote trade and solutions to common problems among the members.

Federal Governments

Australia has a federal government system. In Australia, there are six states. These six states represent the six British colonies that joined to create the Commonwealth of Australia. There are also two territories. Power is split between the central government and the states. The Constitution of Australia is the overriding law of the land. It spells out the rights, privileges, and duties given to each level of government. The constitution defines how national, state, and local governments will share power.

The Australian states approved the first constitution. That constitution gave the commonwealth government the right to pass laws on certain subjects. It allows the states to keep all other lawmaking rights. This is called a division of powers. The federal government is responsible for such things as agreements with other countries and defense. The states are responsible for things such as education and state police.

AUSTRALIA

_____ 479. **Which is TRUE of a confederate government?**
A. Governing power resides with states.
B. Individual counties do not have much power.
C. The power resides with the central government.
D. Power is split between a central authority and its states.

_____ 480. **Which describes the government of Australia?**
A. federal government
B. unitary government
C. confederate government
D. both unitary and confederate

_____ 481. **Which is an example of a confederation?**
A. Australia
B. European Union
C. Australia and New Zealand
D. Commonwealth of Nations

_____ 482. **In what government type is power split between a central government and the states?**
A. unitary
B. federal
C. autocratic
D. confederate

SS6CG6 The student will compare and contrast various forms of government.
b. Explain how governments determine citizen participation: autocratic, oligarchic, and democratic.

HOW GOVERNMENTS DETERMINE CITIZEN PARTICIPATION

The right of people to participate in their government's decisions rests on how their government is organized. Three ways governments determine citizen participation are autocratic, oligarchic, and democratic. These three forms of government differ. The differences are based on who or how many rule or operate the government.

Autocracy

An autocratic form of government means one self-appointed ruler holds the political power. The leader makes decisions for his subjects. In some cases, an autocracy could be a miltary dictatorship. Australia does not have this form of government. Although the country has a monarch as head of state, the monarch's role in government is limited. The country's constitution explains the limited powers of the monarch. This arrangement is known as a constitutional monarchy.

AUSTRALIA

Oligarchy

An oligarchy is "rule by the few." A small group of leaders decides the fate of the people. Political power rests with a small group. The group members may come from a common family. The group may also have power because of wealth or military support.

Democracy

A democracy is rule by the people and their ability to vote. People elect their officials and decide who will lead them. Voters decide who will stay in power. Voters may even vote on laws and changes in a constitution.

In Australia, an elected government runs the country. Australians who are over 18 years of age must vote in an election every four years. Failure to vote can result in a fine and a hearing in court. Voters in Australia elect members of Parliament (MPs). The MPs represent the people's interests in making laws. The MPs choose a prime minister to lead the country. The prime minister recommends a governor-general to the Queen. The Queen chooses a governor-general to perform duties as head of state and to represent her in Australia.

_____ 483. **Which gives the people the most voice in making laws?**

    A. oligarchy

    B. autocracy

    C. theocracy

    D. democracy

_____ 484. **In which form of government might a military dictator hold the power?**

    A. oligarchy

    B. autocracy

    C. democracy

    D. confederacy

_____ 485. **Which statement BEST describes an oligarchy?**

    A. The citizens elect their leaders.

    B. A small group runs the government.

    C. The judicial branch controls political power.

    D. Self-appointed ruler holds the political power.

PREDOMINATE FORMS OF DEMOCRATIC GOVERNMENT

Two major forms of democratic governments–parliamentary and presidential–are designed to represent and protect the rights of the people.

Parliamentary

An elected parliament represents the people and holds the power in a parliamentary democracy. The elected officials create and pass the laws of the land. They share the power. The executive officials and legislature share the same constituency. The constituency is the people who voted for them.

Australia has a parliamentary form of democratic government. The legislative branch is led by Parliament. The people of Australia elect parliament's members. The members of Parliament choose the **prime minister** to be the head of the government. The prime minister is the most powerful person in the government. The monarch, as head of state, appoints a governor-general to represent the crown in Australia. The governor-general is chosen based on the recommendation of the prime minister.

Presidential

In a presidential democracy, the citizens elect the members of the legislature, but they also elect the chief executive, known as the president. The president serves as the head of state. The president also runs the government on a day-to-day basis and heads the military. However, the president does not make the laws. The legislature has the job of making laws. The president serves for a fixed amount of time, and then elections are held again. The legislature does not have the power to force an early election, and the president does not have the power to dissolve the legislature. The United States is an example of a country with a presidential democracy.

_____ **486. Who represents the Queen in Australia's government?**

    A. senate

    B. president

    C. prime minister

    D. governor-general

_____ **487. Who has the most political power in the Australian government?**

    A. the monarch

    B. prime minister

    C governor-general

    D. High Court judge

_____ **488. Which branch of government makes laws in Australia?**

    A. judicial

    B. monarch

    C. executive

    D. legislative

AUSTRALIA

THE FEDERAL PARLIAMENTARY DEMOCRACY OF AUSTRALIA

Form of Leadership

Australia's six states represent the six British colonies united to create the Commonwealth of Australia. These six states approved a constitution. The constitution gives the federal government the right to pass laws on certain subjects. It also allows the states to convene a state parliament and pass certain laws.

Any land within Australia's national border that is not claimed by one of the states is called a *territory*. Territories cannot convene their own government or pass laws. The Commonwealth makes the laws for the territories.

Queen Elizabeth II is the head of state for Australia. The Queen lives in England, not Australia. She does not run the country. The Queen signs laws and is the commander-in-chief of the army, navy, and air force. The Queen does approve elections. The Queen is not busy at any of these jobs, however. Australia's prime minister recommends someone to represent the Queen in Australia. This person, the governor-general, serves the Queen, represents her in Australia, and fulfills her duties and responsibilities there.

The head of government is the prime minister. This person is the leader of the political party with the most members in the Commonwealth Parliament. The person in this position is the most powerful political figure in Australia.

Type of Legislature

In Australia, an elected government operates the country. Every four years, Australians who are over age 18 vote for the people who will be in Parliament. People who are elected go to Parliament in Canberra, the national capital. The Parliament meets several times a year. Parliament makes laws that affect how Australians live. There are two houses of Parliament. These are called the House of Representatives and the Senate.

Australia is divided into areas called *electorates*. Each electorate has about the same number of people living in it. The people who live in each electorate vote for a person to go to Parliament to represent them. That elected person becomes the MP of the House of Representatives for that area. There is one seat in the House of Representatives for each electorate.

The other house of Parliament is the Senate. People of each state, the Northern Territory, and the Australian Capital Territory elect twelve people to be their senators. No matter how big or small a state or territory, each has the same number of senators.

After an election, the political party that wins the most seats in the House of Representatives becomes the government. The winning party's leader becomes the prime minister. The prime minister is the head of the government. The party with the second highest number of seats in the House of Representatives is called the "Opposition." That party's leader is "the leader of the Opposition."

When a member of Parliament first suggests a law, it is called a *bill*. The bill is explained, discussed, and often changed. If the House members vote to pass the bill, it goes to the Senate. There the process repeats. If the bill passes the Senate vote, the bill becomes an "Act of Parliament." The governor-general signs the act, and it becomes a law that Australians must obey.

AUSTRALIA

The Role of the Citizen

Australians have an important role in their government. Since they have a democratic form of government, the voters choose the lawmakers. In Australia, voters must be 18 years old or over to vote. Voting is compulsory. That means that everyone that is eligible to vote is required to vote unless there is a good reason, such as illness. Australians can be fined or may have to go to court if they do not vote.

Australians vote for members of Parliament, or MPs. The leader of the political party that gets the most votes becomes the prime minister.

Voters do not vote for the head of state. The Queen holds that position. The prime minister recommends a person to the Queen to serve as her representative. That person becomes the governor-general. Citizens do not vote for the Queen, the governor-general, or even the judges on the High Court.

Australians enjoy many freedoms. They have freedom of religion and freedom of speech. They have the freedom to choose their own jobs, and they can travel around the country or to other countries. Australians can vote for the leaders that make laws and lead the country. Their level of freedom is similar to what people have in the United Kingdom and the United States.

_____ **489. What responsibility do Australians have after their 18th birthday?**
A. voting
B. marriage
C. military service
D. running for office

_____ **490. Which official do citizens of Australia vote into office?**
A. monarch
B. prime minister
C. governor-general
D. member of Parliament

Use the phrases in the following box to answer question 491.

- approves elections
- signs bills into law
- is commander-in-chief of the military
- acts as head of state for Australia

_____ **491. What do these phrases explain?**
A. duties of the Queen in Australia
B. duties of the Australian prime minister
C. actions taken by judges in the High Court of Australia
D. actions that are not a part of the Australian government

Use the following diagram to answer questions 492-495.

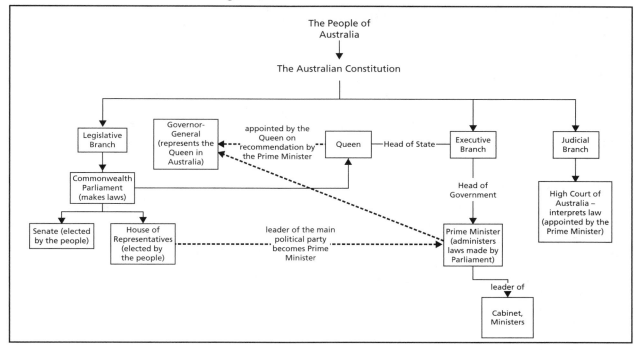

The Organization of the Australian Government

492. **In which branch of government is the governor-general?**
    A. judicial
    B. executive
    C. territorial
    D. legislative

493. **What are the three parts of the Australian Parliament?**
    A. executive, judicial, and legislative branches
    B. High Court, Parliament, and prime minister
    C. government, the constitution, and the people
    D. the Queen, House of Representatives, and the Senate

494. **Which has the most power in the Australian government?**
    A. the Queen
    B. the Senate
    C. the constitution
    D. the people of Australia

495. **Who administers laws made by the Commonwealth Parliament in Australia?**
    A. queen
    B. prime minister
    C. governor-general
    D. members of Parliament

AUSTRALIA

ECONOMIC UNDERSTANDINGS

> **SS6E8 The student will analyze different economic systems.**
> a. Compare how traditional, command, and market, economies answer the economic questions of 1 -what to produce, 2-how to produce, and 3-for whom to produce.

DIFFERENT ECONOMIC SYSTEMS

Scarcity refers to the limited supply of something. Every country must deal with the problem of scarcity because no country has everything that its people want and need. Every country must develop an economic system to determine how to use its limited resources to answer the three basic economic questions: *What* goods and services will be produced? *How* will goods and services be produced? *Who* will consume the goods and services? The way a society answers these questions determines its *economic system*.

Traditional Economy

In a *traditional economy*, customs and habits of the past are used to decide what and how goods will be produced, distributed, and consumed. In this system, each member of the society knows early in life what his or her role in the larger group will be. Because the jobs are handed down from generation to generation, there is very little change in the system over the generations.

In a traditional economy, people are depended on to fulfill their traditional role. If some people are not there to do their part, the system can break down. Farming, hunting and gathering, and cattle herding are often a part of a traditional economy. This type of economy was found in the culture of the Aborigines in Australia.

Command Economy

In a centralized *command economy*, government planning groups make the basic economic decisions. They determine such things as which goods and services to produce, the prices of those goods and services, and wage rates. Individuals and corporations generally do not own businesses or farms; these are owned by the government. Workers at a business are told what to produce and how much to produce in a given time. The expectation is that everyone in the country will be able to have the goods they need when they need them.

The government of Australia controlled one part of the economy in the past. Government-owned companies controlled telecommunications. The government set the price for having a phone, the cost of calls, and wages that were the same in all parts of the country. In 1989, the company was made into a private business with stockholders owning the company.

Market Economy

In a decentralized *market economy*, decisions are guided by changes in prices that occur between individual buyers and sellers in the marketplace. Other names for market systems are *free enterprise*, *capitalism*, and *laissez-faire*. In a market economy, individuals or corporations generally own businesses and farms. Each business or farm decides what it wants to produce.

Australia operates in a market economy. It is considered one of the most free economies in the world. Businesses operate without too many rules from the government. People are free to start a business and can do so quickly. Courts use the laws of Australia to protect the property rights of citizens.

AUSTRALIA

_____ **496. In Australia, who decides which goods will be produced and sold?**
   A. citizens
   B. the monarch
   C. business owners
   D. the prime minister

_____ **497. What type of economic system was used by the Aborigines?**
   A. capitalism
   B. market economy
   C. command economy
   D. traditional economy

> **SS6E8 The student will analyze different economic systems.**
> b. Explain how most countries have a mixed economy located on a continuum between pure and market and pure command.

MIXED ECONOMY

There are no pure command or market economies. All modern economies have characteristics of both systems and are, therefore, ***mixed economies***. However, most economies are closer to one type of economic system than another. In a truly free market economy, for example, the government would not be involved at all. There would be no laws to protect workers from unfair bosses. There would be no rules to make sure that credit cards were properly protected. Many societies have chosen to have some rules to protect consumers, workers, and businesses. These rules reduce the freedoms that businesses have, but they also protect the workers and consumers.

The following diagram shows world economies on a scale. The ones on the left are the most restricted. The ones on the right are the most free. Australia has one of the most free economies in the world. It ranks higher even than the United States. It is known for its good courts and laws that protect property owners.

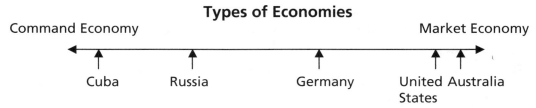

Types of Economies

Command Economy   Market Economy

Cuba   Russia   Germany   United   Australia
                                                States

_____ **498. Which country shown in the diagram has the freest economy?**
   A. Cuba
   B. Germany
   C. Australia
   D. United States

_____ **499. Because most economies have characteristics of the command and market economy, we say they are**
   A. free.
   B. hybrid.
   C. mixed.
   D. communist.

AUSTRALIA

THE ECONOMIC SYSTEM USED IN AUSTRALIA

Australia has one of the freest economies in the world. It is a mixed economy, a market economy with very few rules to restrict the market. The government does not own major industries or businesses. Prices are set by the agreement of buyers and sellers rather than by government rules.

In Australia, people are free to own their own businesses and property. Business owners decide what they want to produce. In the same way, farmers decide what products they will produce and how much of the products to produce. Buyers and sellers are able to agree on prices. Competition between sellers helps to keep the prices good for buyers.

Business owners and consumers can depend on good laws to protect them. The courts are considered fair and honest. Bribery is rare, and it is punished by strict laws.

It is very easy to start a business in Australia. In some countries it can take months to a year or more to start a business. In Australia, the paperwork usually takes less than a week.

_____ **500. What protects businesses and consumers well in Australia?**

     A. buyers and sellers

     B. business owners and consumers

     C. fair and honest courts and good laws

     D. none of these

_____ **501. Who sets the price for goods in Australia?**

     A. Buyers and sellers agree upon a price.

     B. The governor-general sets prices for most goods.

     C. Parliament sets a price for all goods in the country.

     D. Prices for goods brought from China are set by the government.

HOW SPECIALIZATION MAKES TRADE POSSIBLE BETWEEN COUNTRIES

When workers in a factory are working on different jobs, **specialization** occurs. There are workers who buy the raw materials and supplies. Other workers run the machinery to create the products. There may be people who specialize in keeping up with the money, paying bills and salaries. Other workers are involved in selling the product and delivering it. Within the business, no one person can know how to do all the jobs. The factory runs best when each person learns his or her part well. Those employees can get faster at doing their jobs and learn ways to handle problems and work more efficiently.

Work divided in this way is described as a **_division of labor_**. Even if your grandmother bakes her own bread, she probably does not grow the wheat, harvest the wheat, and grind it into flour. She also doesn't build her own oven to cook the bread. Instead, people like your grandmother earn money doing other things. She can then pay for the flour and the oven. She can use her own skills to bake the bread herself.

The economy of countries works in a similar way. Australia, for example, has many natural resources. Coal and iron ore are important to the industries of China. Australia has spent time and money to learn the best ways to get these resources from the ground. Australians can trade these natural resources to China. What does Australia get in return? Goods produced in Chinese factories are brought into Australia. Washing machines, televisions, computers, and household goods are among the many products that can be made more cheaply in China than in Australia.

_____ **502. Which is an example of specialization?**

      A. A business makes and sells goods for a profit.

      B. Two people come to an agreement to trade goods they produced.

      C. A factory builds only one product and finds ways to build it better and less expensively.

      D. A country buys all the goods it needs from other countries and does not produce any of its own.

_____ **503. Why do businesses specialize?**

      A. because they can sell more types of goods

      B. so they can produce goods at a slower pace

      C. so the workers will not become experts in their jobs

      D. because they can produce more goods in less time and for less money

> **SS6E9 The student will give examples of how voluntary trade benefits buyers and sellers in Australia.**
> b. Compare and contrast different types of trade barriers, such as tariffs, quotas and embargos.

TYPES OF TRADE BARRIERS: TARIFFS, QUOTAS, AND EMBARGOS

Trade is the voluntary exchange of goods and services among people and countries. Trade and voluntary exchange occur when buyers and sellers freely and willingly engage in market transactions. When trade is voluntary, both parties benefit and are better off after the trade than they were before the trade.

Countries sometimes try to limit trade with other countries by creating **trade barriers**. The most common types of trade barriers are **tariffs** and **quotas**. A tariff is a tax on imports. A quota is a limit placed on the number of imports that may enter a country.

Another kind of trade barrier is an **embargo**. An embargo is a government order stopping trade with another country. An embargo might be put into place in order to put pressure on another country.

Australia has tried to encourage trade with other countries. It wants other countries to sell goods to Australians, and it wants those countries to buy Australian products. So, there are few trade barriers in the country. When there are tariffs, they are very low. Farmers of wheat and some other crops are given some special treatment by the government. Rules are in place to help Australian farmers have an advantage over foreign farmers in sales to Australian companies. These rules make foreign products cost more.

Australia has participated in embargoes. In 1998, for instance, it put an embargo on weapons being shipped to Yugoslavia. At the time, there was war in that country. Australia wanted to help end the fighting. It refused to sell weapons to either side in the war.

AUSTRALIA

_____ **504. What action did Australia take to try to stop fighting in Yugoslavia?**

      A. quota

      B. trade

      C. tariff

      D. embargo

_____ **505. Why are tariffs low in Australia?**

      A. Australia needs the extra tax money from tariffs.

      B. Australia wants to encourage trade with other countries.

      C. Australia wants to limit the production of goods to keep prices high.

      D. Australia does not want to get involved in the business of other countries.

SS6E9 The student will give examples of how voluntary trade benefits buyers and sellers in Australia.

c. Explain why international trade requires a system for exchanging currency between nations.

INTERNATIONAL TRADE AND A SYSTEM FOR EXCHANGING CURRENCY BETWEEN NATIONS

**Currency** is the money people use to make trade easier. In the United States, we use U.S. dollars (USD or $) to buy goods and services. When Americans work at a job, they are paid in dollars. Most of the time, when you are in a different country, you cannot buy goods and services with currency from your own country. What do you do? You trade it in, or exchange it. With each exchange, however, the bank charges a fee. A business that exchanges a lot of money will pay many fees.

In Australia, the currency is the Australian dollar. Australian dollars are used to pay workers and to buy and sell goods and services. Suppose that gold mined in Australia is needed in California by a jewelry maker. The gold miners want to be paid in Australian dollars. That is what they need to buy food at the grocery store and to pay their families' bills. The jeweler in California has American dollars to spend. In order for the sale to happen, the buyer must trade American dollars for Australian dollars. Banks will exchange money in this way for a small fee.

_____ **506. What is the currency used by people in Australia?**

      A. euros

      B. rubles

      C. dollars

      D. pounds

_____ **507. Why do people have to exchange currency?**

      A. to help banks increase their fees

      B. to transport goods from one country to another

      C. to do business with people from other countries

      D. to make sure that buyers and sellers are treated fairly

AUSTRALIA

a. Explain the relationship between investment in human capital (education and training) and gross domestic product (GDP).

INVESTMENT IN HUMAN CAPITAL AND THE GROSS DOMESTIC PRODUCT

The **Gross Domestic Product (GDP)** of a country is the total value of all the final goods and services produced in that country in one year. The GDP is one way to tell how rich or how poor a country is. The GDP can also be used to tell if the economy of a country is getting better or worse. Raising the GDP of the country can mean a higher standard of living for the people in the country.

To increase the GDP, countries must invest in **human capital**. Human capital includes education, training, skills, and health care of the workers in a business or country.

Australia has invested heavily in human capital. Children are required to attend school from age 6 to about age 18. The taxpayers pay for schooling of all children. The literacy rate of Australia is nearly 100 percent. The workforce is very well trained and educated. The health care system in Australia is very good. Most Australians can expect to be well cared for by the country's doctors, nurses, and hospitals. All of these factors have improved the standard of living over time. In fact, Australia's standard of living is one of the highest in the world, and its GDP ranks with the richest countries of Western Europe.

_____ **508. Which is an example of investment in human capital?**
   A. cash
   B. factories
   C. highways
   D. health care

_____ **509. What has helped Australia to have a high GDP?**
   A. high tax rates
   B. educated workers
   C. new factories and businesses
   D. immigrants with low-paying jobs

INVESTMENT IN CAPITAL AND THE GROSS DOMESTIC PRODUCT

The Gross Domestic Product (GDP) of a country is the total value of all the final goods and services produced in a country in one year. To increase the GDP, countries must invest in **capital goods**. Capital goods are the factories, machines, technologies, buildings, and property needed by businesses to operate. If a business is to be successful, it cannot let its equipment break down or have its buildings fall apart. New technology can help a business produce more goods for a cheaper price.

The free-market approach to the economy forces companies to make capital investments. If a company does not keep its machinery up-to-date, other companies will be able to produce similar goods for a better price. Companies must update their technology too. Australia's businesses use advanced technology to make their companies work more efficiently.

_____ 510. **Which is an example of investing in capital goods by a company?**

    A. providing health insurance for workers

    B. buying robots to build products more quickly

    C. giving employees a chance to learn new skills

    D. keeping an old machine to see if it will last a bit longer

_____ 511. **What has been one result of Australia's investment in capital goods?**

    A. The GDP is decreasing.

    B. The standard of living is declining.

    C. Australia has a high standard of living but a low GDP.

    D. Australia's standard of living and GDP are among the highest in the world.

SS6E10 The student will describe factors that influence economic growth and examine their presence or absence in Australia.

c. Describe the role of natural resources in a country's economy.

THE ROLE OF NATURAL RESOURCES IN A COUNTRY'S ECONOMY

A country has different kinds of resources that can help its people produce goods and services. Human resources are the education and skills that people have to produce goods and services. Capital resources are the things like machines and equipment that people need to produce goods and services. Another kind of resource is **natural resources**. These are sometimes thought of as "gifts of nature." One natural resource is fertile soil, such as on the farms of Australia. Water is another natural resource. Water is available in some parts of Australia, but it is very limited in much of the country.

Natural resources are important to countries. Without natural resources of their own, countries must import the natural resources that they need. This adds to the cost of goods and services. A country is better off if it can use its own natural resources to supply the needs of its people. If a country has many natural resources, it can trade them to other countries for goods and services. It can also use the natural resources to create goods that can be traded to other countries.

Arable land is a valuable resource in Australia. Farmers in Australia are able to grow enough crops that they can feed Australians and have enough left to trade to other countries. Land also provides pasture for beef cattle. The beef cattle are another important export.

Minerals in Australia are a major export. Coal, iron ore, copper, tin, gold, silver, uranium, nickel, tungsten, mineral sands, lead, zinc, diamonds, natural gas, and petroleum are examples. Australia is the world's leader in bauxite, an ore used to get aluminum. Sales of these natural resources bring in money from around the world. One-third of the exports from Australia go to China and Japan.

_____ 512. **Which is an example of a natural resource?**
    A. gold
    B. factories
    C. highways
    D. education

_____ 513. **Which natural resource is a major export of Australia?**
    A. water
    B. timber
    C. iron ore
    D. rain forest

AUSTRALIA

SS6E10 The student will describe factors that influence economic growth and examine their presence or absence in Australia.

d. Describe the role of entrepreneurship.

THE ROLE OF ENTREPRENEURSHIP

The person or people who provide the money to start and operate a business are called *entrepreneurs*. These people risk their own money and time because they believe their business ideas will make a profit. Entrepreneurs must organize their businesses well for them to be successful. Entrepreneurs bring together natural, human, and capital resources to produce goods or services to be provided by their businesses.

Australia is a world leader in entrepreneurs. One in every 12 adults owns his or her own business. The country has many opportunities for a successful business. There are abundant raw materials. There is a highly educated workforce. There is wealth that can be used to buy materials needed to start a business.

The laws in Australia are good for business. They protect entrepreneurs and their property. It is easy to start a business, and there are few rules to restrict the business.

Entrepreneurs are good for Australia. Their businesses keep the economy moving. They provide jobs for other workers. When they make a profit, they pay taxes to keep the government in operation.

_____ **514. Which is a reason entrepreneurs are good for Australia?**

    A. They have many good ideas.

    B. Their businesses provide jobs for other workers.

    C. Their businesses keep natural resources in Australia.

    D. They need to have space for their businesses to operate.

_____ **515. Which is a reason entrepreneurs like Australia?**

    A. Workers have low skills.

    B. Courts protect property rights.

    C. There is little money to invest.

    D. There are many rules from the government.

HISTORICAL UNDERSTANDINGS

SS6H8 The student will describe the culture and development of Australia prior to contact with Europeans.

a. Describe the origins and culture of the Aborigines.

ORIGIN AND CULTURE OF THE ABORIGINES

Aborigines are the native people of Australia. Just as Native Americans lived in North and South America before the European explorers, Aborigines lived in Australia. The Aborigines occupied Australia for at least 40,000 years. They arrived from Southeast Asia and entered the continent from the north. Australia, Tasmania, and New Guinea were one large landmass at that time.

The word *aborigines* means "the people who were here from the beginning." The Aborigines developed efficient ways to adapt to the harsh Australian environment. Their way of life was slow to change. They built containers for storing water and built wells to connect with underground water. They were hunters and gatherers and ate animals, wild nuts, fruits, and berries. They were nomadic, moving from place to place in search of food.

Archaeology has revealed some Aboriginal inventions. Aborigines created some of the earliest rock art as well as the first boomerangs, ground axes, and grindstones in the world. There is no written record of prehistoric Aborigines. What we know of the ancient Aborigines is found in archaeological evidence. The Aborigines kept their history by telling stories that were passed down from generation to generation.

Before the Europeans arrived in 1788, 250,000 to 500,000 people lived in Australia. The Aborigines settled in the same places as present-day Australians, where the climate was most pleasant and water was available. In the tropical north, most Aborigines lived along the coasts and rivers.

Their religious structure was divided into two "moieties." The moiety system divided all the members of a tribe into two groups based on a connection with "totems." The totems were certain animals, plants, or other things in the environment. A person was born into a moiety group and stayed in that group throughout her or his life. A person in one moiety had to marry a person of an opposite moiety.

The traditional social structure of the Aborigines consisted of a tribe or "language group" of as many as 500 people. A tribe included bands called "hordes," of 10 to 20 people. Hordes joined for daily food gathering and hunting.

_____ **516. From where did the Aborigines enter the Australian continent thousands of years ago?**
   A. Africa
   B. Antarctica
   C. New Zealand
   D. Southeast Asia

_____ **517. Which weapon did Aborigines invent?**
   A. swords
   B. slingshots
   C. boomerangs
   D. arrows and bows

AUSTRALIA

_____ **518. Which social group of the Aborigines was made of 10 to 20 people?**
A. tribes
B. hordes
C. kinships
D. moieties

_____ **519. Which describes the Aborigines?**
A. miners
B. seamen
C. nomads
D. ranchers

> **SS6H9 The student will explain the impact European exploration and colonization had on Australia.**
>
> a. Explain the reasons for British colonization of Australia; include the use of prisoners as colonists.

The first Europeans to sail into Australian waters arrived in 1606. During the next 164 years, ships from several nations reached the continent. In 1770, English Captain James Cook claimed the Australian east coast for England when he landed at Botany Bay. This site is near the present-day city of Sydney. Cook named eastern Australia "New South Wales." English sailors mapped the coast of Australia and Tasmania.

PRISONERS AS COLONISTS IN AUSTRALIA

The American Revolution resulted in independence of the American colonies from **Great Britain**. The Georgia colony in North America had been used as a penal (prison) colony for Great Britain at one time. After Great Britain lost colonies in North America, it began to look for other locations for prisoners. Australia seemed like a good choice. It had no colonies from other countries. There seemed to be few indigenous people, and it was in a region where Great Britain did not have any other colonies.

From 1788 to 1823, the colony of New South Wales was officially a penal colony consisting mainly of convicts, marines, and the marines' wives. About 20 percent of the first convicts were women. The British transported prisoners to Australia until 1868. By then, many free immigrants had settled in the region. They were building trading posts, farms, and businesses.

Great Britain saw that Australia was a good location to base its navy in the South Pacific. Its location would make it possible for British ships to make repairs and get supplies. There were opportunities for trade between Asia, Australia, and the Americas. In addition, the British government did not want the French to get a foothold on the continent. The countries of Europe were jealous of each other. The Europeans believed that if their countries had colonies, they would be better off.

Nonprisoner colonization continued. Major coastal settlements became seven independent colonies. By 1861, officials created the boundaries between the colonies that are still used today. The Commonwealth of Australia was established on January 1, 1901. Melbourne served as the national capital until Canberra was completed in 1927.

AUSTRALIA

_____ 520. **The prisoners used to colonize Australia in the late 1700s were primarily from which country?**
A. China
B. France
C. Mexico
D. Great Britain

_____ 521. **Which war made the government of Great Britain look to Australia as a penal colony?**
A. War of 1812
B. Seven Years' War
C. American Revolution
D. French and Indian War

_____ 522. **What part of the first prisoners sent to Australia were women?**
A. 10 percent
B. 20 percent
C. 30 percent
D. 50 percent

_____ 523. **What was the original name Captain James Cook gave to the colony of Australia?**
A. Melbourne
B. South England
C. New South Wales
D. Commonwealth of Australia

SS6H9 The student will explain the impact European exploration and colonization had on Australia.
b. Explain the impact of European colonization of Australia in terms of diseases and weapons on the indigenous peoples of Australia.

THE IMPACT OF EUROPEAN DISEASES AND WEAPONS ON THE INDIGENOUS PEOPLE OF AUSTRALIA

The British settlers had an immediate impact on Aboriginal life. European settlers took over good sources of water, fisheries, and productive land. Settlers turned land used by the Aborigines into colonial towns, farms, and mining operations. Some Aboriginal people welcomed the colonists. Some thought whites were the spirits of the dead. Others tried to protect their hunting lands and homes.

The most damaging things the Europeans brought to Australia were diseases. Smallpox, for instance, was a new disease for the Aborigines. They had no immunity to the disease. Smallpox began to sicken and kill large numbers of Aborigines. It is estimated that half of the indigenous people of Australia died of diseases brought by Europeans.

The British guns gave the colonists a major advantage in fights. Many Aboriginal people living near settlements were killed or forced to leave. Those Aboriginal people who survived the British expansion often tried to remain near their original homeland. Others began to live on the edges of colonial settlements.

AUSTRALIA

The introduction of cattle and sheep to the area required that settlers build fences, clear trees, and raise crops for the livestock, which changed the landscape. The lands that they used were the home of the Aborigines. The armed British were able to push aside the Aborigines and use their land.

As the number of British settlements expanded, Aboriginal people turned to violence to protect their land. A gold rush in the 1850s attracted thousands of new settlers to Australia. That resulted in more conflicts with Aboriginal people and hundreds more deaths. In some areas, white farmers formed revenge groups. These groups responded to the killing of sheep and cattle by murdering Aboriginal women and children. In the remote outback, ranchers needed Aboriginal labor to work their cattle and sheep farms. Ranchers asked surviving local Aboriginal populations to work as stockmen and domestic workers.

_____ 524. **What was the greatest threat to the Aborigines after the Europeans began settling Australia?**
A. guns used in battles
B. diseases Europeans carried with them
C. animals Europeans brought with them
D. mining and excavation tools used to extract minerals

_____ 525. **What event in the mid-19th century led to the killing of hundreds of Aborigines?**
A. gold rush
B. release of prisoners
C. settlement of coastal cities
D. establishment of sheep and cattle farms

_____ 526. **Which was an effect of British settlement of Australia?**
A. Aborigines remained in their homelands.
B. Many Aborigines became factory workers in order to survive.
C. Thousands of Aborigines died of smallpox and other diseases.
D. Aborigines were elected to representative positions in the colonial government.

SOCIAL STUDIES

SKILLS PRACTICE TEST

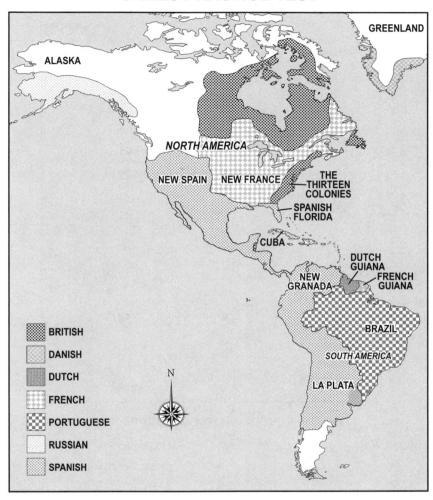

Use the map to answer questions 1-2.

1. Which European countries claimed the most territory in South America in 1763?

   A. France and Spain

   B. Portugal and Spain

   C. Brazil and La Plata

   D. Portugal and the Netherlands (Dutch)

2 Which European countries claimed small portions of South America in 1763?

   A. Portugal and Spain

   B. Brazil and La Plata

   C. New Granada and La Plata

   D. the Netherlands (Dutch) and France

PLEASE GO ON TO THE NEXT PAGE.

SOCIAL STUDIES

SKILLS PRACTICE TEST

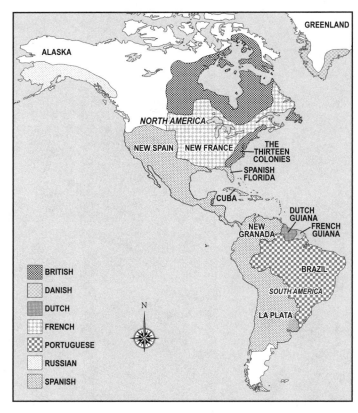

Use the map to answer questions 3-5.

3. What was the Spanish territory southeast of New Spain?

   A. Alaska

   B. Louisiana

   C. British Honduras

   D. New Granada

4. Spanish Florida was north of which colony?

   A. Cuba

   B. Louisiana

   C. Rupert's Land

   D. Thirteen Colonies

5. Which of the following statements is TRUE based on information in the map?

   A. British and French territory was growing in South America in 1763.

   B. The Spanish and Portuguese had the largest land claims in the New World in 1763.

   C. The British, French, Spanish, and Portuguese claimed equal amounts of land in South America.

   D. The Portuguese and Spanish were fighting for control of the lands in Central America and the Caribbean.

SOCIAL STUDIES

SKILLS PRACTICE TEST

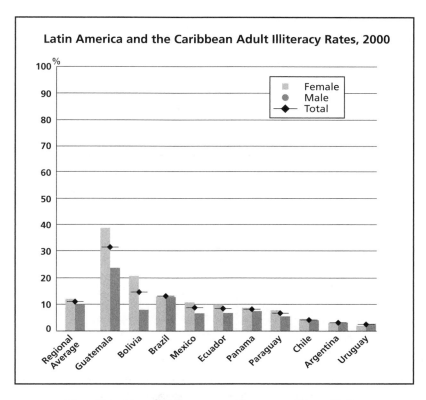

Latin America and the Caribbean Adult Illiteracy Rates, 2000

Use the graph to answer the questions 6-8.

6. Which country had the highest illiteracy rate?

    A. Brazil

    B. Uruguay

    C. Argentina

    D. Guatemala

8. Which question could be answered using the graph?

    A. Which Caribbean country has the highest literacy rate?

    B. What country in South America has the highest illiteracy rate?

    C. How has the literacy rate in Bolivia changed in the past five years?

    D. What was the average rate of illiteracy in Latin America and the Caribbean in 2000?

7. Which country had the greatest difference between boys' and girls' literacy rates?

    A. Brazil

    B. Uruguay

    C. Argentina

    D. Guatemala

SOCIAL STUDIES

SKILLS PRACTICE TEST

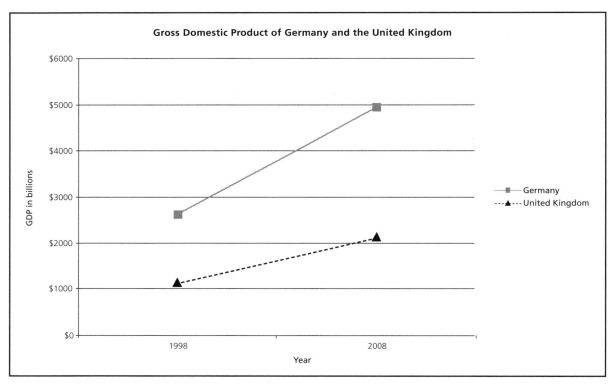

Gross Domestic Product of Germany and the United Kingdom

Use the graph to answer questions 9-11.

9. Which country had the greatest gain in GDP from 1998 to 2008?

   A. Germany

   B. United Kingdom

   C. They are the same

   D. Unable to tell from this graph

10. What was the approximate GDP of the United Kingdom in 1998?

   A. $1,000

   B. $1,000,000

   C. $1,000,000,000

   D. $1,000,000,000,000

11. Which is true about the GDP of Germany and the United Kingdom?

   A. The GDP of both countries held steady.

   B. The GDP of both countries grew at about the same rate.

   C. Germany's GDP was growing at a faster rate than the United Kingdom.

   D. Germany's GDP was growing at a slower rate than the United Kingdom.

12. Which would be the BEST research question for a sixth grader's report on Europe?

    A. What is the capital of Russia?

    B. What was the history of Europe?

    C. What were the main causes of World War II?

    D. How are Americans and Europeans alike, and how are they different?

Use the events in the box to answer questions 13-14.

> I. Apple Computer invented the iPod with the ability to download songs over the Internet.
>
> II. The Internet was common in people's homes.
>
> III. Apple Computer sold its one-millionth song for iPod over the Internet.
>
> IV. Home computers became common in Americans' homes.

13. Which shows the events listed above in correct order?

    A. I, III, IV, II

    B. III, IV, I, II

    C. II, IV, I, III

    D. IV, II, I, III

14. Which would be needed in order to use this information to create a timeline?

    A. dates for each event

    B. the history of the Apple Computer company

    C. more events in the history of electronic music

    D. information on how long it takes to download music

SOCIAL STUDIES

SKILLS PRACTICE TEST

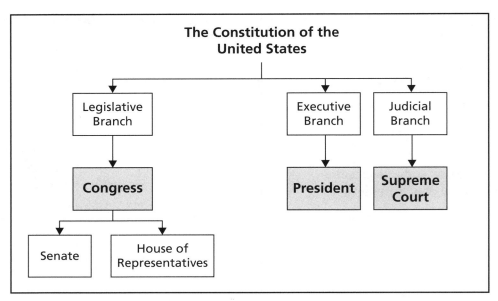

Use the diagram to answer questions 15-18.

15. What is the purpose of this diagram?

    A. to show how the U.S. government is organized

    B. to identify the leaders of the U.S. government

    C. to show which branch of government is most powerful

    D. to identify the type of government used in other countries

16. What branch of government is divided into two parts?

    A. the Constitution

    B. the judicial branch

    C. the executive branch

    D. the legislative branch

17. Who is the leader in the executive branch of government?

    A. Congress

    B. the President

    C. the Constitution

    D. the Supreme Court

18. Why is the Constitution at the top level of this chart?

    A. to show that it cannot be changed

    B. to show that it controls the things below it in the diagram

    C. because most of the Constitution was written in 1787, and the president was recently elected

    D. because the Constitution was written by the Founding Fathers and is more important than any other document

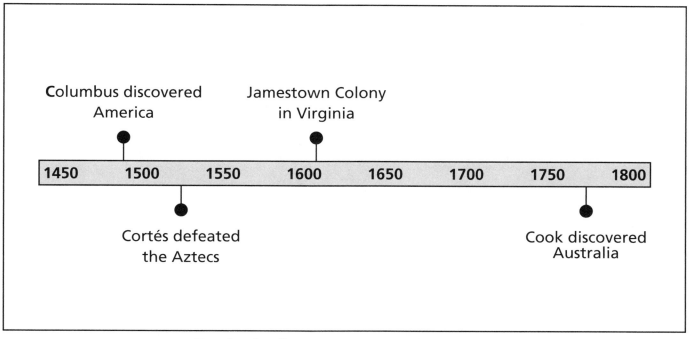

Use the timeline to answer questions 19-22.

19. In what century did Christopher Columbus land in the New World?

    A. 13th

    B. 14th

    C. 15th

    D. 16th

20. About how many years passed between Columbus's voyage and the discovery of Australia by Cook?

    A. about 350

    B. exactly 300

    C. not quite 300

    D. much more than 350

21. When did Cortés defeat the Aztecs?

    A. 1500

    B. 1550

    C. about 1520

    D. about 1540

22. Which event happened LAST?

    A. Jamestown was settled.

    B. Cook discovered Australia.

    C. Cortés defeated the Aztecs.

    D. Columbus discovered America.

SOCIAL STUDIES

SKILLS PRACTICE TEST

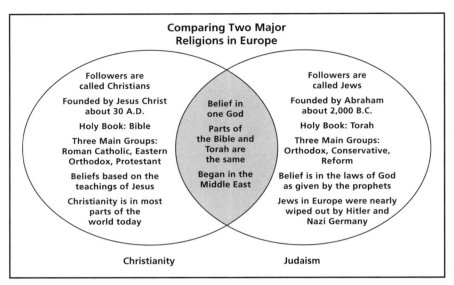

Comparing Two Major Religions in Europe

Followers are called Christians

Founded by Jesus Christ about 30 A.D.

Holy Book: Bible

Three Main Groups: Roman Catholic, Eastern Orthodox, Protestant

Beliefs based on the teachings of Jesus

Christianity is in most parts of the world today

Belief in one God

Parts of the Bible and Torah are the same

Began in the Middle East

Followers are called Jews

Founded by Abraham about 2,000 B.C.

Holy Book: Torah

Three Main Groups: Orthodox, Conservative, Reform

Belief is in the laws of God as given by the prophets

Jews in Europe were nearly wiped out by Hitler and Nazi Germany

Christianity   Judaism

Use the Venn diagram to answer questions 23–26.

23. Which of the religions began in the Middle East?

    A. Judaism

    B. Christianity

    C. both of them

    D. neither of them

24. What is one difference between the two religions?

    A. Each has a belief in one God.

    B. Each began in the Middle East.

    C. Some holy writings are the same.

    D. Beliefs are based on the teachings of Jesus.

25. Which question can be answered using this diagram?

    A. What are the major religions in Europe?

    B. Which religion has the most followers in Europe?

    C. Who were the founders of Christianity and Judaism?

    D. What cities are considered "holy" to Christians and Jews?

26. Which is an OPINION about two of the religions in Europe?

    A. Judaism is the older of the two religions.

    B. Christians base their beliefs on the teachings of Jesus.

    C. Christians and Jews each believe that there is only one God.

    D. The Jewish synagogues are the most beautiful churches in Europe.

27. Which must be included on a bar graph for it to be useful for sharing information?

    A. graph paper

    B. a computer printer

    C. labels for each axis

    D. different colored bars

28. Which reference book would be BEST to locate a map of Australia?

    A. atlas

    B. almanac

    C. thesaurus

    D. dictionary

29. Which BEST describes the purpose of an almanac?

    A. to be a source of maps for locations in the world

    B. to suggest synonyms and antonyms of given words

    C. to give definitions and origins of a language's words

    D. to provide an annual update of useful facts and statistical information

30. Which model gives the BEST representation of the location of places on Earth's surface?

    A. globe

    B. atlas map

    C. foldable map

    D. highway map

SOCIAL STUDIES

SKILLS PRACTICE TEST

Use the map to answer questions 31-35.

31. What German state capital is located closest to latitude 48°N and longitude 12°E?

   A. Berlin

   B. Munich

   C. Freiburg

   D. Magdeburg

32. What is the approximate distance, in miles, from Berlin to the Polish border?

   A. 50 miles

   B. 75 miles

   C. 100 miles

   D. 200 miles

33. What symbol is used to identify the German capital city on the map?

   A. a star

   B. a circle

   C. a circle within a circle

   D. a star with a circle around it

34. What BEST describes this type of map?

   A. climate map

   B. physical map

   C. political map

   D. topographic map

35. What question could be answered using this map?

   A. What are Germany's main ports?

   B. Where are Germany's major airports?

   C. Where are the major highways in Germany?

   D. What are the major languages spoken in Germany?

SOCIAL STUDIES

SKILLS PRACTICE TEST

Study both maps. Use the maps to answer questions 36–39.

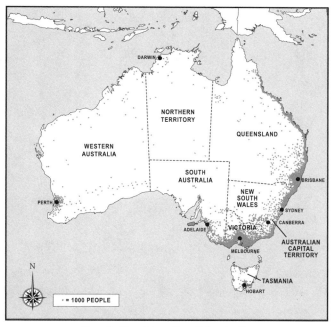

Population Density of Australia

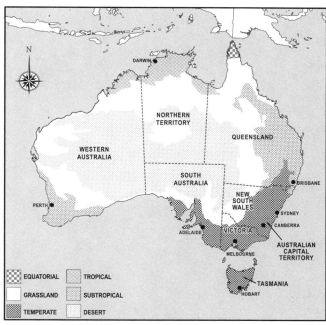

Climate Zones in Australia

36. What does a dot on the population density map represent?

   A. city or town

   B. 1,000 people

   C. crowded location

   D. location of special place

37. Where is the largest concentration of people in Australia?

   A. in South Australia

   B. in the Northern Territory

   C. in central Western Australia

   D. in New South Wales and Victoria

38. Where is the coolest climate in Australia?

   A. Tasmania

   B. Queensland

   C. South Australia

   D. Northern Territory

39. Which city has the warmest climate and the least populated area?

   A. Darwin

   B. Sydney

   C. Brisbane

   D. Melbourne

SOCIAL STUDIES

SKILLS PRACTICE TEST

Study both maps. Use the maps to answer questions 40-41.

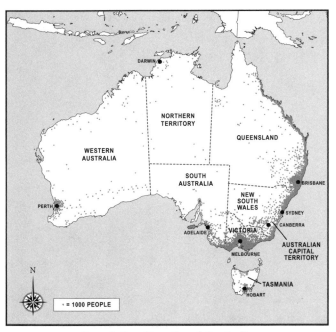

Population Density of Australia

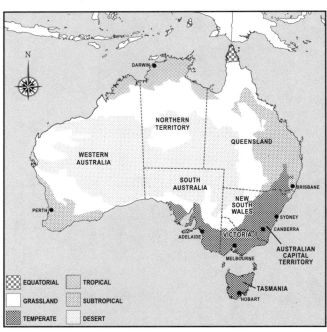

Climate Zones in Australia

40. Which describes where people live in Australia?

   A. Australians tend to live far apart, and the climate varies with the altitude.

   B. Most Australians live along the western coast of Australia where the climate varies.

   C. Most Australians live along the southeast coast where there is a temperate climate.

   D. Australians are spread across their country, and they enjoy a warm and humid climate.

41. Which of these maps is MOST LIKELY to need updating in the next twenty years?

   A. the climate zone map

   B. the population density map

   C. Both maps will need updating.

   D. Neither map should need to be updated.

SOCIAL STUDIES

SKILLS PRACTICE TEST

Use the graph below to answer questions 42-45.

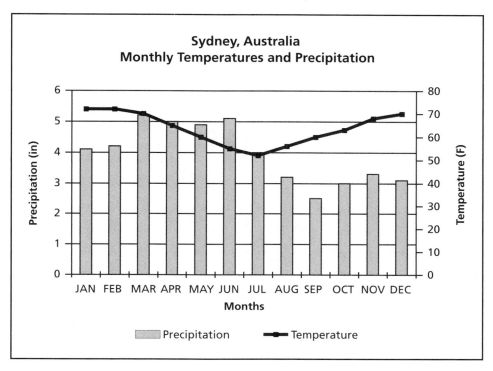

42. Which is the coolest month in Sydney, Australia?

    A. July

    B. April

    C. August

    D. December

43. In which month does Sydney, Australia, usually get more than 5 inches of rain?

    A. July

    B. March

    C. January

    D. September

44. What is the driest month in Sydney, Australia?

    A. July

    B. March

    C. January

    D. September

45. Which is generally true of temperatures in Sydney from July to December?

    A. They are increasing.

    B. They are decreasing.

    C. They stay about the same.

    D. They follow the same pattern as January to June.

Use the map to answer questions 46-50.

46. Which city is approximately 200 miles from Rome?

    A. Naples, Italy

    B. Taranto, Italy

    C. Vatican City

    D. Sassari, Sardinia

47. What fact about Italy's location would be MOST helpful to Italian merchants trading with other countries?

    A. There is an oil terminal in Sicily.

    B. It is surrounded on three sides by seas.

    C. There are many natural resources in the country.

    D. It is far from other countries with a similar climate.

48. Which coordinates are closest to Genoa, Italy?

    A. 43°N, 9°E

    B. 44°N, 9°E

    C. 44°N, 7°E

    D. 43°N, 7°E

49. Which direction from Rome is Venice?

    A. west

    B. east

    C. north

    D. south

50. Which describes how the Po River flows?

    A. north to south across the center of Italy

    B. east to west across the southern tip of Italy

    C. west to east across the northern part of Italy

    D. south to north through the southern part of Italy

PLEASE STOP! STOP!

Student Name: _____

Assignment: _____

Period: _____

Marking Instructions:
- Use a No. 2 pencil (no ink or ballpoint pens)
- Fill the circles in completely
- Erase completely to change your answer
- Make no stray marks

Example:

A B C D
1 ○ ● ○ ○

Score:

Student ID Number

	0○	0○	0○	0○	0○	0○	0○	0○	0○
1○	1○	1○	1○	1○	1○	1○	1○	1○
2○	2○	2○	2○	2○	2○	2○	2○	2○
3○	3○	3○	3○	3○	3○	3○	3○	3○
4○	4○	4○	4○	4○	4○	4○	4○	4○
5○	5○	5○	5○	5○	5○	5○	5○	5○
6○	6○	6○	6○	6○	6○	6○	6○	6○
7○	7○	7○	7○	7○	7○	7○	7○	7○
8○	8○	8○	8○	8○	8○	8○	8○	8○
9○	9○	9○	9○	9○	9○	9○	9○	9○

	A B C D		A B C D		A B C D		A B C D		A B C D
1	○ ○ ○ ○	11	○ ○ ○ ○	21	○ ○ ○ ○	31	○ ○ ○ ○	41	○ ○ ○ ○
2	○ ○ ○ ○	12	○ ○ ○ ○	22	○ ○ ○ ○	32	○ ○ ○ ○	42	○ ○ ○ ○
3	○ ○ ○ ○	13	○ ○ ○ ○	23	○ ○ ○ ○	33	○ ○ ○ ○	43	○ ○ ○ ○
4	○ ○ ○ ○	14	○ ○ ○ ○	24	○ ○ ○ ○	34	○ ○ ○ ○	44	○ ○ ○ ○
5	○ ○ ○ ○	15	○ ○ ○ ○	25	○ ○ ○ ○	35	○ ○ ○ ○	45	○ ○ ○ ○
6	○ ○ ○ ○	16	○ ○ ○ ○	26	○ ○ ○ ○	36	○ ○ ○ ○	46	○ ○ ○ ○
7	○ ○ ○ ○	17	○ ○ ○ ○	27	○ ○ ○ ○	37	○ ○ ○ ○	47	○ ○ ○ ○
8	○ ○ ○ ○	18	○ ○ ○ ○	28	○ ○ ○ ○	38	○ ○ ○ ○	48	○ ○ ○ ○
9	○ ○ ○ ○	19	○ ○ ○ ○	29	○ ○ ○ ○	39	○ ○ ○ ○	49	○ ○ ○ ○
10	○ ○ ○ ○	20	○ ○ ○ ○	30	○ ○ ○ ○	40	○ ○ ○ ○	50	○ ○ ○ ○

SOCIAL STUDIES

LATIN AMERICA AND CANADA

1. What was the capital city of the Aztec empire?

    A. Mexico City

    B. Montezuma

    C. Tenochtitlan

    D. Machu Picchu

2. The best time for people to borrow money is when

    A. interest rates are low.

    B. interest rates are rising.

    C. their credit scores have dropped.

    D. they do not have a steady source of income.

3. Why is it important for a country to invest in human capital?

    A. It needs money in order to pay its workers.

    B. Workers enjoy getting extra training and job opportunities.

    C. The country's economy is more successful when workers have good training and health care.

    D. Businesses are not responsible for the training and health care of the workers they employ.

4. Which did Montezuma and Atahualpa have in common?

    A. They were Spanish conquistadors.

    B. They were freedom fighters in Latin America.

    C. Christopher Columbus discovered them in the Bahamas.

    D. They were leaders of Native American people conquered by the Spanish.

SOCIAL STUDIES

LATIN AMERICA AND CANADA

Use the map below to answer questions 5-6.

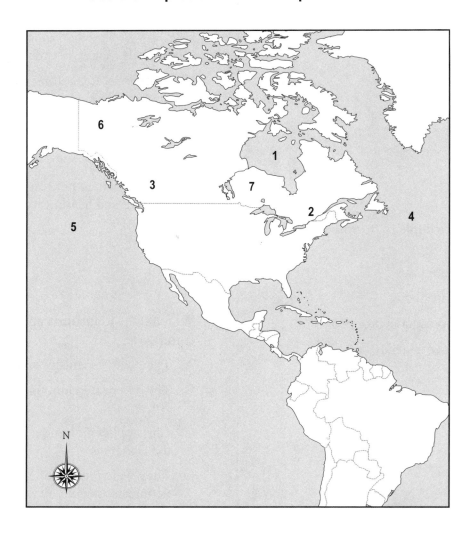

5. Which feature is closest to the "2" on the map?

   A. Great Plains

   B. Lake Superior

   C. Rocky Mountains

   D. St. Lawrence River

6. Which feature is located nearest the "7" on the map?

   A. Lake Huron

   B. Canadian Shield

   C. Rocky Mountains

   D. St. Lawrence River

SOCIAL STUDIES

LATIN AMERICA AND CANADA

Use the graph to answer question 7.

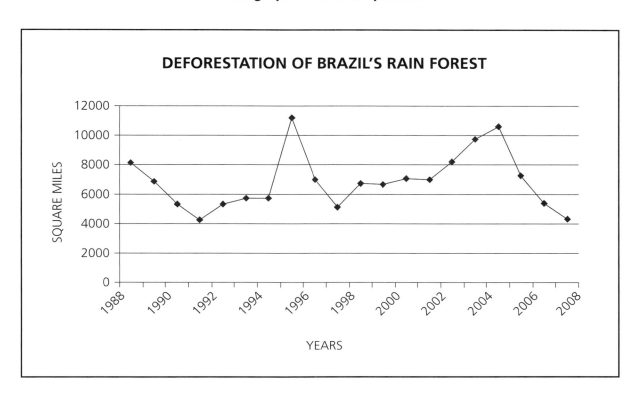

DEFORESTATION OF BRAZIL'S RAIN FOREST

7. What trend was there in deforestation of the Brazilian rain forest from 1996 to 2004?

   A. The rate of deforestation was increasing.

   B. The rate of deforestation was decreasing.

   C. Deforestation levels stayed about the same.

   D. Deforestation levels were lower than they were in the 1980s.

8. Which is MOST important to helping Brazilian businesses trade with other countries in the world?

   A. There are seven major seaports along Brazil's Atlantic coast.

   B. The Amazon River allows ships to travel inland to the Andes.

   C. Brazil shares a border with very few South American countries.

   D. Brazil is able to purchase goods from other countries that it cannot make on its own.

SOCIAL STUDIES

LATIN AMERICA AND CANADA

9. What are the three main cultural influences on the people of Latin America and the Caribbean?

   A. Africans, Mulattoes, Catholics

   B. Africans, Europeans, Native Americans

   C. Mestizos, Native Americans, Europeans

   D. Native Americans, Mulattoes, Europeans

Use the map to answer questions 10-11.

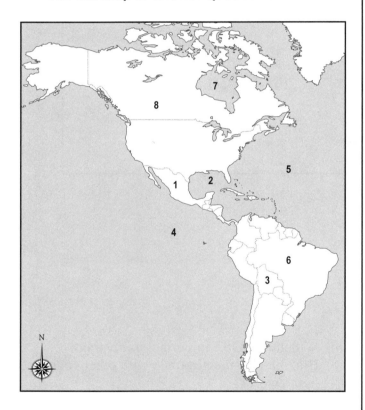

10. What number on the map marks Mexico?

    A. 1

    B. 3

    C. 6

    D. 8

11. What area is marked by a "2" on the map?

    A. Hudson Bay

    B. Pacific Ocean

    C. Atlantic Ocean

    D. Gulf of Mexico

12. Which two European countries contributed most to the languages of Canada?

    A. Spain and Portugal

    B. France and Portugal

    C. Great Britain and Spain

    D. Great Britain and France

LATIN AMERICA AND CANADA

13. What did the Zapatistas do in Mexico to show that they were against the North American Free Trade Agreement (NAFTA)?

    A. They attacked the Capitol in Mexico City.

    B. They took over several towns in southern Mexico.

    C. They formed friendships with groups in other countries supporting NAFTA.

    D. They worked with the government on agreements to improve the rights of poor Mexicans.

14. Which is an example of specialization?

    A. A business makes many different types of goods.

    B. A country buys all the goods it needs from other countries and does not produce any of its own.

    C. A business focuses on producing one or two types of goods and leaves the production of other goods to other businesses.

    D. A violin-maker completes the entire process of making a violin from cutting a tree for wood to producing his own strings.

15. One of the main purposes of the North American Free Trade Agreement (NAFTA) was to

    A. increase trade by creating a large free-trade zone.

    B. create tariffs between Canada, Mexico, and the United States.

    C. decrease the standard of living for some people while raising it for others.

    D. keep people in one country from buying goods from the other two countries.

16. Which was an effect of the Cuban Revolution on the relationship between Cuba and the United States?

    A. Americans bought more Cuban sugar and cigars.

    B. Cuba's economy became stronger and more independent.

    C. The U.S. government put an embargo on trade with Cuba.

    D. The tourist industry in Cuba grew because of increased visits by Americans.

17. In which form of government would the "will of the people" MOST likely be the rule of law?

    A. autocracy

    B. oligarchy

    C. traditional

    B. democracy

18. Which is a way that people in Quebec are trying to protect their French language and culture?

    A. French is the official language of Quebec.

    B. The Canadian government prints laws only in French.

    C. Laws state the businesses in Quebec must be bilingual.

    D. Quebec's citizens are not allowed to speak French in public.

19. In which economic system do people make economic decisions based on changes in prices that occur between buyers and sellers?

    A. mixed

    B. market

    C. command

    D. traditional

20. Which country imprisoned Toussaint L'Ouverture for his work to free slaves in the Caribbean?

    A. Haiti

    B. France

    C. Portugal

    D. Great Britain

SOCIAL STUDIES

LATIN AMERICA AND CANADA

Use the graph to answer question 21

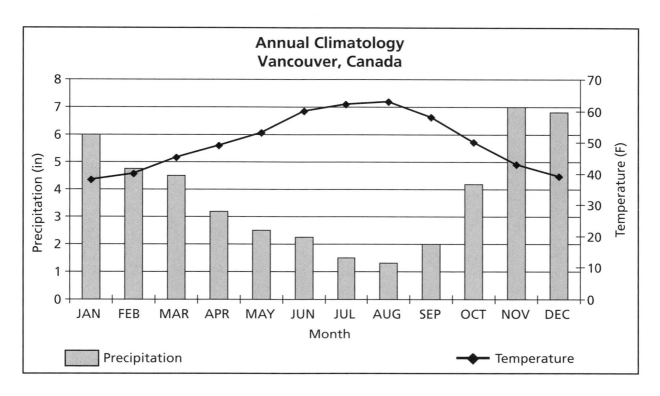

**Annual Climatology
Vancouver, Canada**

Precipitation

Temperature

21. Which is true about the climate in Vancouver, Canada?

   A. Winter months in Vancouver are the driest of the year.

   B. Vancouver's summer months are usually its hottest and driest.

   C. Winter months in Vancouver are no wetter than the summers.

   D. Vancouver's summer months are usually its hottest and wettest.

22. Which statement is TRUE about how the president in a presidential democracy is different from the prime minister in a parliamentary democracy?

   A. The prime minister is the head of state for the country, but the president is not.

   B. The prime minister is the chief executive and head of the military, but the president is not.

   C. The prime minister is elected directly by the people, but the president is elected by the legislature.

   D. The prime minister is chosen from the members of parliament, but the president runs for office separately.

23. What is one reason that businesses from different countries have to exchange currencies?

   A. Exchanging currencies helps to increase profit.

   B. Most people want to use American dollars for trade.

   C. Currency is used to buy and sell goods and services.

   D. Different countries have different currencies.

24. How did the Spanish government have an influence on the spread of the Roman Catholic Church in the New World?

   A. The Catholic Church controlled Spain.

   B. Spanish royalty did not support the Catholic Church.

   C. The Catholic Church paid to build missions to Christianize the native population.

   D. Churches from other parts of the world did not send missionaries to the New World.

25. Which is an example of a quota used as a trade barrier by the United States against another country?

   A. agreement by a U.S. company to buy timber from Canada

   B. not allowing Americans to buy any goods from the country until the country stops fighting with its neighbor

   C. limiting the number of foreign cars that can be purchased by Americans in order to increase sales of U.S.-made cars

   D. charging an extra tax on sugar imported from other countries to help American sugar cane farmers sell more of their sugar in the United States

26. Which is an effect of slavery that influences Latin America today?

   A. Many Latin Americans have ancestors from Africa.

   B. Slavery exists in few Latin American countries.

   C. Latin America has no people with ancestors from Africa.

   D. The people of Latin America accept slavery as part of their lives.

SOCIAL STUDIES

LATIN AMERICA AND CANADA

27. Which statement about political parties is true about Cuba and is NOT true of Mexico?

    A. There are many political parties.

    B. There is only one legal political party.

    C. The leader of a political party cannot be president.

    D. Those running for office may not be in the Communist Party.

28. What was the Columbian Exchange?

    A. sending food and people from the Old World to the New World

    B. sending animals and plants from the Old World to the New World

    C. the moving of animals, plants, people, and diseases from Central and South America to North America

    D. the moving of animals, plants, people, and diseases from the Old World to the New World and from the New World to the Old

29. Which is a way that entrepreneurs help increase the Gross Domestic Product (GDP) of a country?

    A. by writing laws to protect personal property

    B. by creating businesses that give people jobs

    C. by closing businesses that are making too much money

    D. by working to decrease the amount of goods and services sold in a country

30. How is power distributed in a unitary government?

    A. One ruler makes all the decisions for a country.

    B. Smaller units of government, like counties, control the central government.

    C. A central government assigns power and duties to smaller units of government within the country.

    D. The central government does not have much power over the smaller units of government in the country.

SOCIAL STUDIES

31. Why do most Mexicans and Venezuelans live in urban areas?

   A. Rural areas do not have good climates.

   B. There is much arable land in these countries.

   C. There are more jobs in the factories and businesses of the cities.

   D. Rural areas have more opportunity for good education and health care.

32. Which natural resources help the economies of some countries in Latin America?

   A. forests, oil, water

   B. steel, natural gas, fertile soil

   C. fertile soil, forests, mountains

   D. cheap labor, hydroelectric power, oil

33. How does investment in capital goods by a business help a country increase its Gross Domestic Product (GDP)?

   A. The GDP of a country goes down when businesses earn more profit.

   B. Businesses that invest in capital goods are able to provide a better place for their workers to work.

   C. Highly trained workers help the businesses make more money by finding better ways to help the businesses work.

   D. When a business invests in capital goods, it can produce more goods at a better price and increase the profit that it makes.

SOCIAL STUDIES

LATIN AMERICA AND CANADA

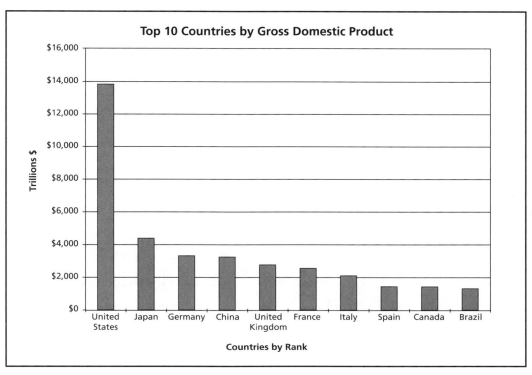

Top 10 Countries by Gross Domestic Product

Use the graph to answer questions 34-35.

34. How does the GDP of Brazil compare to that of the United States?

   A. The GDPs of both countries are about the same.

   B. The GDP of the United States is about double that of Brazil.

   C. Brazil's GDP is about ten times greater than that of the United States.

   D. The GDP of the United States is about ten times greater than Brazil's GDP.

35. What was the approximate GDP of Canada?

   A. $1 trillion

   B. $1.6 trillion

   C. $160 trillion

   D. $1600 trillion

SOCIAL STUDIES

LATIN AMERICA AND CANADA

36. Which statement describes the economy of Brazil?

    A. Brazil has a pure market economy.

    B. Brazil has a pure command economy.

    C. Brazil has a mostly command economy. However, the government allows some farmers to sell some of their goods on their own.

    D. Brazil has a mixed economy. It works mostly as a market economy, but the government does control some key businesses.

37. How did Canada gain its independence from Great Britain?

    A. It won the Canadian Revolution.

    B. The monarch split the United Kingdom.

    C. Canada is still controlled by Great Britain and has limited independence.

    D. Agreements were made over many years that gradually gave Canada its independence.

38. Why is the southern part of Canada the region where most Canadians live?

    A. It is closest to the United States.

    B. It has the most favorable climate.

    C. Most of the ports are in southern Canada.

    D. Mountains cover most of northern Canada.

39. Which term describes how political power is distributed in Canada?

    A. unitary government

    B. federal government

    C. aristocratic government

    D. confederation government

SOCIAL STUDIES

LATIN AMERICA AND CANADA

40. Why are Spanish and Portuguese the main languages of Latin America?

    A. People from Spain and Portugal colonized Latin America.

    B. People in Latin America found Spanish and Portuguese easy to learn.

    C. The Roman Catholic Church did not allow people to speak English or French.

    D. Indigenous people switched to these languages to make communication easier.

41. Which of the following would be MOST helpful to improving a country's standard of living?

    A. deceasing the literacy rate

    B. increasing the literacy rate

    C. reducing the number of factories

    D. creating more low-paying jobs on farms

42. Which condition makes it easy for Canada to trade with the United States?

    A. The countries share a border over 3,000 miles long.

    B. Canada has easy access to seven major ports on three oceans.

    C. The countries have abundant natural resources and a long growing season.

    D. Canada has many natural resources and goods that are not available in the United States.

SOCIAL STUDIES

LATIN AMERICA AND CANADA

Sources of Sulfur Dioxide (SO₂) in the Air

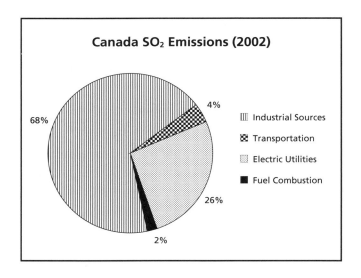

Canada SO₂ Emissions (2002)

68%
4%
26%
2%

- ▥ Industrial Sources
- ▩ Transportation
- ▦ Electric Utilities
- ■ Fuel Combustion

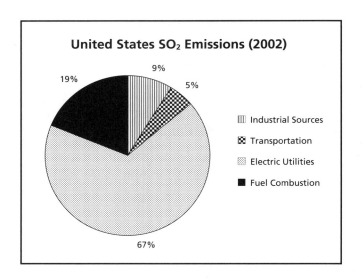

United States SO₂ Emissions (2002)

9%
19%
5%
67%

- ▥ Industrial Sources
- ▩ Transportation
- ▦ Electric Utilities
- ■ Fuel Combustion

Use the graphs to answer questions 43-44.

43. A purpose of these graphs is to show

   A. which country produces the most sulfur dioxide pollution.

   B. the sources of sulfur dioxide pollution in the United States and Canada.

   C. a comparison of the air pollution rates in the United States and Canada.

   D. that Canada creates more sulfur dioxide pollution than the United States.

44. Which source of pollution was the greatest producer of SO₂ in Canada?

   A. transportation

   B. electric utilities

   C. fuel combustion

   D. industrial sources

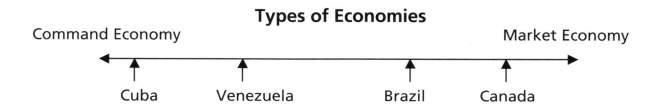

Types of Economies

Command Economy   Market Economy

Cuba   Venezuela   Brazil   Canada

Use the diagram to answer questions 45-46.

45. Which country has an economic system closest to a pure command economy?

   A. Cuba

   B. Brazil

   C. Canada

   D. Venezuela

46. Which country's businesses have the least government control?

   A. Cuba

   B. Brazil

   C. Canada

   D. Venezuela

SOCIAL STUDIES

LATIN AMERICA AND CANADA

47. What is an advantage of a savings account over a checking account?

    A. Savings accounts are easier to get.

    B. Savings accounts can be used to guarantee loans.

    C. Savings accounts pay a higher rate of interest.

    D. Savings accounts provide more protection for your money.

48. The land of which modern country was part of the Inca Empire?

    A. Chile

    B. Panama

    C. Uruguay

    D. Venezuela

49. In which general direction did Pizarro travel from Panama to reach the Inca Empire?

    A. east

    B. west

    C. north

    D. south

Inca Empire, 1532

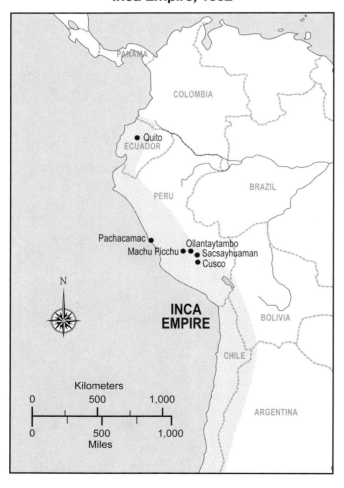

Use the map to answer questions 48-50.

50. Which question could be answered using the map?

    A. What was the distance from Quito to Cusco?

    B. Who was the ruler of the Inca Empire when Pizarro arrived?

    C. In which direction was the Aztec Empire from the Inca Empire?

    D. Which of its neighbors had the Inca Empire conquered before 1530?

PLEASE STOP! STOP!

Student Name:_____

Assignment: _____

Period:_____

Marking Instructions:
- Use a No. 2 pencil (no ink or ballpoint pens)
- Fill the circles in completely
- Erase completely to change your answer
- Make no stray marks

Example:

   A   B   C   D
1 ○ ● ○ ○

Score:

Student ID Number

0○	0○	0○	0○	0○	0○	0○	0○	0○
1○	1○	1○	1○	1○	1○	1○	1○	1○
2○	2○	2○	2○	2○	2○	2○	2○	2○
3○	3○	3○	3○	3○	3○	3○	3○	3○
4○	4○	4○	4○	4○	4○	4○	4○	4○
5○	5○	5○	5○	5○	5○	5○	5○	5○
6○	6○	6○	6○	6○	6○	6○	6○	6○
7○	7○	7○	7○	7○	7○	7○	7○	7○
8○	8○	8○	8○	8○	8○	8○	8○	8○
9○	9○	9○	9○	9○	9○	9○	9○	9○

    A   B   C   D
1 ○ ○ ○ ○   11 ○ ○ ○ ○   21 ○ ○ ○ ○   31 ○ ○ ○ ○   41 ○ ○ ○ ○

2 ○ ○ ○ ○   12 ○ ○ ○ ○   22 ○ ○ ○ ○   32 ○ ○ ○ ○   42 ○ ○ ○ ○

3 ○ ○ ○ ○   13 ○ ○ ○ ○   23 ○ ○ ○ ○   33 ○ ○ ○ ○   43 ○ ○ ○ ○

4 ○ ○ ○ ○   14 ○ ○ ○ ○   24 ○ ○ ○ ○   34 ○ ○ ○ ○   44 ○ ○ ○ ○

5 ○ ○ ○ ○   15 ○ ○ ○ ○   25 ○ ○ ○ ○   35 ○ ○ ○ ○   45 ○ ○ ○ ○

6 ○ ○ ○ ○   16 ○ ○ ○ ○   26 ○ ○ ○ ○   36 ○ ○ ○ ○   46 ○ ○ ○ ○

7 ○ ○ ○ ○   17 ○ ○ ○ ○   27 ○ ○ ○ ○   37 ○ ○ ○ ○   47 ○ ○ ○ ○

8 ○ ○ ○ ○   18 ○ ○ ○ ○   28 ○ ○ ○ ○   38 ○ ○ ○ ○   48 ○ ○ ○ ○

9 ○ ○ ○ ○   19 ○ ○ ○ ○   29 ○ ○ ○ ○   39 ○ ○ ○ ○   49 ○ ○ ○ ○

10 ○ ○ ○ ○   20 ○ ○ ○ ○   30 ○ ○ ○ ○   40 ○ ○ ○ ○   50 ○ ○ ○ ○

SOCIAL STUDIES

EUROPE

1. Which are examples of Romance languages?

    A. French and Italian

    B. Russian and Polish

    C. English and French

    D. English and German

Use the statements in the box to answer question 2.

- The lawmaking bodies are divided into two houses.
- All have some part of their lawmaking body elected by the people.
- Each divides the jobs of head of state and head of government (chief executive).

---

2. Which statement explains what these sentences are about?

    A. They describe the governments of European countries.

    B. They tell how the countries of Europe choose their leaders.

    C. They explain how the EU countries must set up their parliaments.

    D. They are ways that the governments of Germany, Russia, and the United Kingdom are alike.

3. What have Europeans done to try to solve the problem of so many languages being spoken on the continent?

    A. outlawed the use of languages spoken by only a few people

    B. decided not to trade with people who do not speak the same language

    C. passed laws saying English is the only official language of the European Union

    D. made schoolchildren learn one or two other languages besides their native language

4. In which form of government would the fewest number of people be involved in making the rule of law?

    A. oligarchy

    B. autocracy

    C. traditional

    B. democracy

5. How is power distributed in a unitary government?

    A. No one group or person has control of the government.

    B. Smaller units of government, like counties, control the central government.

    C. A central government assigns power and duties to smaller units of government within the country.

    D. The central government does not have much power over the smaller units of government in the country.

SOCIAL STUDIES

EUROPE

Use the statements in the box to answer question 6.

> - constitutional monarchy
> - parliamentary democracy
> - unitary government

6. The statements above describe the government of which country?

   A. Italy

   B. Russia

   C. Germany

   D. Great Britain

7. In which type of economy do individuals have the most freedom?

   A. mixed

   B. market

   C. command

   D. traditional

8. What part of the Treaty of Versailles was most damaging to the German economy after World War I?

   A. Germany lost its colonies.

   B. The German emperor was to be put on trial.

   C. Germany had to pay the Allies large sums of money.

   D. Germans were not allowed to have a large army and navy.

9. Which country was the leader of the Eastern Bloc?

   A. Germany

   B. Soviet Union

   C. United States

   D. United Kingdom

10. Which were two terms used to describe the dividing line between eastern and western, communist and noncommunist areas?

    A. NATO and Warsaw Pact

    B. Berlin Wall and Iron Curtain

    C. Allied Powers and Axis Powers

    D. Nazi Germany and Free Germany

11. Why is it important for a country to invest in human capital?

    A. It needs money in order to pay its workers.

    B. Workers enjoy getting extra training and job opportunities.

    C. Businesses cannot do all the training needed by workers to be successful.

    D. A country's economy is more successful when workers have good education and health care.

SOCIAL STUDIES

EUROPE

12. Which condition helped the United Kingdom become a leader in world trade?

   A. Two percent of the people are farmers, and there is a lot of arable land.

   B. It is home to the world's busiest airport and has seven other large airports.

   C. It is an island with a mild climate and is located near many other countries.

   D. Urban areas are heavily populated and most jobs are found in the urban areas.

13. Why would a company spend money to buy new machines for its factories rather than continue to use older machines that were still working?

   A. Older machines cannot be run well by younger workers.

   B. Older machines do not produce as much pollution as newer ones.

   C. New machines might help the company produce more goods at a lower price.

   D. New machines would cost the company a lot of money but would provide jobs for workers.

14. Which is a reason the European Union was created?

   A. to isolate Russia and make it more difficult for it to trade

   B. to practice reaching consensus among European countries

   C. to promote the French franc as a common currency for Europe

   D. to make Europe more competitive in world markets and to solve common problems

15. Which is an example of investing in capital goods by a company?

   A. constructing a new factory

   B. keeping old delivery trucks

   C. training workers to do their jobs better

   D. keeping old computers in order to save money

SOCIAL STUDIES

EUROPE

16. What environmental disaster occurred in 1986 in Chernobyl, Ukraine?

    A. a nuclear reactor explosion

    B. acid rain caused by engine exhaust

    C. "the great smoke" from coal-burning factories

    D. the death of forests due to water pollution from mining

17. One difference between the German and Russian languages is that German

    A. does not use the Cyrillic alphabet.

    B. is spoken by fewer people than Russian.

    C. has not been spoken in Europe since World War II.

    D. is spoken in only one country in Europe, and Russian is spoken in several.

18. What has helped Italian merchants become successful traders?

    A. The location of the Alps mountains defends Italy against other countries.

    B. The islands of Sicily and Sardinia are not far from the coast of western Italy.

    C. Warm air from the Sahara desert creates a warm, dry summer for most of Italy.

    D. Italy's location on the Mediterranean Sea provides access to Africa, Asia, and Europe.

SOCIAL STUDIES

EUROPE

Use the map below to answer questions 19-21.

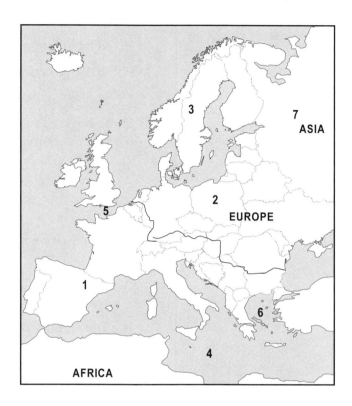

19. Which feature is located near the "7" on the map?

   A. Rhine River

   B. Ural Mountains

   C. Pyrenees Mountains

   D. Scandinavian Peninsula

20. Which physical feature is located near the "2" on the map?

   A. European Plain

   B. English Channel

   C. Iberian Peninsula

   D. The Alps Mountains

21. Which number marks the English Channel?

   A. 1

   B. 3

   C. 5

   D. 7

EUROPE

22. Which pairing of sacred text and religion is correct?

    A. Judaism – Torah

    B. Christianity - Talmud

    C. Muslim – Old Testament

    D. Roman Catholic – Koran

23. Which is a literate adult in Europe LEAST likely to have?

    A. good health care

    B. a high-paying job

    C. modern technology

    D. uneducated children

24. What type of government did Czar Nicholas II have in Russia?

    A. republic

    B. autocracy

    C. oligarchy

    D. democracy

25. What is a main reason for people to exchange currency?

    A. to have foreign money

    B. to use American dollars to trade

    C. to make more money by trading currency

    D. to buy and sell goods and services with other countries

26. Which situation might keep an embargo against a country from being successful?

    A. People in the country suffer because trading has stopped.

    B. The country does not need to trade with other counties.

    C. The country is able to find other trading partners not in the embargo.

    D. People in the country don't care whether their country trades with other countries.

SOCIAL STUDIES

EUROPE

27. Put the following events in the order in which they happened.

    | I. | Hitler was named chancellor of Germany. |
    | II. | Germany invaded Poland. |
    | III. | Germans were unhappy because of high unemployment and poverty. |
    | IV. | France and Great Britain declared war on Germany. |

    A. I, II, IV, III

    B. II, IV, III, I

    C. IV, III, I, II

    D. III, I, II, IV

28. How does having natural resources help the economy of a country?

    A. The country is able to produce all the goods and services that it needs.

    B. The country saves money because it does not have to import natural resources.

    C. Companies can export natural resources without having to create goods to sell.

    D. Companies spend more money because they must buy the natural resources needed to create more goods.

29. Which was a cause of the Russian Revolution?

    A. The czar was executed.

    B. There were food shortages in Russia.

    C. The Germans showed signs of surrender.

    D. Soldiers did not know how to use their weapons.

30. What actions did the United Nations take as a result of the Holocaust?

    A. It divided Palestine and Germany.

    B. It defeated Hitler and freed the Jews.

    C. It helped the Jews find jobs and shelter.

    D. It created a Jewish state and made genocide a crime.

31. Put the following events in the order in which they occurred.

    | I. | The Spanish conquered the Aztecs and the Incas. |
    | II. | The Pope sent Europeans to remove Muslims from the Holy Land. |
    | III. | Christopher Columbus explored the Bahamas. |
    | IV. | Spain controlled the Philippines. |

    A. I, II, III, IV

    B. II, III, IV, I

    C. II, III, I, IV

    D. IV, I, III, II

EUROPE

32. What marked the end of the Cold War?

    A. the rule of Gorbachev

    B. the creation of Russia

    C. the break-up of the Soviet Union

    D. the destruction of the Berlin Wall

33. One reason that the British Commonwealth is called a confederation is that member countries

    A. are voluntary members.

    B. must have a constitution.

    C. have strong central governments.

    D. must do what the majority of the members want to do.

SOCIAL STUDIES

EUROPE

Use the following graph to answer questions 34-36.

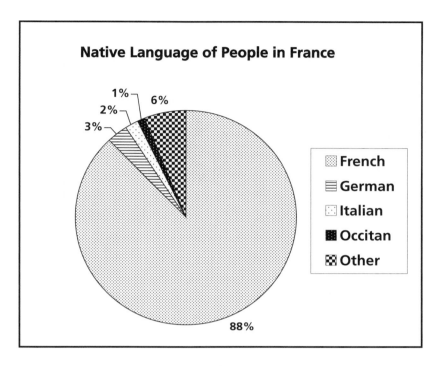

Native Language of People in France

1%
2%
3%
6%

French
German
Italian
Occitan
Other

88%

34. Which question can be answered using the graph?

    A. How many Bretons live in France?

    B. How many people in France speak French?

    C. How are the Occitan native-speakers treated by French native-speakers?

    D. What percentage of people in France have Italian as their native language?

35. What is the smallest language group in France
    A. Arabic

    B. English

    C. Occitan

    D. German

36. What percentage of people in France speak Italian as a native language?

    A. 2 percent

    B. 12 percent

    C. 88 percent

    D. 0.20 percent

SOCIAL STUDIES

EUROPE

Use the map to answer questions 37-39.

37. Which country is located at the "3" on the map?

    A. Italy

    B. Spain

    C. Poland

    D. Russia

38. Which number on the map marks the country of Poland?

    A. 3

    B. 5

    C. 6

    D. 8

39. Which country is north of Italy?

    A. Spain

    B. Russia

    C. Ukraine

    D. Germany

SOCIAL STUDIES

EUROPE

40. Which is an example of human capital?

    A. cash

    B. factories

    C. education

    D. highways

41. Which is an example of an entrepreneur?

    A. a manager of a hospital

    B. a person who runs a government-owned coal mine

    C. a roofer who works for a business owned by an individual

    D. a person who uses her money and time to start a business selling cell phones

42. Why did Prince Henry the Navigator want to send ships south to Africa?

    A. He hoped to learn more about marine life.

    B. He wanted to prove the world was not flat.

    C. He felt his father, the king, would be proud.

    D. He wanted a route around Africa to the Asian markets.

43. Which religion did Prince Henry the Navigator hope to spread?

    A. Islam

    B. Hinduism

    C. Buddhism

    D. Christianity

44. What type of people were the first British colonists in Australia?

    A. sailors

    B. captains

    C. prisoners

    D. conquistadors

45. How did nationalism play a part in Europe's competition to colonize Africa and Asia?

    A. Europeans felt a need to "civilize" other parts of the world.

    B. European missionaries were trying to spread their religion.

    C. Smaller countries wanted more land to accommodate growing populations.

    D. Having colonies made countries feel more important and successful than other countries.

SOCIAL STUDIES

EUROPE

46. Which country's unification led to the collapse of the Soviet Union?

    A. Russia

    B. Germany

    C. Yugoslavia

    D. United Kingdom

47. What was the largest country created from the former Soviet Union?

    A. Russia

    B. Poland

    C. Germany

    D. Sovietestan

48. Which religion has the largest number of followers in Europe?

    A. Islam

    B. Judaism

    C. Hinduism

    D. Christianity

SOCIAL STUDIES

EUROPE

Comparison of Parliamentary and Presidential Systems of Government

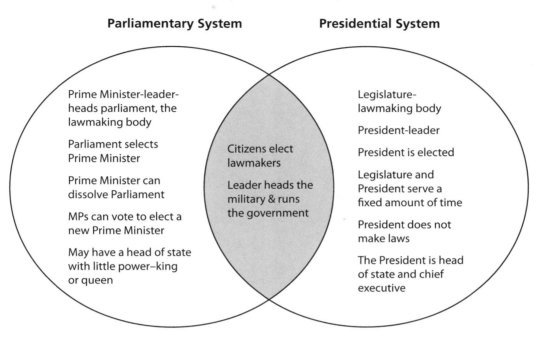

Parliamentary System

Prime Minister-leader-heads parliament, the lawmaking body

Parliament selects Prime Minister

Prime Minister can dissolve Parliament

MPs can vote to elect a new Prime Minister

May have a head of state with little power–king or queen

Citizens elect lawmakers

Leader heads the military & runs the government

Presidential System

Legislature-lawmaking body

President-leader

President is elected

Legislature and President serve a fixed amount of time

President does not make laws

The President is head of state and chief executive

Use the diagram to answer questions 49-50.

49. In what way are the prime minister and the president alike in this diagram?

A. The lawmaking body appoints them.

B. They make the laws for their countries.

C. They can dissolve the lawmaking body.

D. They are in charge of the military and control the government.

50. Who has the most government power in the parliamentary system?

A. a citizen

B. the monarch

C. the prime minister

D. a member of parliament

PLEASE STOP! STOP!

Student Name:_____

Assignment: _____

Period:_____

Marking Instructions:
- Use a No. 2 pencil (no ink or ballpoint pens)
- Fill the circles in completely
- Erase completely to change your answer
- Make no stray marks

Example:

	A	B	C	D
1	○	●	○	○

Score:

Student ID Number

0○	0○	0○	0○	0○	0○	0○	0○	0○
1○	1○	1○	1○	1○	1○	1○	1○	1○
2○	2○	2○	2○	2○	2○	2○	2○	2○
3○	3○	3○	3○	3○	3○	3○	3○	3○
4○	4○	4○	4○	4○	4○	4○	4○	4○
5○	5○	5○	5○	5○	5○	5○	5○	5○
6○	6○	6○	6○	6○	6○	6○	6○	6○
7○	7○	7○	7○	7○	7○	7○	7○	7○
8○	8○	8○	8○	8○	8○	8○	8○	8○
9○	9○	9○	9○	9○	9○	9○	9○	9○

	A	B	C	D			A	B	C	D			A	B	C	D			A	B	C	D			A	B	C	D
1	○	○	○	○		11	○	○	○	○		21	○	○	○	○		31	○	○	○	○		41	○	○	○	○
2	○	○	○	○		12	○	○	○	○		22	○	○	○	○		32	○	○	○	○		42	○	○	○	○
3	○	○	○	○		13	○	○	○	○		23	○	○	○	○		33	○	○	○	○		43	○	○	○	○
4	○	○	○	○		14	○	○	○	○		24	○	○	○	○		34	○	○	○	○		44	○	○	○	○
5	○	○	○	○		15	○	○	○	○		25	○	○	○	○		35	○	○	○	○		45	○	○	○	○
6	○	○	○	○		16	○	○	○	○		26	○	○	○	○		36	○	○	○	○		46	○	○	○	○
7	○	○	○	○		17	○	○	○	○		27	○	○	○	○		37	○	○	○	○		47	○	○	○	○
8	○	○	○	○		18	○	○	○	○		28	○	○	○	○		38	○	○	○	○		48	○	○	○	○
9	○	○	○	○		19	○	○	○	○		29	○	○	○	○		39	○	○	○	○		49	○	○	○	○
10	○	○	○	○		20	○	○	○	○		30	○	○	○	○		40	○	○	○	○		50	○	○	○	○

SOCIAL STUDIES

AUSTRALIA

1. From where did the Aborigines enter the Australian continent thousands of years ago?

   A. Africa

   B. Antarctica

   C. New Zealand

   D. Southeast Asia

2. Why are natural resources important to Australia's economy?

   A. Australia has natural resources that are not valuable to other countries.

   B. People in Australia have been unable to get to their natural resources in order to trade.

   C. There are too many natural resources in Australia for the businesses there to use them.

   D. Australians can trade their natural resources to other countries for goods that they want and need.

3. Why do Australians have to exchange currency in order to trade with other countries?

   A. Australian banks need the fees.

   B. It ensures buyers and sellers are treated fairly.

   C. Transporting goods to other countries is expensive.

   D. Businesses in other countries do not use Australian dollars.

4. Which natural resource is important to Australia's economy?

   A. iron ore

   B. modern factories

   C. excellent highways

   D. education of workers

5. Which was an effect of British settlement of Australia?

   A. Aborigines remained in their homelands.

   B. Many Aborigines became factory workers in order to survive.

   C. Thousands of Aborigines died of smallpox and other diseases.

   D. Aborigines were elected to representative positions in the colonial government.

6. Why are most of Australia's cities on the eastern and southeastern coast of the country?

   A. The central part of the country is too wet.

   B. The western coast is thick with tropical rain forest.

   C. The climate is temperate, and there is good rainfall.

   D. Northern Australia is too cold in winter for ports to stay open.

SOCIAL STUDIES

AUSTRALIA

7. A large number of the early settlers in Australia were

    A. Jesuits.

    B. pilgrims.

    C. prisoners.

    D. conquistadors.

8. Which statement is TRUE about the economic system in Australia?

    A. It is difficult for individuals to start their own businesses.

    B. Government rules and laws make starting a business in Australia very risky.

    C. Laws are in place to protect the rights and property of people who want to start their own businesses in Australia.

    D. Few Australians are willing to use their money and time to start businesses because the government is likely to take their businesses away.

9. Which is an example of investing in capital goods by a company?

    A. providing extra training for workers

    B. buying computers to build products more quickly

    C. giving employees an improved health insurance plan

    D. keeping older trucks instead of replacing them with newer, more efficient ones

10. How were the Aborigines affected by the British colonization of Australia in the nineteenth century?

    A. Aboriginal farmers had to change the crops they grew.

    B. Diseases spread and killed most the Aborigines.

    C. Opal and diamond mines helped to make the Aborigines wealthy.

    D. Laws were put into place to make sure that rights of the Aborigines were protected.

11. Which action by the Australian government would make its economy less like a mixed economy and more like a pure market economy?

    A. a limit on sugar imports of 50 tons per year

    B. a 10 percent tax on all fish bought from Asian countries

    C. the decision to let supply and demand set the price of fuel

    D. the addition of a $100 fee for all computers imported into the country

12. Which country's culture had the greatest effect on the language and religion of Australia?

    A. Spain

    B. Portugal

    C. United States

    D. United Kingdom

SOCIAL STUDIES

AUSTRALIA

13. What was one advantage the British had over the Aborigines as they explored and colonized Australia?

    A. The British knew ways to survive in the outback.

    B. The British had powerful weapons such as guns and cannons.

    C. The British knew how to find water in the dry parts of Australia.

    D. The British had ships that could sail from one continent to another.

14. Who administers laws made by the Commonwealth Parliament in Australia?

    A. queen

    B. prime minister

    C. governor-general

    D. members of Parliament

15. Which best describes the geography of Australia?

    A. lakes and rivers across the southwest

    B. mountainous with scattered tropical lowlands

    C. large tropical zone in the central region of the country

    D. large semiarid, dry region with temperate climates in the southeastern coastal areas

16. Which weapon did the Australian Aborigines invent?

    A. atlatl

    B. cannon

    C. slingshot

    D. boomerang

17. Which is true of Australia's market economy?

    A. The government sets the prices for goods and services.

    B. Australia does not trade with countries outside of Asia.

    C. The monarchy owns most farms and sets the prices for food.

    D. Consumers decide which goods will be produced and which services offered.

18. What event in the mid-19th century led to the killing of hundreds of Aborigines?

    A. a gold rush

    B. the release of prisoners

    C. settlement of coastal cities

    D. establishment of sheep and cattle farms

SOCIAL STUDIES

AUSTRALIA

19. Which gives the citizens the most voice in making the laws of their country?

    A. autocracy

    B. oligarchy

    C. theocracy

    D. democracy

Read the statement in the box. Use the information to answer question 20.

> Three Australians began a company selling opal jewelry. They bought a small warehouse as the place to start the business. They purchased opals and silver from local mines. They hired art students to create new and original designs.

20. The three Australians in the passage are examples of

    A. entrepreneurs.

    B. capital resources.

    C. human resources.

    D. natural resources.

21. Which is an effect of a low literacy rate in a country?

    A. Citizens are generally wealthier.

    B. Citizens can expect to live longer.

    C. Citizens have a lower standard of living.

    D. Citizens compete better in the world economy.

22. Because most economies have characteristics of the command and market economy, we say they are

    A. free.

    B. mixed.

    C. hybrid.

    D. communist.

SOCIAL STUDIES

AUSTRALIA

Use the graph to answer question 23.

23. Which is located at the place marked with a "2" on the map?

    A. Coral Sea

    B. Ayers Rock

    C. Great Barrier Reef

    D. Great Victoria Desert

SOCIAL STUDIES

AUSTRALIA

Use the graph to answer question 24.

24. Which feature is marked by the "?" on the map?

    A. Canberra

    B. Coral Sea

    C. Ayers Rock

    D. Tasman Sea

25. Which activity was a common part of the life of the Aborigines?

    A. mining

    B. writing

    C. farming

    D. hunting

SOCIAL STUDIES

AUSTRALIA

26. Which is the most likely effect of a country investing in the education and training of its citizens?

    A. The GDP will no longer be important because the citizens are educated.

    B. The GDP will go down because the cost of education and training is very high.

    C. The GDP will stay about the same because education and training do not affect it.

    D. The GDP will rise because workers that are better educated can find ways to do their jobs better.

27. What is the main reason few people live in the Great Victoria Desert?

    A. It is too hot and dry.

    B. There are winter floods.

    C. Australians prefer city life.

    D. The area has not been explored.

28. Which describes the government of Australia?

    A. federal government

    B. unitary government

    C. confederate government

    D. both unitary and confederate

29. Which nearby country is most important to Australia for trade?

    A. China

    B. India

    C. South Africa

    D. United States

30. Which is the reason most Australians practice Christianity?

    A. It is illegal to practice other religions in Australia.

    B. Most of the original European settlers were Christian.

    C. Australian Aborigines practiced Christianity before the Europeans arrived.

    D. The monarchy requires Australians to be members of the Anglican Church.

31. Which statement BEST describes an oligarchy?

    A. The citizens elect their leaders.

    B. A small group runs the government.

    C. The judicial branch controls political power.

    D. A self-appointed ruler holds the political power.

SOCIAL STUDIES

AUSTRALIA

Organization of the Australian Government

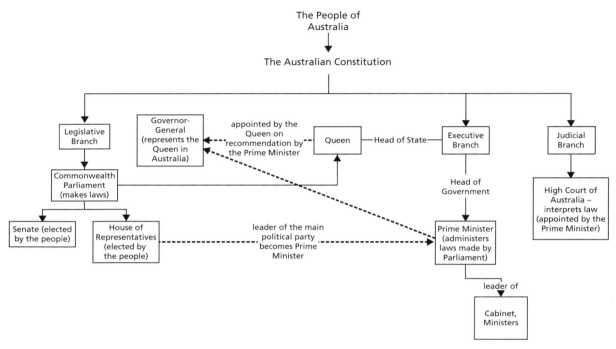

Use the diagram to answer questions 32-34.

32. The Commonwealth Parliament is in which part of the government?

    A. executive branch

    B. judicial branch

    C. legislative branch

    D. none of these

33. What is the role of the governor-general in Australia?

    A. acts as head of government

    B. represents the Queen in Australia

    C. waits for recommendations from the prime minister

    D. be the leader of the political party with the most representatives in Parliament

34. Which has the most power in the Australian government?

    A. the Queen

    B. the Senate

    C. the constitution

    D. the people of Australia

SOCIAL STUDIES

AUSTRALIA

35. What is one difference between the Australian prime minister and the president of the United States?

    A. The president is the head of state, and the prime minister is not.

    B. The president is selected from the elected members of the legislative branch.

    C. The prime minister is selected from the elected members of the legislative branch and the president is chosen by the Senate.

    D. The president is selected from the elected members of the legislative branch and the prime minister is chosen by the governor-general.

36. The prime minister in Australia is also the

    A. Queen's representative in Australia.

    B. person who serves as governor-general.

    C. chief judge of the High Court of Australia.

    D. leader of the political party with the most seats in Parliament.

37. Which is an example of a confederation?

    A. Australia

    B. European Union

    C. Australia and New Zealand

    D. Commonwealth of Nations

38. Which is an example of capital goods?

    A. gold

    B. factories

    C. highways

    D. health care

39. Which BEST describes a result of British colonization of Australia?

    A. Australia is a modern, independent country with close ties to Great Britain.

    B. Australia is an old-fashioned country that is very dependent on Great Britain.

    C. Australia is a modern, independent country, but it has few ties with Great Britain.

    D. Australia is an old-fashioned country that is governed by the Queen of Great Britain.

40. Which condition helps Australia have a strong market economy?

    A. The courts are fair and honest, and there are good laws.

    B. Buyers have little money and few choices in the market.

    C. Business owners have many rules to follow and high taxes.

    D. none of these

SOCIAL STUDIES

AUSTRALIA

41. What has helped Australia to have a high GDP?

A. high tax rates

B. tariffs on imports

C. modern factories and technology

D. immigrants with low-paying jobs

42. Which is an important role of entrepreneurs in the Australian economy?

A. They sell stocks in the stock market.

B. They provide new jobs for Australian workers.

C. They close factories that are not making much money.

D. They are needed to lead the largest companies in the country.

43. Which is an example of specialization?

A. A business sells goods for a profit.

B. Two people come to an agreement to trade goods they produced.

C. A factory builds one product and finds ways to build it better and less expensively.

D. A country buys all the goods it needs from other countries and does not produce any of its own.

Use the statements in the box to answer question 44.

- The government has laws to protect private property owners.

- Courts enforce laws to protect consumers and businesses.

- Prices for goods and services are set based on what consumers agree to pay.

- The government has few trade barriers such as tariffs or quotas.

44. What type of economy do these statements describe?

A. market

B. command

C. production

D. traditional

45. Tariffs and quotas are alike because they both

A. restrict trade between countries.

B. stop all trade between countries.

C. increase trade between countries.

D. make trade between countries easier.

SOCIAL STUDIES

AUSTRALIA

Read the statement in the box. Use the information to answer question 46.

> In 1998, Australia stopped selling weapons to the people of Yugoslavia. Australia hoped that by stopping trade in this way, it might force an end to the civil war in Yugoslavia.

46. Which best describes the action taken by Australia?

    A. tariff

    B. quota

    C. embargo

    D. specialization

47. How are the prices for goods and services set in Australia?

    A. Buyers and sellers agree upon a price for goods and services.

    B. Parliament sets a price for all goods and services in the country.

    C. The governor-general and the monarch set prices for most goods and services.

    D. Prices for goods brought from China are set by the prime minister and Parliament.

48. What is the currency of Australia?

    A. euro

    B. ruble

    C. Australian peso

    D. Australian dollar

49. Which is a reason that the British wanted to start a colony in Australia?

    A. to have religious freedom

    B. to use it as a penal colony

    C. to reduce the population of London

    D. to expand trade with the Aborigines

50. In which century did the British begin to colonize Australia?

    A. 15th century

    B. 16th century

    C. 17th century

    D. 18th century

PLEASE STOP! STOP!

Student Name: _____

Assignment: _____

Period: _____

Marking Instructions:

- Use a No. 2 pencil (no ink or ballpoint pens)
- Fill the circles in completely
- Erase completely to change your answer
- Make no stray marks

Example:

   A   B   C   D
1 ○   ●   ○   ○

Score:

Student ID Number

	0	0	0	0	0	0	0	0	0
1	○	○	○	○	○	○	○	○	○
2	○	○	○	○	○	○	○	○	○
3	○	○	○	○	○	○	○	○	○
4	○	○	○	○	○	○	○	○	○
5	○	○	○	○	○	○	○	○	○
6	○	○	○	○	○	○	○	○	○
7	○	○	○	○	○	○	○	○	○
8	○	○	○	○	○	○	○	○	○
9	○	○	○	○	○	○	○	○	○

```
         A  B  C  D              A  B  C  D              A  B  C  D              A  B  C  D              A  B  C  D
 1       ○  ○  ○  ○     11       ○  ○  ○  ○     21       ○  ○  ○  ○     31       ○  ○  ○  ○     41       ○  ○  ○  ○
 2       ○  ○  ○  ○     12       ○  ○  ○  ○     22       ○  ○  ○  ○     32       ○  ○  ○  ○     42       ○  ○  ○  ○
 3       ○  ○  ○  ○     13       ○  ○  ○  ○     23       ○  ○  ○  ○     33       ○  ○  ○  ○     43       ○  ○  ○  ○
 4       ○  ○  ○  ○     14       ○  ○  ○  ○     24       ○  ○  ○  ○     34       ○  ○  ○  ○     44       ○  ○  ○  ○
 5       ○  ○  ○  ○     15       ○  ○  ○  ○     25       ○  ○  ○  ○     35       ○  ○  ○  ○     45       ○  ○  ○  ○
 6       ○  ○  ○  ○     16       ○  ○  ○  ○     26       ○  ○  ○  ○     36       ○  ○  ○  ○     46       ○  ○  ○  ○
 7       ○  ○  ○  ○     17       ○  ○  ○  ○     27       ○  ○  ○  ○     37       ○  ○  ○  ○     47       ○  ○  ○  ○
 8       ○  ○  ○  ○     18       ○  ○  ○  ○     28       ○  ○  ○  ○     38       ○  ○  ○  ○     48       ○  ○  ○  ○
 9       ○  ○  ○  ○     19       ○  ○  ○  ○     29       ○  ○  ○  ○     39       ○  ○  ○  ○     49       ○  ○  ○  ○
10       ○  ○  ○  ○     20       ○  ○  ○  ○     30       ○  ○  ○  ○     40       ○  ○  ○  ○     50       ○  ○  ○  ○
```

SOCIAL STUDIES

CRCT PRACTICE TEST

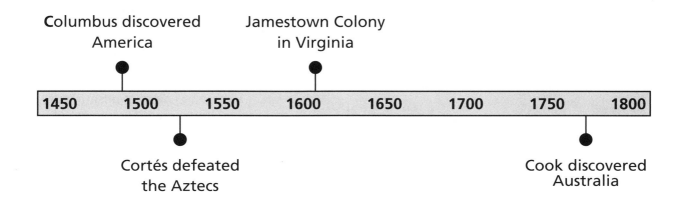

Use the timeline to answer questions 1–4.

1. In what century did Christopher Columbus land in the New World?

   A. 14th

   B. 15th

   C. 16th

   D. not shown

2. About how many years passed between Columbus's voyage and Cook's discovery of Australia?

   A. about 350

   B. exactly 300

   C. not quite 300

   D. much more than 350

3. When did Cortés defeat the Aztecs?

   A. in 1550

   B. after 1540

   C. about 1520

   D. before 1500

4. Which event happened before Cortés defeated the Aztecs?

   A. Jamestown was settled.

   B. Cook discovered Australia.

   C. Columbus discovered America.

   D. none of these

SOCIAL STUDIES

CRCT PRACTICE TEST

5. Which is LEAST likely to be found in Europe today?

   A. capitalism

   B. market economy

   C. command economy

   D. traditional economy

6. What was the Columbian Exchange?

   A. sending food and people from the Old World to the New World

   B. sending animals and plants from the Old World to the New World

   C. the moving of animals, plants, people, and diseases from Central and South America to North America

   D. the moving of animals, plants, people, and diseases from the Old World to the New World and from the New World to the Old World

7. What environmental disaster occurred in 1986 in Chernobyl, Ukraine?

   A. a nuclear reactor explosion

   B. acid rain caused by engine exhaust

   C. "the great smoke" from coal-burning factories

   D. death of forests due to water pollution from mining

8. What was one result of the colonization of Canada by Europeans?

   A. Europeans are no longer welcome in Canada.

   B. Canada's official languages are English and French.

   C. Great Britain has no relationship with Canada in the 21st century.

   D. The Canadian Revolution removed the French and the English from power.

9. One difference between the German and Russian languages is that German

   A. does not use the Cyrillic alphabet.

   B. is spoken by fewer people than Russian.

   C. has not been spoken in Europe since World War II.

   D. is spoken in only one country in Europe, and Russian is spoken in several.

10. Because most economies have characteristics of the command and market economy, we say they are

   A. free.

   B. mixed.

   C. capitalist.

   D. communist.

SOCIAL STUDIES

CRCT PRACTICE TEST

11. Why did Prince Henry the Navigator want to send ships south to Africa?

    A. He hoped to learn more about marine life.

    B. He wanted to prove the world was not flat.

    C. He felt his father, the king, would be proud.

    D. He wanted a route around Africa to the Asian markets.

12. Who claimed Australia for Great Britain?

    A. George III

    B. Captain James Cook

    C. Christopher Columbus

    D. Prince Henry the Navigator

13. What is one effect of slavery that influences Latin America today?

    A. Many Latin Americans have ancestors from Africa.

    B. Slavery exists in few Latin American countries.

    C. Latin America has no people with ancestors from Africa.

    D. The people of Latin America accept slavery as part of their lives.

14. Which two European countries contributed most to the languages of Latin America?

    A. England and Spain

    B. Spain and Portugal

    C. France and Portugal

    D. England and Portugal

SOCIAL STUDIES

CRCT PRACTICE TEST

Use the following map to answer question 15.

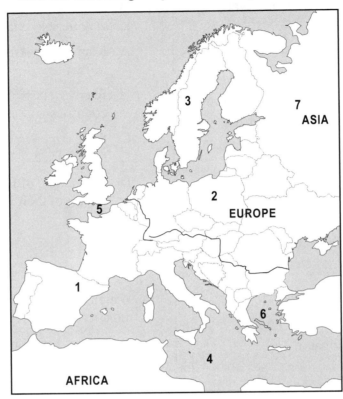

15. Which feature is located near the "3" on the map?

    A. Rhine River

    B. Ural Mountains

    C. Pyrenees Mountains

    D. Scandinavian Peninsula

16. Which condition helped the United Kingdom become a leader in world trade?

    A. Two percent of its people are farmers, and there is a lot of arable land.

    B. The island has a mild climate and is located near many other countries.

    C. It is home to the world's busiest airport and has seven other large airports.

    D. Urban areas are heavily populated, and most jobs are found in the urban areas.

SOCIAL STUDIES

CRCT PRACTICE TEST

Use the map to answer question 17.

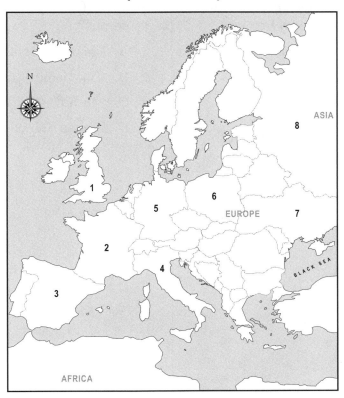

17. Which number on the map marks Russia?

    A. 3

    B. 5

    C. 6

    D. 8

18. What has helped Italian merchants become successful traders?

    A. The location of the Alps mountains is a defense against other countries.

    B. The islands of Sicily and Sardinia are not far from the coast of western Italy.

    C. Warm air from the Sahara desert creates a warm, dry summer for most of Italy.

    D. Italy is located on the Mediterranean Sea with access to Africa, Asia, and Europe.

19. A country that invests in human capital will have a more successful economy because

    A. there will be more money to pay its workers.

    B. workers will learn the skills they need on their own.

    C. businesses will not pay taxes to pay for good schools.

    D. workers who are educated, skilled, and healthy are more productive.

20. Which pairing of sacred text and religion is correct?

    A. Judaism – Torah

    B. Christianity - Talmud

    C. Muslim – Old Testament

    D. Roman Catholic – Koran

SOCIAL STUDIES

CRCT PRACTICE TEST

Use the map to answer question 21.

Australia

21. Which is located at the place marked with a "1" on the map?

    A. Coral Sea

    B. Indian Ocean

    C. Atlantic Ocean

    D. Great Barrier Reef

22. A main purpose of NAFTA was to

    A. increase trade by creating a large free-trade zone.

    B. create tariffs between Canada, Mexico, and the United States.

    C. keep people in one country from buying goods from the other countries.

    D. decrease the standard of living for some people while raising it for others.

23. Which situation might keep an embargo against a country from being successful?

    A. People in the country suffer because trading has stopped.

    B. The country does not need to trade with other counties.

    C. The country is able to find other trading partners not in the embargo.

    D. People in the country don't care whether their country trades with other countries.

24. Which of the countries has the least freedom to do business?

    A. Cuba

    B. Brazil

    C. Canada

    D. about the same in each

25. Which was a cause of the Russian Revolution?

    A. The czar was executed.

    B. There were food shortages in Russia.

    C. The Germans showed signs of surrender.

    D. Soldiers did not know how to use their weapons.

26. What marked the end of the Cold War?

    A. the rule of Gorbachev

    B. the creation of Russia

    C. the break-up of the Soviet Union

    D. the destruction of the Berlin Wall

SOCIAL STUDIES

CRCT PRACTICE TEST

Use the map to answer questions 27-28.

27. Which country is marked by the "5" on the map?

   A. Haiti

   B. Cuba

   C. Bolivia

   D. Venezuela

28. Which number marks the country of Brazil?

   A. 2

   B. 3

   C. 5

   D. 6

SOCIAL STUDIES

CRCT PRACTICE TEST

Use the map to answer questions 29-30.

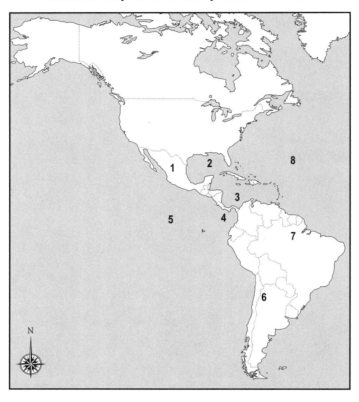

29. Which feature is located near the "6" on the map?

   A. Panama Canal

   B. Atacama Desert

   C. Appalachian Mountains

   D. Sierra Madre Mountains

30. What number marks the Gulf of Mexico?

   A. 1

   B. 2

   C. 3

   D. 5

31. Which solution is a way that the government is trying to reduce pollution in Mexico City?

   A. ignoring cars with exhaust problems

   B. reducing the number of buses and trains

   C. making sure the population continues to grow

   D. increasing the number of cars that produce little or no air pollution

32. What almost caused a nuclear attack between the United States and the Soviet Union?

    A. President Kennedy did not like the leader of the Soviet Union.

    B. The Soviet Union wanted to show the Cubans that they were strong friends.

    C. Castro allowed the Soviet Union to build a nuclear missile launch complex in Cuba.

    D. The United States wanted the sugar cane crop that the Soviet Union was buying from Cuba.

33. What did the Zapatistas do to show they were against NAFTA?

    A. attacked government troops in Mexico City

    B. took over several towns in southern Mexico

    C. formed friendships with groups in other countries with similar goals

    D. worked with the government on agreements to improve the rights of poor Mexicans

34. Which two European countries contributed most to the languages of Canada?

    A. England and Spain

    B. Spain and Portugal

    C. England and France

    D. France and Portugal

35. What is the goal of the independence movement in Quebec?

    A. for Quebec to have its own monarch

    B. for Quebec to be an independent country

    C. to have Quebec become a part of France again

    D. to have the rest of Canada become French-speaking

36. Which term describes how political power is distributed in Brazil?

    A. unitary government

    B. federal government

    C. aristocratic government

    D. confederation government

37. Which statement is TRUE about how the president in a presidential democracy is different from a prime minister in a parliamentary democracy?

    A. The prime minister is the head of state for the country, but the president is not.

    B. The prime minister is the chief executive and head of the military, but the president is not.

    C. The prime minister is elected directly by the people, but the president is elected by the legislature.

    D. The prime minister is chosen from the members of parliament, but the president runs for office separately.

38. Canada has to work with the United States to solve the problem of acid rain because the United States

    A. is the source of much of Canada's air pollution.

    B. purchases many of the goods that Canada produces in its factories.

    C. has reduced the amount of acid rain and understands how to solve the problem.

    D. is careful to keep air pollution from leaving the United States and entering Canada.

39. Which condition makes it easy for Canada to trade with the United States?

    A. The countries share a border over 3,000 miles long.

    B. Canada has easy access to seven major ports on three oceans.

    C. The countries have abundant natural resources and a long growing season.

    D. Canada has many natural resources and goods that are not available in the United States.

Use the statements in the box to answer question 40.

- signs bills into law
- is commander-in-chief of the military
- acts as head of state for Australia
- approves elections

---

40. What do these statements explain?

    A. duties of the Queen in Australia

    B. duties of the Australian prime minister

    C. actions taken by judges in the High Court of Australia

    D. actions that are not a part of the Australian government

41. Who has the most political power in the Australian government?

    A. the monarch

    B. prime minister

    C. governor-general

    D. High Court judge

SOCIAL STUDIES

CRCT PRACTICE TEST

Use the graph to answer questions 42-43.

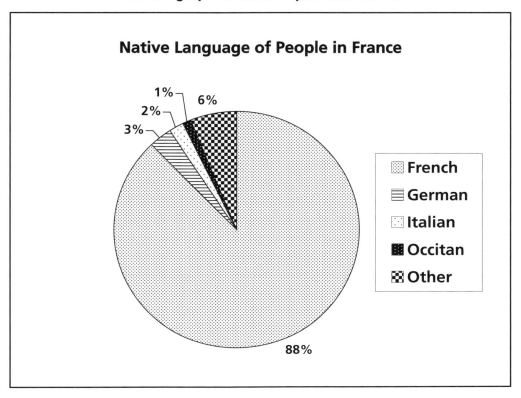

Native Language of People in France

1%
2%
3%
6%
88%

French
German
Italian
Occitan
Other

42. Which question can be answered using the graph?

   A. How many people in France speak Italian?

   B. How many people in France speak French?

   C. What percent of people in France have Occitan as their native language?

   D. What part of the French population speaks English as a second language?

43. What part of the people in France speaks French as their native language?

   A. 3 percent

   B. 12 percent

   C. 88 percent

   D. None

44. What is an advantage of a savings account over a checking account?

   A. Savings accounts are easier to get.

   B. Savings accounts can be used to guarantee loans.

   C. Savings accounts pay a higher rate of interest.

   D. Savings accounts provide more protection for your money.

45. Why are Spanish and Portuguese the main languages of Latin America?

   A. People from Spain and Portugal colonized Latin America.

   B. People in Latin America found Spanish and Portuguese easy to learn.

   C. The Roman Catholic Church did not allow people to speak English or French.

   D. Indigenous people switched to these languages to make communication easier.

46. Which of the following is usually TRUE about a country's literacy rate and its standard of living?

   A. A low literacy rate goes along with a low standard of living.

   B. A low literacy rate goes along with a high standard of living.

   C. Increasing the standard of living means decreasing the literacy rate.

   D. Decreasing the standard of living means increasing the literacy rate.

SOCIAL STUDIES

CRCT PRACTICE TEST

Use the diagram to answer questions 47-48.

Types of Economies

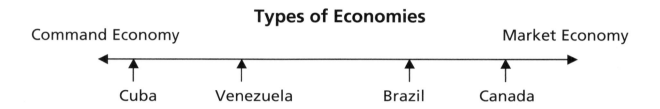

Command Economy   Market Economy

Cuba   Venezuela   Brazil   Canada

47. Which country has an economic system closest to a pure market economy?

   A. Cuba

   B. Brazil

   C. Canada

   D. Venezuela

48. Which country's businesses have the most government control?

   A. Cuba

   B. Brazil

   C. Canada

   D. Venezuela

49. Which is MOST important to helping Brazilian businesses trade with other countries in the world?

   A. The Amazon River allows ships to travel inland to the Andes.

   B. There are seven major seaports along Brazil's Atlantic coast.

   C. Brazil shares a border with very few South American countries.

   D. Brazil does not have many natural resources to trade with other countries.

SOCIAL STUDIES

CRCT PRACTICE TEST

Use the map below to answer questions 50-51.

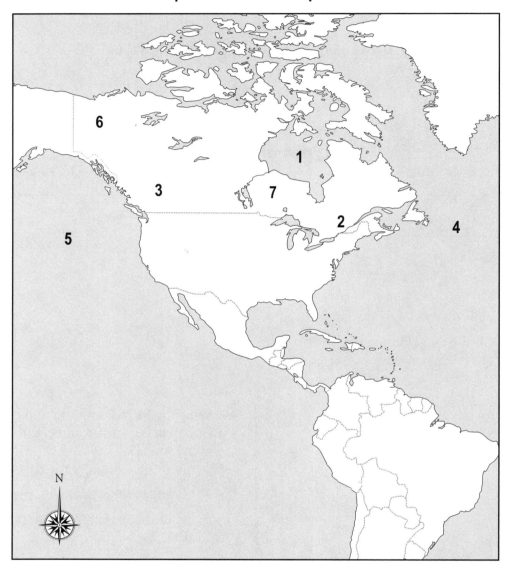

50. Which feature is closest to the "3" on the map?

    A. Lake Superior

    B. Canadian Shield

    C. Rocky Mountains

    D. St. Lawrence River

51. Which feature is located nearest the "1" on the map?

    A. Arctic Ocean

    B. Hudson Bay

    C. Lake Huron

    D. Atlantic Ocean

CRCT PRACTICE TEST

Use the statements in the box to answer question 52.

> • The lawmaking bodies are divided into two houses.
>
> • All have some part of their lawmaking body elected by the people.
>
> • Each divides the jobs of head of state and head of government (chief executive).

52. Which statement explains what these sentences are about?

   A. They describe the governments of European countries.

   B. They tell how the countries of Europe choose their leaders.

   C. They explain how the EU countries must set up their parliaments.

   D. They are ways that the governments of Germany, Russia, and the United Kingdom are alike.

53. In which form of government would the fewest number of people be involved in making the rule of law?

   A. oligarchy

   B. autocracy

   C. traditional

   D. democracy

Use the statements in the word box to answer question 54.

> • constitutional monarchy
>
> • parliamentary democracy
>
> • federation
>
> • great personal freedom

54. The statements above describe the government of which country?

   A. Cuba

   B. Russia

   C. Canada

   D. Great Britain

55. Why is the southern part of Canada the region where most Canadians live?

   A. It is closest to the United States.

   B. It has the most favorable climate.

   C. Most of the ports are in southern Canada.

   D. Mountains cover most of northern Canada.

56. Which type of economy is LEAST likely to be found in the countries of Europe?

   A. mixed

   B. market

   C. command

   D. traditional

57. Why is it important for a country to invest in human capital?

   A. A country needs money in order to pay its workers.

   B. Workers enjoy getting extra training and job opportunities.

   C. Businesses cannot do all the training needed by workers to be successful.

   D. A country's economy is more successful when workers have good education and health care.

58. Why would a company spend money to buy new machines for its factories rather than continue to use older machines that were still working?

   A. Older machines cannot be run well by younger workers.

   B. Older machines do not produce as much pollution as newer ones.

   C. New machines might help the company produce more goods at a lower price.

   D. New machines would cost the company a lot of money but would provide jobs for workers.

59. The United Kingdom is to Parliament as Germany is to

   A. President.

   B. Bundestag.

   C. Chancellor.

   D. Representative.

60. Which is a reason the European Union was created?

   A. to isolate Russia and make it more difficult for it to trade

   B. to practice reaching consensus among European countries

   C. to promote the French franc as a common currency for Europe

   D. to make Europe more competitive in world markets and to solve common problems

PLEASE STOP!

Student Name: _____

Assignment: _____

Period: _____

Marking Instructions:
- Use a No. 2 pencil (no ink or ballpoint pens)
- Fill the circles in completely
- Erase completely to change your answer
- Make no stray marks

Student ID Number

0	0	0	0	0	0	0	0	0
1	1	1	1	1	1	1	1	1
2	2	2	2	2	2	2	2	2
3	3	3	3	3	3	3	3	3
4	4	4	4	4	4	4	4	4
5	5	5	5	5	5	5	5	5
6	6	6	6	6	6	6	6	6
7	7	7	7	7	7	7	7	7
8	8	8	8	8	8	8	8	8
9	9	9	9	9	9	9	9	9

Example:

   A B C D
1 ○ ● ○ ○

Score:

[ ]

	A B C D		A B C D		A B C D		A B C D
1	○ ○ ○ ○	16	○ ○ ○ ○	31	○ ○ ○ ○	46	○ ○ ○ ○
2	○ ○ ○ ○	17	○ ○ ○ ○	32	○ ○ ○ ○	47	○ ○ ○ ○
3	○ ○ ○ ○	18	○ ○ ○ ○	33	○ ○ ○ ○	48	○ ○ ○ ○
4	○ ○ ○ ○	19	○ ○ ○ ○	34	○ ○ ○ ○	49	○ ○ ○ ○
5	○ ○ ○ ○	20	○ ○ ○ ○	35	○ ○ ○ ○	50	○ ○ ○ ○
6	○ ○ ○ ○	21	○ ○ ○ ○	36	○ ○ ○ ○	51	○ ○ ○ ○
7	○ ○ ○ ○	22	○ ○ ○ ○	37	○ ○ ○ ○	52	○ ○ ○ ○
8	○ ○ ○ ○	23	○ ○ ○ ○	38	○ ○ ○ ○	53	○ ○ ○ ○
9	○ ○ ○ ○	24	○ ○ ○ ○	39	○ ○ ○ ○	54	○ ○ ○ ○
10	○ ○ ○ ○	25	○ ○ ○ ○	40	○ ○ ○ ○	55	○ ○ ○ ○
11	○ ○ ○ ○	26	○ ○ ○ ○	41	○ ○ ○ ○	56	○ ○ ○ ○
12	○ ○ ○ ○	27	○ ○ ○ ○	42	○ ○ ○ ○	57	○ ○ ○ ○
13	○ ○ ○ ○	28	○ ○ ○ ○	43	○ ○ ○ ○	58	○ ○ ○ ○
14	○ ○ ○ ○	29	○ ○ ○ ○	44	○ ○ ○ ○	59	○ ○ ○ ○
15	○ ○ ○ ○	30	○ ○ ○ ○	45	○ ○ ○ ○	60	○ ○ ○ ○

19

GLOSSARY

A

Aborigines the indigenous or native people of Australia; "the people who were here from the beginning"

acid rain clouds or rain containing sulfur dioxide, carbon dioxide, and nitrogen oxides that cause problems in the environment

algal bloom a rapid increase in lake algae, caused by phosphorus pollution; can kill plant and animal life

Allied Powers the alliance of Great Britain, France, Russia, and the United States during World War I

arable farmable; a description applied to land that is capable of being farmed

autocratic government a government with a single ruler with unlimited power

B

Basic Law the constitution of Germany

blackout a time when all electricity to a region is cut off

British Commonwealth weak association of member countries once part of the British Empire; also called the Commonwealth of Nations

British pound the currency of the United Kingdom

budget a plan for spending and savings based on estimated income and expenses

Bundesrat the less-powerful upper house of the German parliament, which represents the interests of the state governments

Bundestag the powerful lower house of the German parliament; elects the chancellor

bush the remote countryside of Australia

C

capital goods goods which include the factories, machines, technologies, buildings, and property needed for a business to operate

capitalism a decentralized market economy

Central Powers the alliance of Germany, Austria-Hungary, the Ottoman Empire, and Bulgaria in World War I

chancellor head of state running day-to-day operations of government in some democracies, like Germany

chief executive a leader who heads the military, enforces laws, and keeps a country running day to day

clear-cutting cutting all the trees in an area

Cold War a period of distrust and misunderstanding between the Soviet Union and its former allies in the West, particularly the United States

colony a foreign area controlled by a country and contributing to its wealth

Columbian Exchange the moving of animals, plants, people, and diseases between the Old and New Worlds

command economy an economy in which centralized planning groups decide what and how goods and services will be produced, distributed, and consumed

Commonwealth of Nations weak association of member countries once part of the British Empire; also called the British Commonwealth

communist describes a government that owns or controls most farms and businesses

confederation government a form of government based on a voluntary agreement under which separate countries work together

conquistador Spanish conqueror

constitutional monarchy a government in which the king or queen is head of state with little real power, as limited by a constitution

credit the ability to borrow money

Crusades military expeditions sent from 1096 to 1272 by various popes to capture the Holy Land from Muslim Turks

Cuban Missile Crisis a tense time in 1962 when nuclear war seemed possible after the Soviet Union placed missiles in Cuba and the United States demanded their removal

currency money used in a particular country to buy goods and services

Cyrillic alphabet writing system (differing from the Roman alphabet) used to write Russian and other Slavic languages

czar absolute rule of Russia before 1917

D

deforestation the process of clearing forests, selling the timber, and using the cleared land for other purposes

demand how many people want the goods available and what they are willing to pay for them

direct democracy a democratic form of government requiring a vote by all citizens for every government decision

E

economic depression a hard time in the economy when businesses, banks, factories close and people lose their jobs; buying and selling almost stops

economic system the way a country decides what goods and services will be produced, how they will be produced, and who will consume them

embargo a government order stopping trade with another country to put pressure on the government of that other country

entrepreneur one who risks his or her own money, time, ideas, and energy to start and run a business

euro the currency of the European Union

European Union (EU) a group of 27 European countries united to bring more advantages to members that might not be available to the smaller nations; the EU works to improve trade, education, farming, and industry among the members

exchange rate the price of one nation's currency in terms of another nation's currency

expenses the costs related to running a business

exports goods sold to other countries

F

federal government a form of government in which power is divided between a central government and smaller divisions, such as states

Federation Council that part of Russia's Federal Assembly that represents state government; approves presidential appointments

financial investment savings put into a bank account, certificate of deposit, stock, bond, or mutual fund that pays a future benefit such as interest

free economy describes an economy where businesses can operate without too many rules from the government

free enterprise a decentralized market economy

free-trade zone an area where there are no tariffs among participating countries; for example, North America (NAFTA) or the European Union

G

genocide the planned killing of a race of people

Germanic languages includes languages like German or English originating from Germanic tribes; largest European language group; found in northwest and central Europe

Great Britain the united countries of England, Scotland, and Wales, a union that dates from the early 1700s

Great Smog four days of intense smog in London in 1952, which alerted people to poor air quality

Great War European conflict from 1914 to 1918; also known as World War I and "the war to end all wars"

Gross Domestic Product (GDP) the total value of all the final goods and services produced in a country in one year

Gulf Stream a current of warm water from the Gulf of Mexico that moves north across the Atlantic, warming Ireland and the United Kingdom

H

head of state   in a parliamentary system, the symbolic leader of a country

Holocaust   the systematic killing of 6 million Jews and others by the Nazis before and during World War II

House of Commons   the powerful, representative lawmaking body of the United Kingdom's Parliament; controls the budget

House of Lords   the less-powerful, advisory lawmaking body of the United Kingdom's Parliament

human capital   workers of a business or country including their education, training, skills, and health

I

illiteracy rate   the percentage of a country's people who cannot read and write

imports   goods purchased from other countries

income   money coming in for a person or into a business

indigenous population   the first people known to inhabit an area

industrialized countries   countries that depend more on manufacturing than farming; generally have a high standard of living

interest   a fee for the use of money

investing   putting money into a bank account, stock, bond, or mutual fund that pays interest

L

laissez-faire   a decentralized market economy

Latin America   countries of Central and South America and the Caribbean having Spanish or Portuguese as their primary language

law of supply and demand   determines price based on amount of goods available, how many consumers want the goods, and what they are willing to pay

life expectancy   the average number of years a person in a country may be reasonably expected to live

literacy rate   the percentage of a country's people who can read and write

literate   able to read and write

M

market economy   an economy in which changes in price guide what and how goods and services will be produced, distributed, and consumed

mestizo   in Latin America, one whose ancestors were both European and Native American

militarism   using strong armies and threats of war

mixed economy   an economy that blends characteristics of both command and market economies, but falls closer to one form or the other

monarch   a king or queen, symbol of a country; "the Crown"

monolith   what you see of a single large rock sticking out of the earth

MP   member of parliament, elected as a representative of the people in a parliamentary system of democracy

mulatto   in Latin America, one whose ancestors were both African and European

N

NAFTA   North American Free Trade Agreement, which was signed in 1994 by the United States, Canada, and Mexico eliminating tariffs

Nahuatl   Aztec language

nationalism   the love of one's country

North Atlantic Treaty Organization (NATO) an alliance of the United States, Canada, and its western European allies; formed after World War II

Nazi Party   National Socialist Party of Germany's Adolf Hitler

O

oligarchic government   a government that is ruled by a few

Ottoman Empire   Turkey and its colonies

outback   the dry interior of the continent of Australia

293

P

parliamentary system type of democratic government where citizens elect MPs who choose a prime minister as chief executive

penal describes a prison

peso the Mexican or Cuban currency

phosphorus a chemical used in fertilizer, pesticides, toothpaste, detergents, and explosives that can pollute water

physical capital factories, machines, technologies, buildings, and property needed for a business to operate

physical capital investment purchasing physical capital (capital goods)

Pope leader of the Roman Catholic Church

presidential system type of democratic government where citizens elect members of the legislature and also the chief executive, known as the president

prime minister the head of state in a parliamentary system of democracy, responsible for running the day-to-day operations of government

profit money left after business expenses are subtracted from business income

Q

Quechua the Inca language

quota (1) in a centralized command economy, being told by the government what and how much to produce in a certain time; (2) a limit placed on the number of imports that may enter a country

R

real Brazilian currency

real investment the purchase of a new home by a person or the purchase of physical capital by a business

representative democracy a democratic form of government in which the citizens elect representatives to make government decisions

Romance languages includes languages like French, Italian, Spanish, Portuguese, and Romanian, which come from Latin, the ancient Roman language; found in south and west of Europe

ruble the Russian currency

S

Santeria a Cuban religion based on African traditional beliefs

savings income not spent

scarcity limited supply of something

Scramble for Africa the division of much of Africa among European countries between 1885 and 1910

separatist a person who wants Quebec to be an independent country from Canada

service jobs jobs that involve providing services to people rather than products

slag leftover rock from the smelting process

Slavic languages includes Russian; found in central and eastern Europe; sometimes written with Cyrillic alphabet

smokeless zones areas of London where, in order to improve air quality, only smokeless fuels can be used

Soviet Union a powerful communist country that supported the Castro government in Cuba

specialization the division of labor; work is divided into parts for workers, factories, or countries to become expert at producing certain goods

State Duma the elected body of Russia's Federal Assembly; controls the budget and makes laws; approves prime minister selected by the president

stock market crash occurs when the value of stocks falls quickly and deeply

supply the amount of goods available

T

tariff a tax on imports

third world countries developing nations that do not have much industry and that depend upon farming; have lower standard of living than industrialized countries

trade the voluntary exchange of goods and services among people and countries benefitting both parties

trade barriers ways of limiting trade by tariffs, quotas, or embargoes

traditional economy an economy in which customs and habits of the past decide what and how goods and services are produced, distributed, and consumed

U

unitary government   a form of government in which a central government operates all levels of government in a country

urban   referring to cities

V

viceroy   Spanish governor of conquered American lands

W

welfare state   government that guarantees certain benefits to the unemployed, poor, disabled, old, and sick, such as is done in the Basic Law of Germany

World War I   European conflict from 1914 to 1918; also known as the Great War and "the war to end all wars"

World War II   worldwide conflict lasting from 1939 to 1945

Z

Zapatistas   a guerrilla group who supported improved living conditions for indigenous Mexicans; they have resorted to harassment, sabotage, and forcible takeovers of local governments

INDEX

INDEX

INDEX

INDEX

INDEX

301

Order Form
CRCT Test Prep

Clairmont Press

Phone: 1-800-874-8638   Fax: 1-800-874-9190   E-mail: gacrct@clairmontpress.com
1494 Bellflower Court   Lilburn, Georgia 30047

Ship to:

_____
Name   Position

_____
School/District

_____
Street Address   (not PO Box)

_____
City   State   Zip Code

_____
Telephone

_____
E-mail Address

Bill to:

_____
Name   Position

_____
School/District

_____
Street Address or PO Box

_____
City   State   Zip Code

_____
Purchase Order Number

Item #	Quantity	Title/Description	Price	Total
978-1-56733-099-1		**6th Grade** CRCT Test Prep TEACHING THE GEORGIA PERFORMANCE STANDARDS		
978-1-56733-098-4		**7th Grade** CRCT Test Prep TEACHING THE GEORGIA PERFORMANCE STANDARDS		
978-1-56733-097-7		**8th Grade** CRCT Test Prep TEACHING THE GEORGIA PERFORMANCE STANDARDS		

* Shipping and handling charges:
• For orders of less than $500.00, add 10% for standard shipping and $5.95 for handling.
• For orders of $500.00 or more, add 10% for standard shipping and handling.

Subtotal	
Shipping and Handling*	
TOTAL	

You may charge this order to your VISA® or MasterCard®

Card type (please check one):   ☐ MasterCard   ☐ VISA   Signature _____

Credit Card Number:
☐☐☐☐ ☐☐☐☐ ☐☐☐☐ ☐☐☐☐   Expiration Date: ☐☐ / ☐☐   CVV code on back of card ☐☐☐☐
                                              M M   Y Y

Credit Card Billing Address: _____
                              Street   City   State   Zip

150+ Copies	$ 9.00 each*
100-149 Copies	$10.00 each*
30-99 Copies	$11.00 each*
11-29 Copies	$13.00 each*
5-10 Copies	$15.00 each*

Minimum Order is 5 books. Above pricing applies to total number of books ordered (a combination of all grade levels) with a minimum order of five (5) books.

TEACHERS: The answers to all questions and tests can be found at **www.clairmontpress.com**

Click on GA CRCT Test Prep and complete **registration** for the password. Passwords are e-mailed after approval.

* Prices are subject to change without notice. Please contact Clairmont Press to confirm pricing and availabilty.

010113